Fodor's Pocket Guides

NEW YORK CITY

Welcome to New York City

New York City pulses with an irresistible and irrepressible energy. It's also loud, crowded, abrasive, and expensive—but there's nowhere on Earth quite like it. History meets hipness in this global center of entertainment, fashion, media, and finance. World-class museums, recognizable skyscrapers and bridges, celebrated theater, buzzy restaurants, and ethnic enclaves beckon at every turn.

From humble beginnings as a Dutch trading post known as New Amsterdam in 1625, New York City has grown to encompass five boroughs, each with their own appeal. Manhattan may have the most heavy hitters in terms of sights, but Brooklyn's trendy eateries, bars, and maker culture have elevated the vast borough across the East River into a global brand. The Bronx is synonymous with the Yankees and waves of immigrants have turned Queens into a sensational hub of ethnic eats from Greek to Indian to Chinese and more.

The city can feel overwhelming when you're standing in Grand Central Terminal at rush hour or in the middle of Times Square but step away from major arteries like 42nd Street and Broadway, and hushed tree-lined neighborhoods like the West Village, Brooklyn Heights, and the Upper West Side present a much more intimate side of city living.

And, truly, the city is increasingly livable these days, despite recent spikes in crime and inflation. Streets are regularly closed off to cars and glorious waterfront parks now line every borough, providing vital green spaces beyond leafy Central Park—many with staggering skyline views to boot. And while prices have gone up everywhere, some of the city's best experiences are still absolutely free, like riding the Staten Island Ferry to see the Statue of Liberty or walking across the majestic Brooklyn Bridge.

As you plan your upcoming travels to New York City, please confirm that places are still open and let us know when we need to make updates by writing to us at corrections@fodors.com.

Contents

MAPS

Chapter 1

EXPERIENCE NEW YORK CITY

10 ULTIMATE EXPERIENCES

New York City offers terrific experiences that should be on every traveler's list. Here are Fodor's top picks for a memorable trip.

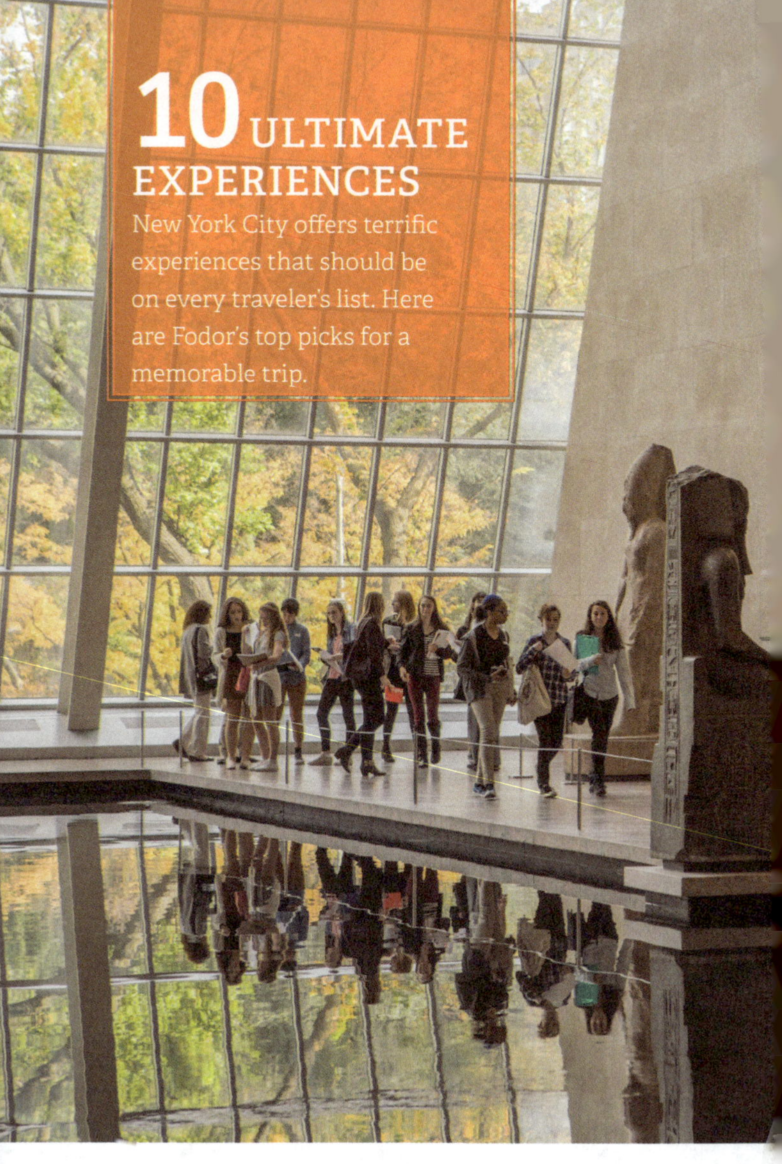

1 See art at the Met

The sprawling Metropolitan Museum of Art houses 5,000 years of human creativity—from the ancient Egyptian Temple of Dendur to Warhol's *Mao*. *(Ch. 7)*

2 Discover your past

Through interactive exhibits, photographs, audio recordings, and artifacts, Ellis Island and the Statue of Liberty remind us that we are a nation of immigrants. *(Ch. 3)*

3 Ride the ferry

The Staten Island Ferry offers great views of both Lower Manhattan and the Statue of Liberty—all for free. The trip is especially romantic at night. *(Ch. 3)*

4 Pay your respects

The reflecting pools at the National 9/11 Memorial at the World Trade Center were built where the Twin Towers once stood and are a tribute to America's fallen heroes. *(Ch. 3)*

5 Marvel at Grand Central Terminal

A magnificent transportation hub, Grand Central Terminal's Beaux-Arts main hall has a 120-foot-high blue ceiling with a sparkling mural of constellations. *(Ch. 6)*

6 Stroll in Central Park

Central Park consists of nearly 850 acres of green space—from manicured lawns to groves of trees. It's an urban oasis that doubles as New Yorkers' shared backyard. *(Ch. 7)*

7 Visit Harlem

Harlem has stood at the heart of Black culture since the start of the 20th century. Its cultural and dining legacies live on today, along with its neighborhood charm. *(Ch. 7)*

8 Catch a show

New York is synonymous with Broadway—the dozens of theaters in the area around Times Square are home to some of the greatest performances on Earth. *(Ch. 6)*

9 Listen to an opera

Lincoln Center is the performing-arts hub for jazz, opera, and ballet. It's also worth a visit for architecture buffs. *(Ch. 7)*

10 Walk to Brooklyn

The Brooklyn Bridge is the prettiest bridge in New York and walking across it is a rite of passage, delivering some of the best views of Manhattan, Brooklyn, and the harbor. *(Chs. 3, 8)*

WHAT'S WHERE

1 Lower Manhattan. This area includes the Financial District and TriBeCa. Landmarks include The Seaport and Wall Street. Luxe shops dominate SoHo, while Chinatown teems with dim-sum joints.

2 The Village and Lower East Side. Artists, NYU students, LGBTQ+ people, and celebrities all call this historic area home, while the Lower East Side has lots of live music and indie shops.

3 Union Square and Chelsea. Union Square Park hosts the city's best greenmarket. Chelsea is full of galleries and the Meatpacking District is home to the High Line.

4 Midtown. See Times Square in all its neon and Broadway theater glory. Midtown from 5th Avenue to the East River has grand hotels, shopping, and the Empire State Building.

5 Upper East and West with Harlem. The Metropolitan Museum of Art and the American Museum of Natural History are major draws, as is Central Park. Harlem has fantastic restaurants and historic sites.

6 The Outer Boroughs. Brooklyn is known for its neighborhoods like Williamsburg and DUMBO. Queens is a collection of diverse communities and the Bronx is home to Yankee Stadium and the Bronx Zoo.

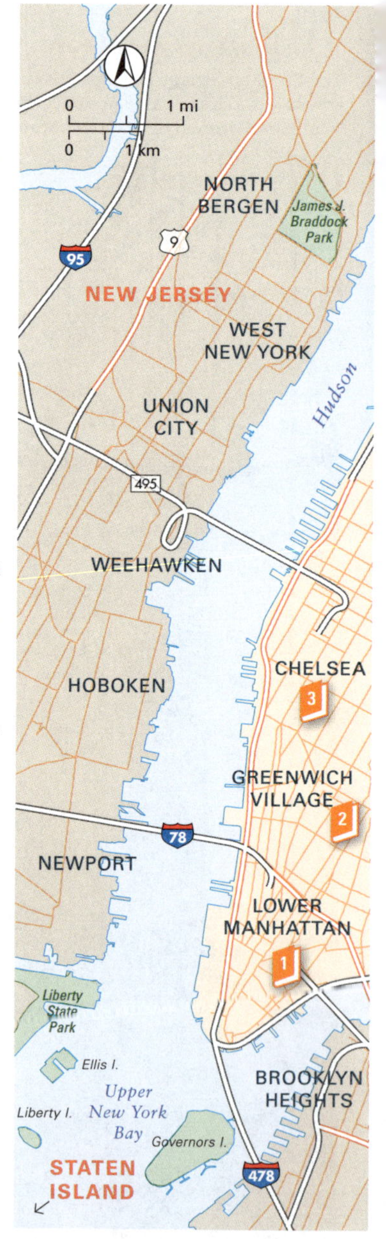

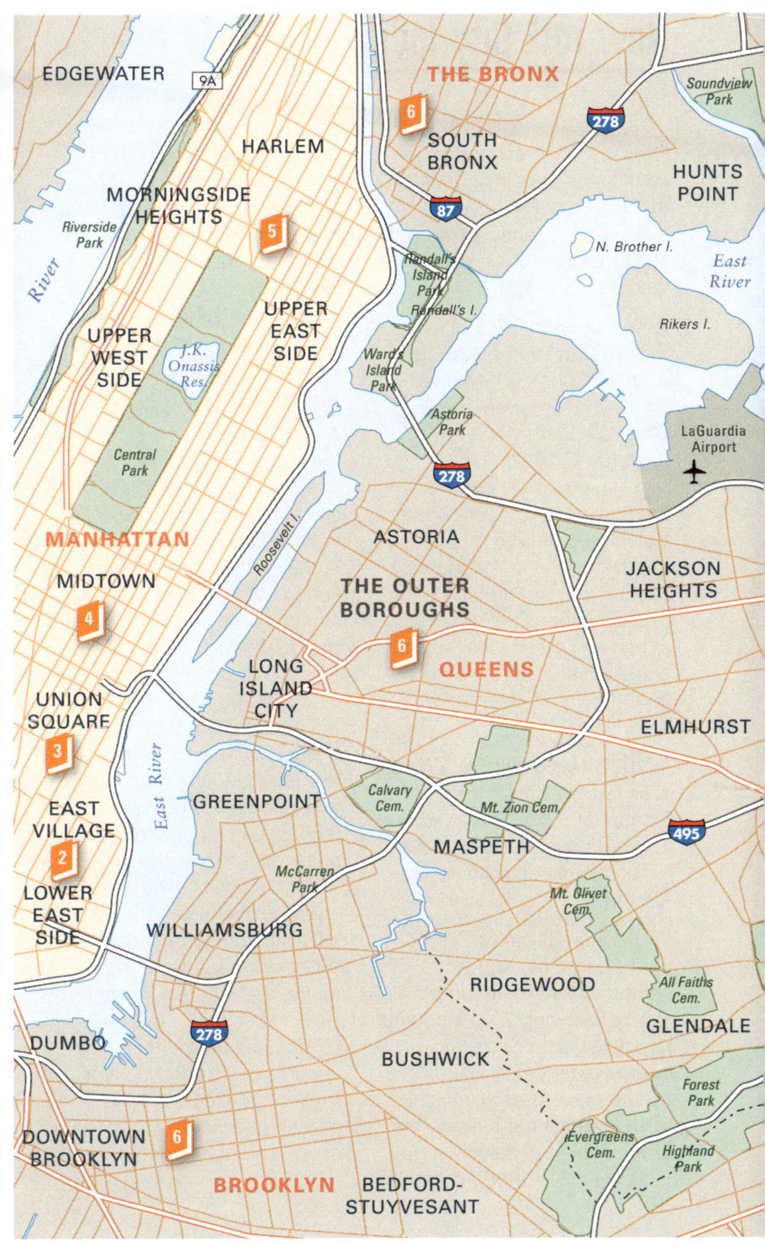
EDGEWATER
9A
THE BRONX
6
SOUTH BRONX
278
Soundview Park
HUNTS POINT
HARLEM
MORNINGSIDE HEIGHTS
Riverside Park
River
5
87
N. Brother I.
East River
Randall's Island Park
Randall's I.
Rikers I.
UPPER EAST SIDE
UPPER WEST SIDE
J.K. Onassis Res.
Ward's Island Park
Astoria Park
LaGuardia Airport
Central Park
278
Roosevelt I.
MANHATTAN
ASTORIA
MIDTOWN
THE OUTER BOROUGHS
JACKSON HEIGHTS
4
6
QUEENS
LONG ISLAND CITY
UNION SQUARE
ELMHURST
3
East River
GREENPOINT
Calvary Cem.
Mt. Zion Cem.
EAST VILLAGE
495
MASPETH
2
McCarren Park
LOWER EAST SIDE
Mt. Olivet Cem.
WILLIAMSBURG
RIDGEWOOD
All Faiths Cem.
GLENDALE
DUMBO
278
BUSHWICK
Forest Park
DOWNTOWN BROOKLYN
6
Evergreens Cem.
Highland Park
BROOKLYN
BEDFORD-STUYVESANT

New York City Today

POLITICS

New York City remains a confluence of political ideals that lean toward the liberal side, while balancing the egos and ambitions of its elected officials.

Governor Kathy Hochul, who took over in 2021 following Andrew Cuomo's controversial resignation, was elected New York State's first female governor in 2022. Democrat Hochul has shown her political savvy in many arenas, including efforts to rebuild the state economy postpandemic. She's prioritized tenant rights, affordable housing, climate action and green jobs, better educational opportunities, and the statewide teacher workforce.

In 2022, Democrat Eric Adams took over as mayor from Democrat Bill de Blasio, both of whom campaigned on plans for economic equality across the city.

CRIME AND SAFETY

Since taking office, Adams has prioritized restoring public safety following 2021's notable uptick in crime. So far, it seems to be working: 2022 numbers were largely back to 2019 levels and 2023 saw the city's highest decrease in gun violence since 1995. Incidents of theft remain high, however, from pickpocketing to shoplifting; in fact, retail theft has become so widespread, many stores now lock their goods up on shelves. Visitors should expect increased police presence on the subway, streets, train stations, and popular gathering places.

THE MIGRANT CRISIS

A more pressing issue now is the surge in migrants. While New York has always received and absorbed thousands of new arrivals every year, those numbers started spiking in spring 2022 as border states began bussing migrants from the US–Mexico border into the city. By one estimate, over 150,000 had arrived by the end of 2023, with the majority in need of shelter. Due to a local law that mandates every homeless person who requests a bed be provided one—New York is the only major US city to offer a legal "right to shelter"—officials have scrambled to find affordable-housing solutions. As a result, many hotels, former jails, and schools have been repurposed as shelters. It's not uncommon to see migrants lined up outside buildings awaiting services or setting up sidewalk encampments.

ECONOMY

The COVID-19 pandemic hit New York hard and fast, bringing much of the city to a heartbreaking standstill in mid-March 2020. Before the pandemic, New York had seen its tourism numbers skyrocket year after year. The surge brought about the city's biggest hotel expansion in a generation, attracting a host of new brands—from high-end boutiques to budget chains—all across the city. When tourism plummeted in 2020, some businesses closed temporarily; others, sadly, closed permanently.

With the support of city and state subsidies that helped keep many tourism-related companies afloat during the pandemic's darkest months, visitor numbers began to inch up once again in 2021, and many of those "paused" businesses reopened. For comparison: in 2019 the city welcomed a record-breaking 66 million visitors. But in 2020, there were only about 22 million; in 2021, 33 million. In 2022 that number jumped to 56 million and in 2023, it was back up to 61.8 million, 93% of prepandemic levels. New York City Tourism + Conventions, the city's tourism bureau, now expects 64.5 million in 2024.

That said, inflation has hit NYC hard. Restaurants are more expensive than they were—even pre- or during the pandemic—and Broadway tickets are increasingly hard to come by at good-value prices. Taxis and ride-sharing apps have also gotten much more expensive, as the city keeps adding new surcharges to almost every ride. Budget accordingly. As of June 2024, the implementation of congestion pricing for cars traveling below 60th Street ($15 for passenger cars, as well as $2.50 for rideshares and $1.25 for taxis, which tourists can expect to see on their totals) has been put on an indefinite hold (though it could still happen at a later date).

CANNABIS

As of 2022, it's now legal for adults 21 years and older to buy and smoke recreational cannabis in New York State. You're allowed three ounces of cannabis and up to 24 grams of concentrated cannabis for personal use. As of this writing, 44 legal shops have opened in NYC. However, "illegal" shops have opened seemingly on every block. Since people can smoke or vape wherever smoking tobacco is allowed, expect to smell pot everywhere, all day long.

What to Eat and Drink in New York City

BURGERS

Burgers are a New York staple, starting with fast-food varieties (like 5 Napkin Burger) to hole-in-the-wall discoveries (like Midtown's Burger Joint) to high-end burgers made with foie gras and black truffles.

OYSTERS

Almost every upscale restaurant in the city has oysters on the menu; you'd be missing out not to try a few. You can also head to the historic Grand Central Oyster Bar in Grand Central Terminal to slurp some back in a retro venue that dates back to 1913.

BAGELS AND LOX

It doesn't get more classic New York than a bagel piled high with cream cheese, lox, tomatoes, onions, and capers. Fortunately, you'll find consistently delicious bagels all over the city. One of the most historic purveyors is Russ & Daughters, serving since 1914.

PIZZA

New Yorkers take their pizza seriously, and choosing a favorite pizzeria is an extremely personal matter. But a special few stand out from the rest, like neighboring Brooklyn spots Juliana's and Grimaldi's. They're two of the city's best for coal-fired pizza—both are casual, and neither take reservations.

HOT DOGS

Hot dogs are among NYC's most ubiquitous and affordable eats. Franks run the gamut from quick eats to kosher to gourmet. Carts and trucks all over town serve 'em up boiled on a basic bun (New Yorkers typically top them with mustard and onions, not ketchup). For something fancier, head to Crif Dogs in the East Village for deep-fried, bacon-wrapped dogs with creative toppings (its back door also leads to Please Don't Tell).

Pasta

PASTA
For traditional, handmade pastas, the Theater District is a safe bet, and spots like Tony's di Napoli serve huge, family-style portions. Head to the West Village (perhaps to Via Carota) and Williamsburg (local fave Lilia) for more nuanced, creative, and utterly delicious pasta.

PASTRAMI SANDWICHES
When Harry Met Sally might have immortalized Katz's Delicatessen on the silver screen, but this place has been a New York institution since 1888. But there are plenty of great old and new delis serving hand-carved pastrami, corned beef, brisket, knishes, hot dogs, and matzo ball soup. (Don't forget the pickles.)

DIM SUM
The ultimate weekend brunch, dim sum is a Chinatown staple. Bring a group, and prepare to feast on dim sum classics, like dumplings, rice rolls, scallion pancakes, and the original egg rolls stuffed with veggies and chicken at go-to spots like Jing Fong and Nom Wah Tea Parlor.

MEXICAN FOOD
Drawing inspiration from Mexico City, Oaxaca, Baja, and the Yucatán, New York City's Mexican restaurants are a cut above. Choices span everything from inexpensive-and-fantastic street tacos (sometimes from food trucks) to long-running Tex-Mex joints, to upscale spots all around the five boroughs.

New York City's Best Museums

MUSEUM OF MODERN ART
MoMA is Manhattan's oldest museum dedicated to modern art. The collection is rich in 20th-century masterworks, including pieces by Kahlo, Pollock, Nevelson, Van Gogh, and Matisse.

NEUE GALERIE
The Neue Galerie, a time capsule of Austrian elegance, offers an impressive supply of Schieles and Klimts—including *Portrait of Adele Bloch Bauer I*, Klimt's masterpiece in gold—not to mention a mean sacher torte in its Café Sabarsky.

GUGGENHEIM MUSEUM
Founded by Solomon Guggenheim, is filled with work by luminaries like Kandinsky and Calder—all displayed inside Frank Lloyd Wright's sculptural spiral building, an icon of New York architecture.

TENEMENT MUSEUM
For a step back to various points in time on the Lower East Side, book one of the experiences that revolve around the partially restored 19th-century buildings that comprise the Tenement Museum. Options include apartment tours and neighborhood walks.

9/11 MUSEUM
Beside the twin pools that form the 9/11 Memorial Plaza is the glass pavilion of the 9/11 Memorial Museum (part of the complex known as the National 9/11 Memorial & Museum). The museum descends some seven stories down to the bedrock the Twin Towers were built on, and the vast space displays a poignant, powerful collection of artifacts, memorabilia, photographs, and multimedia exhibits.

WHITNEY MUSEUM OF AMERICAN ART
The Whitney offers contemporary and historical perspectives on American art while continually redefining what contemporary and American art is. Its Renzo Piano–designed building is an agile backdrop.

BROOKLYN MUSEUM
Those in the know visit the Brooklyn Museum for its collections of Egyptian, American decorative, and African arts. The museum also attracts visitors for its smashing contemporary shows.

THE JEWISH MUSEUM
The Jewish Museum is much more than a contemporary art museum. With innovative exhibits like a virtual reality design exhibition or Leonard Cohen retrospective, this museum pushes boundaries.

METROPOLITAN MUSEUM OF ART
A vast, encyclopedic institution, the Met is one of the world's great museums and has an extensive collections of human artifacts. But it's not the dusty, creaky, Museum Mile institution you might imagine; instead, it delivers thoughtful exhibitions of history, art, design, and objects, not to mention the Met Gala, the city's most glamorous party.

QUEENS MUSEUM
It makes sense that the most diverse place on Earth would have a museum to represent the true meaning of diversity. The Queens Museum's programming ranges from traditional art shows to participative performance across all mediums, demographics, and locations in the borough.

What to Buy in New York City

BOOKS
New York is a literary town that's inspired countless writers. Bookstores like the Strand and McNally Jackson celebrate the written word with such gusto that some may even put down their phones for a few minutes.

DESIGNER GOODS
Every major designer maintains lavish flagships in New York. Even if you're not ready to splurge, it's still worth popping into their boutiques for the design alone, like the Rem Koolhaas–designed Prada flagship in SoHo, the Hermès flagship on Madison Avenue, and the dazzling Cartier on 5th Avenue. You can also one-stop shop at Bergdorf Goodman, the swanky department store that carries them all.

VINTAGE CLOTHING
Channel the legacy of stylish New Yorkers and go vintage at the city's secondhand stores. Try Beacon's Closet, which gets swarmed with hipsters on the weekends, or Housing Works, which benefits people living with and affected by HIV/AIDS. Both have multiple locations throughout the city. (Some of the best can be found in Brooklyn.) Screaming Mimis in the West Village is a long-established hot spot. Another great bet is Brooklyn's 10ft. Single by Stella Dallas, which has an array of vintage goods from the recent past and a huge selection of mid-century cocktail dresses, coats, and menswear.

SOUVENIRS GALORE
The crowded sidewalks of Chinatown beckon for all sorts of reasons, especially for inexpensive souvenirs like bulk-discount T-shirts, knockoff handbags, and all manner of phone accessories. Sure, you can load up on keychains and tote bags here like nowhere else in the city, but don't be shy about browsing inside Chinatown's authentic herb and tea stores for souvenirs you won't find anyplace else.

HOME DECOR
New York is full of quirky and one-of-a-kind design and decor shops. For fun kitchen supplies, Fishs Eddy is a must-visit for upcycled vintage plates and silverware as well as novelty kitchen

MoMA Design Store

items. For high design, look no further than the MoMA Design Store, with outlets on 53rd Street or on Spring Street in SoHo, which has everything from jewelry to pet accessories. For exquisite ephemera, drop by one of John Derian's East Village or West Village location for decoupage ceramics and glassware handmade in New York.

LOCAL CRAFTS

To find one-of-a-kind creations by local artisans and designers, there's no better place to shop than Artists & Fleas. Launched in 2003, the multimerchant marketplace now has multiple locations in Williamsburg, Chelsea Market, and at pop-ups around town. You can find everything from clutches printed with cheeky phrases to custom clocks made from old hardcover books.

New York City in Every Season

Brooklyn Botanic Garden

SPRING

New York explodes into riotous color in spring, as tulips, magnolia trees, and cherry blossoms burst out everywhere from city parks to brownstone pocket gardens. New Yorkers come out of hibernation in droves to witness the city in bloom, especially the pink popcorn cherry blossoms at the Brooklyn Botanic Garden, which typically start flowering by early April. It's also the start of baseball season, with home openers for both of New York's Major League teams, the Yankees and the Mets, around the first week of April. Come May, major art fairs descend on Manhattan, with megawatt contemporary and fine art on display from Frieze New York to TEFAF; Chelsea galleries like Pace usually schedule splashy—and free—art openings for this period, too. If you're lucky, one of the city's professional basketball or hockey teams will be angling for a playoff berth by late May, further energizing the city. While the weather can be fickle—do expect some rain—it can also be downright glorious, with crisp, clear days leading to cooler nights: ideal conditions for long walks in Central Park or along the High Line. Given how sublime the season often is, the period from mid-March through Memorial Day can be expensive. Early June can yield better hotel rates, if you're flexible on dates.

Coney Island

SUMMER

New York summers are swelteringly hot. Temperatures typically start amping up in June and continue their highs through early September. While few new Broadway shows open during this period, hugely popular outdoor movie and performing-arts festivals fill the gap. The Tribeca Film Festival kicks off the calendar, bringing upwards of 250 films and 1,000-plus screenings to Lower Manhattan (and beyond) in early June. Soon after, prominent 5th Avenue museums open their doors for free from 6 pm to 9 pm for the Museum Mile Festival. The city's beloved annual Mermaid Parade marks the official start of summer by bringing everyone to the Coney Island boardwalk around June 21; Pride Weekend follows with a float-filled parade through Greenwich Village during the last weekend in June. Come July and August, evenings under the stars beckon. Crowds spread out picnic blankets for classic movies in Bryant Park; sway and groove to live music at BRIC Celebrate Brooklyn! under the Prospect Park Bandshell; and take in star-powered Shakespeare plays at the Delacorte Theater in Central Park. And, when the heat really becomes unbearable, Coney Island and Rockaway Beach are just a subway ride away.

New York City in Every Season

Central Park

FALL

Ask any New Yorker what their favorite season is, and they'll likely say fall. The weather is at its best, filled with temperate, blue-sky days suffused with lingering light, from right after Labor Day until early November. The leaves turn dazzling shades of copper and red in Central Park and the city buzzes with new Broadway shows; museum exhibitions; and opera, ballet, and classical music productions, most of which open by the end of September. New Yorkers also take Halloween seriously: locals deck out their brownstone stoops with incredible displays in the weeks leading up to October 31, especially in Greenwich Village, site of the world's largest Halloween Parade, which brings thousands of wildly costumed participants to the streets. Next up: millions of spectators gather along the route of the 26.2-mile New York City Marathon on the first Sunday in November to cheer on the more than 50,000 runners hoofing it across all five boroughs. The season caps off with Macy's Thanksgiving Day Parade, with its renowned helium balloons bobbing above Midtown. The combination of exceptional weather and major happenings makes this period one of the most expensive times to visit, but it's always worth it.

Rockefeller Center

WINTER

The festive period from Thanksgiving through New Year's Eve is New York at its most magical. The annual Rockefeller Center Tree Lighting officially kicks off the season in early December. Fifth Avenue department stores like Tiffany & Co. and Saks Fifth Avenue go all out with lavish decorations. In Brooklyn, Dyker Heights puts on a Christmas light show like nowhere else. Up in the Bronx, the annual Holiday Train Show at the New York Botanical Garden is one of the city's top seasonal attractions, especially for families. All of this sparkle means that prices are usually at their peak between Thanksgiving and Christmas Eve.

After the ball drops in Times Square, winter really sets in. January days are short and you might face bone-chilling winds or even a snowstorm. But you'll also benefit from the city's lowest hotel prices, uncrowded attractions, and two-for-one tickets to select Broadway performances during winter Broadway Week. It's also a great time to go skating at the Central Park, Bryant Park, or Prospect Park rinks. The city starts to come back to life around Lunar New Year—falling between late-January and late-February—when Chinatown celebrates with food vendors, colorful decorations, and an elaborate parade through Lower Manhattan.

What to Read and Watch

JUST KIDS BY PATTI SMITH

In her National Book Award–winning memoir, artist, poet, and punk-rock-movement founder Patti Smith creates a beautiful love letter both to her friend, Robert Mapplethorpe, and to the New York City of their shared youth. Smith captures the mood of being young in the city in the 1960s and '70s, and all those fleeting, poignant moments that exist right on the brink of change, success, and heartbreak.

THE WEARY BLUES BY LANGSTON HUGHES

Hughes's poetry here is about Harlem—its life forces, culture, art, and music—during its 1920s renaissance. The young poet borrowed blues and jazz elements to write poetry about Black music and life in a way that had seldom been done before, and his work is at once personal, lyrical, and a resounding voice for the Black experience at the time.

THE GOLDFINCH BY DONNA TARTT

This Dickensian feat of a novel spans Manhattan from the dark corners of the East Village to the wealthy enclave of the Upper East Side and everywhere in between. Linked to the book's other characters through one major tragedy (and subsequent smaller ones), the novel's antihero is full of moral contradictions and personality flaws, but his journey (from a preteen into adulthood) is fascinating, and it's impossible not to want to follow along.

SOUR HEART BY JENNY ZHANG

Jenny Zhang's heartfelt story collection links together the experiences of first- and second-generation Chinese Americans living throughout Queens and Brooklyn. Her sharp, funny writing describes what it's like to grow up in a country that your parents aren't quite a part of—with the weight of their expectations on your shoulders—and illustrates a human experience important to the New York (and American) story.

THE BONFIRE OF THE VANITIES BY TOM WOLFE

Through a central crime told from several points of view of the people involved (a Wall Street trader living on Park Avenue, a bullish assistant district attorney, and an alcoholic tabloid journalist), this satirical novel strives to encapsulate much of the mood of 1980s New York City: less-than-pretty aspects of racism, classism, vapid excess, and bitter greed. While it's funny and full of farce, Wolfe used his skills as a journalist to base much of the novel on real happenings and characters.

WHEN HARRY MET SALLY

Written by the late, great native New Yorker Nora Ephron, this Billy Crystal and Meg Ryan classic tops the list because it's terrific both as a romantic comedy *and* as an essential New York movie. Much like the pair's long-running friendship and budding romance in the film, this movie is savvy and fun, filled with citywide wanderings (including its classic scene at Katz's Deli), and culminating with a desperate, romantic run through Manhattan on New Year's Eve.

DO THE RIGHT THING

With his *Chronicles of Brooklyn* series, renowned filmmaker Spike Lee dedicates a whole slew of fantastic movies (*He Got Game, She's Gotta Have It, Red Hook Summer*) to life and Black culture in this outer borough, one of the all-time best being 1989's *Do the Right Thing*. Starring a young Spike Lee himself, Brooklyn's Bed-Stuy neighborhood on a hot summer day is the setting for a poignant film about racial tension, police brutality, and community.

WEST SIDE STORY

The original musical drama about love, feuds, and racial clashes in the 1950s takes place on New York's Upper West Side, a demographically different neighborhood then than it is today. The 1961 movie is a classic, and Puerto Rican singer and actor Rita Moreno gives one of the films best performances in her supporting role as Anita. (Moreno returned for another *West Side Story* appearance in Steven Spielberg's 2021 remake.)

HOME ALONE 2: LOST IN NEW YORK

There's something magical about New York City at Christmastime, and New York Christmas movies, when done right (*Miracle on 34th Street, Elf, You've Got Mail*), give you warm-and-fuzzy feelings about both the holiday season and the city. *Home Alone 2* is especially fun because of how much New York you get through Kevin's explorations and antics: Rockefeller Center, Central Park, the Empire State Building, and the Plaza Hotel all make their way into this family-friendly screwball film.

PARIAH

In writer-director Dee Rees's first feature film, a young Black woman growing up in Fort Greene, Brooklyn (where it was largely filmed), explores identity and belonging through sexuality, family, and the greater community. Adepero Oduye, the young actress playing Alike, gives a touching performance,

What to Read and Watch

in a beautiful film about sexual identity and coming of age in Brooklyn.

EMPIRE

This musical drama focuses on a large entertainment company that functions much like a royal dynasty, and not without the same amount of complications and drama. Though much of the actual filming happened in Chicago, everything about *Empire*, from the scandals and power grabs to the fashion and hip-hop interludes, reflects New York.

SEX AND THE CITY

This classic HBO show was groundbreaking in its time for featuring a group of cosmopolitan (and cosmopolitan-drinking) women talking about sex and dating in a frank and refreshing way. Besides the infuriatingly large apartments, its depictions of New York and its themes around the turn of the millennium are entertaining and expansive.

FRIENDS

Irreverent but addictive, this light comedy-drama about twenty- to thirtysomethings living around Greenwich Village (in unrealistically nice apartments) ran for 10 seasons in the '90s and early 2000s. Still one of the most popular sitcoms ever, *Friends* follows the theme of New York shows that are about little else but the intertwining lives of its New York characters and the city itself.

SEINFELD

The original "show about nothing" is really a sitcom about NYC. It features comedian Jerry Seinfeld and his pals as they get themselves into sometimes unfortunate, always hilarious, and usually quintessential New York situations—like mishaps at the Puerto Rican Day Parade, Macy's Day Parade, NYC Marathon, as well as conflicts over parking spaces, bad neighbors and roommates, even 212 versus 646 area codes.

THE MARVELOUS MRS. MAISEL

In this Amazon comedy-drama series set in NYC in the late 1950s and early 1960s, Miriam Maisel (aka Mrs. Maisel), a Jewish Upper East Side housewife and mother of two, discovers she has a knack for comedy. She starts doing her schtick downtown, at whatever Village club will actually let a woman do a stand-up gig. Local haunts like La Bonbonniere, Village Vanguard, and Old Town Bar—among many historic neighborhood spots—regularly serve as set locations.

Chapter 2

TRAVEL SMART

Updated by
Arabella Bowen

★ STATE CAPITAL:
Albany

POPULATION:
8,335,897

LANGUAGE:
English

$ CURRENCY:
U.S. dollar

AREA CODES:
212, 332, 347, 646, 718, 917, 929

⚠ EMERGENCIES:
911

DRIVING:
On the right

ELECTRICITY:
120–220 v/60 cycles; plugs have two or three rectangular prongs

TIME:
EST/EDT

WEBSITES:
www.nyctourism.com
new.mta.info

AIRPORTS:
LGA, JFK, EWR

Know Before You Go

It can feel vast, loud, and confusing, yet New York City also can be manageable—yes, it really can. There are some simple and brilliant ways not only to survive each new day in the big city, but also to navigate and even enjoy its magnificent chaos. Best of all, the effort is well worth it, as the Big Apple is like nowhere else on earth.

GET ORIENTED

Manhattan is best navigated by studying the street grid. Forget north and south, and think uptown and downtown, along the avenues. Avenues are mostly one-way, with odd numbers pointing downtown and even numbers heading uptown. Streets run crosstown (roughly east and west), generally linking the East River to the Hudson River. Their directions vary, but mostly odd-numbered streets are westbound. The area below 14th Street is older and doesn't follow the grid so neatly; many streets are on funny diagonals and have names rather than numbers. Broadway is the big boulevard that diagonally connects Lower Manhattan to Inwood and the Harlem River. Fifth Avenue separates east from west street addresses (e.g., 25 East 39th Street stands across 5th Avenue from 25 West 39th Street).

IT'S (RELATIVELY) SAFE

NYC has always had its fair share of crime, though statistically it's been one of the safer big U.S. cities over the years. That changed during the pandemic, however. Crime spiked in 2021, most noticeably in downtown neighborhoods like Greenwich Village. Fortunately, 2022 and 2023 largely saw a decline to 2019 levels. Theft remains a real concern though: be extra vigilant of pickpockets in crowded areas and don't wear headphones on the street. The subway has also seen a major uptick in crime and has become a hangout spot for homeless people. Police presence has increased, but it's still an issue. Take care when you ride and splurge for a taxi or rideshare late at night.

PRACTICE SIDEWALK ETIQUETTE

Although it may seem obvious, NYC sidewalks are busy shared public thoroughfares along which pedestrians converge and occasionally collide. Think of them more like foot highways—made for motion, not stopping—and walk on the right side of the sidewalk, as you would drive on the right side of the road. We beg you, don't get too caught up in your selfies, and never, ever walk with your eyes glued to your phone.

KNOW YOUR NEIGHBORHOODS

Every NYC neighborhood has a character of its own. From Chinatown and Times Square to Lincoln Center and all the way to Coney Island, each pocket can captivate visitors. Among the most notable are Greenwich Village for its historically bohemian scene; TriBeCa and SoHo for their boutiques, galleries, and cobblestones; and Williamsburg for its trendy restaurants. Visitors thirsty for nightlife might prefer the East Village or Lower East Side; while theater lovers will appreciate Midtown Manhattan.

THE INS AND OUTS OF DINING OUT

Fine dining is always on the menu in Manhattan, where scoring a table at a hot new eatery can top off a foodie's perfect trip. The most reliable way to snag that dream table is to reserve it well in advance, either directly with the restaurant, or with an app like OpenTable or Resy. Since COVID, many eateries now offer covered outdoor seating. For last-minute attempts at a fully booked restaurant, show up in person during nonpeak dining hours (i.e., not at 12:30 or 8 pm), be very kind to the almighty host, be flexible, and hope for a cancellation (or see if you can eat at the bar). FYI: some NYC restaurants still accept cash only.

PLAN AHEAD

Just like locking in a great restaurant reservation, catching the best NYC entertainment means planning ahead. So if your dream visit hinges on catching a top Broadway show, buy that ticket first, then buy your NYC flights to plan your trip around it. This applies to any show or attraction with high demand and timed-ticket reservations. Last-minute tickets can sometimes be had through TKTS discount booths, and the NYC CityPASS (🌐 *www.citypass.com*) lets you skip the line (and save money on admission) at several top attractions.

AIRPORT TIPS

JFK Airport is about an hour's taxi ride with a flat rate of $70 to Manhattan plus surcharges and tolls. The AirTrain to the A or E subway, however, is a cheaper alternative, costing just $11.15 total and taking around 90 minutes to Midtown Manhattan. From Newark (EWR) Airport, wise travelers skip pricey New Jersey taxis and instead take the AirTrain to Newark Airport Station, then transfer to an NJ Transit train into New York Penn Station for $16. For LaGuardia, a taxi is best, since only buses (not trains) provide its measly mass-transit option; though at least there's now the Q70 "Select Bus Service," which runs express from Manhattan, Brooklyn, and Long Island. Shared rides can be arranged via Lyft or Uber. Or take an airport shuttle bus like GO Airlink NYC or Newark Airport Express (around $40 one-way). Just be aware that all of NYC's airports are remote, so build in at least an hour more than you think you'll need.

Getting Here and Around

If you're flying into one of the three major airports that service New York—John F. Kennedy (JFK), LaGuardia (LGA), or New Jersey's Newark Liberty (EWR)—pick your mode of transportation for getting to Manhattan before your plane lands. Tourists typically either take a car service or head to the taxi line, but those aren't necessarily the best choices, especially during rush hour. Public transportation, especially if you're traveling light and without young children, is a swift, inexpensive option.

Once you're in Manhattan, getting around can be a breeze when you get the hang of the subway system. Better yet, if you're not in a rush and the weather's cooperating, just walk—it's the best way to discover the true New York. Not quite sure where you are or how to get where you're headed? Ask a local. You might be surprised at how friendly the city's inhabitants are, debunking their reputation for rudeness. In the same getting-there-is-half-the-fun spirit, there are also boat and bus journeys that let you see the city from a whole new perspective.

Air

Generally, most international flights go in and out of John F. Kennedy or Newark Liberty airport, while domestic flights go in and out of both of these, as well as LaGuardia Airport.

AIRPORTS

The major air gateways to New York City are LaGuardia Airport (LGA) and John F. Kennedy International Airport (JFK) in the borough of Queens, and Newark Liberty International Airport (EWR) in the state of New Jersey.

TRANSFERS—CAR SERVICES AND RIDESHARING

Car services can be a great convenience, because, upon request, the driver can meet you in the baggage-claim area and help with your luggage (though more likely, the driver will wait in the car to rendezvous with you in a designated airport-pickup zone). Airport flat rates are often comparable to taxi fares, but some car services charge for parking and wait time at the airport. To eliminate these expenses, other car services require you to telephone their dispatcher (or order a taxi through an app, like Curb) when you land so they can send the next available car to pick you up.

The New York City Taxi and Limousine Commission rules require all car services to be licensed and pick up riders only by prior arrangement; if possible, call 24 hours in advance for reservations or at least a half day before your flight's departure. Drivers of nonlicensed vehicles ("gypsy cabs" or black cars) often solicit fares outside the terminal in baggage-claim areas. Don't take them: you run the risk of an unsafe ride in a vehicle that might not be properly insured, and you will almost certainly pay more than the going rate.

Reserving a car with Lyft, Uber, or other ride-sharing services is another option—just be sure you know which airport terminal and passenger zone you're at before setting the pickup location.

TRANSFERS—TAXIS AND SHUTTLES

Outside the baggage-claim area at each of New York's major airports are yellow-cab stands where a uniformed dispatcher connects passengers with taxis. Cabs are not permitted to pick up fares anywhere else in the arrivals area, so if you want a taxi, take your place in line. Shuttle services generally pick up passengers from designated spots along the curbs.

GO Airlink NYC and SuperShuttle run vans and some buses from JFK, LaGuardia, and Newark airports to popular spots like Grand Central Terminal, the Port Authority Bus Terminal, Penn Station, and hotels in Manhattan. Fares start around $40 one-way per person to or from JFK or LGA. Those rates are significantly cheaper than taking a taxi if you're on your own but probably not if there are two or more of you sharing the cost.

If you choose to use such services, keep in mind that customers' satisfaction with them is very mixed; online reviews often complain of significant waits for vans to both arrive and reach their destinations. In any case, allow extra time for the shuttle's other pickups and drop-offs along the way.

TRANSFERS BETWEEN AIRPORTS

There are several transportation options for connecting to and from area airports, including shuttles, AirTrain and mass transit, and car service or taxi. GO Airlink NYC, SuperShuttle, and ETS Airport Shuttle run share-ride vans between Newark, JFK, and LaGuardia airports. AirTrain provides information on how to reach your destination from any of New York's airports. Note

Getting Here and Around

that if you arrive after midnight at any airport, you might wait a long time for a taxi.

TRANSFERS FROM JFK INTERNATIONAL AIRPORT

The rate for traveling between JFK and Manhattan by yellow cab in either direction is a flat fee of $70 plus surcharges and tolls (which average about $13); peak times incur an additional $5 surcharge. The trip takes 40–60 minutes. Prices are roughly $38–$78 for trips to most other locations in New York City. You should also tip the driver for safe driving and good service (around 10%–20% of the final fare).

JFK's AirTrain ($8.50) connects JFK Airport to the New York City subway (A, E, J, and Z trains) and the Long Island Rail Road (LIRR)—both of which take you to Manhattan or Brooklyn. The AirTrain monorail system runs 24 hours, though it's far less frequent overnight. Not sure which train to take? Check 🌐 *citymapper.com/nyc* or 🌐 *new.mta.info* (or their corresponding apps) for the best route to your destination.

Subway travel between JFK and Manhattan takes about an hour and costs $2.90 in subway fare (plus the $1 fee for a new, refillable MetroCard) plus another $8.50 for the AirTrain. The LIRR travels between JFK's AirTrain stop (Jamaica Station) and Grand Central Station or Penn Station in around 20 minutes for $8.25 (off-peak) or $11.25 (peak), excluding the AirTrain fee. When traveling *from* Manhattan to JFK via subway, take the E train to Sutphin Boulevard, or take the A train to the Howard Beach station; then, in either case, transfer to the AirTrain. If you are riding the A train, be sure to take an A train marked "Far Rockaway" or "Rockaway Park," *not* an A train bound for "Lefferts Boulevard."

TRANSFERS FROM LAGUARDIA AIRPORT

Taxis cost $40–$60 (plus tip and tolls) to most central destinations in New York City, and take at least 30–45 minutes.

You can also take the LaGuardia Link Q70 bus for free to the Woodside–61st Street subway station in Queens (with connections to the 7 train, or to the LIRR, with service to Penn Station) or to the Jackson Heights–Roosevelt Avenue subway stop (where you can transfer to the E, F, M, R, and 7 trains and reach many points in Manhattan and Brooklyn). Once you arrive at either station, pay $2.90 to get on the subway by tapping on with a credit card or contactless device or buying a MetroCard.

Another option is to take the M60 bus to its end point at 106th Street and Broadway on Manhattan's Upper West Side, with connections en route to several New York City Subway lines (2, 3, 4, 5, 6, A, B, C, D, N, and Q trains); you'll need to pay $2.90 on board with a credit card, contactless device, MetroCard or exact change and request a transfer if you plan to continue on. Allow at least 60 minutes for the entire trip to Midtown, and perhaps a bit more during heavy traffic or rain.

TRANSFERS FROM NEWARK AIRPORT

Taxis to Manhattan cost about $90 plus tolls and tip and take 30–45 minutes in normal traffic; inquire with the airport's taxi dispatcher about shared group rates, too. If you're heading to the airport from Manhattan, there's a $20 surcharge on top of the normal taxi rate, plus tolls and a customary tip.

AirTrain Newark, an elevated light-rail system, can take you from the airline terminal to the Newark Liberty International Airport Station. From here, you can take New Jersey Transit (or, for a much higher price, Amtrak) trains heading to New York Penn Station. It's an efficient and low-cost way to get to New York City, particularly if you don't have many in your group and aren't carrying massive amounts of luggage.

Total travel time to New York Penn Station via New Jersey Transit is approximately 30 minutes, and the cost is $16, including the AirTrain fee. By contrast, a similar, slightly faster trip (about 25 minutes) via Amtrak starts at $25. The AirTrain runs every three minutes from 5 am to midnight and every 15 minutes from midnight to 5 am. Note that New Jersey Transit trains first make a stop at the confusingly named Newark Penn Station before they reach New York Penn Station, their final stop. If you're not sure when to get off the train, ask a conductor or fellow passenger.

Newark Airport Express buses travel between the airport and Manhattan, with stops at Port Authority, Bryant Park (at 42nd Street and 5th Avenue), and Grand Central Terminal about every 15–30 minutes until midnight. The trip takes roughly 45 minutes, and the fare is $18.70 (plus $2.50 in administrative and fuel surcharge fees). Buses headed to Newark Airport depart at the same intervals, from the same Manhattan locations.

Getting Here and Around

Boat

The Staten Island Ferry runs across New York Harbor between Whitehall Street (next to Battery Park in Lower Manhattan) and St. George terminal in Staten Island. The free 25-minute ride gives you a view of the Financial District skyscrapers, the Statue of Liberty, and Ellis Island.

NYC Ferry (🌐 *ferry.nyc*) shuttles passengers to the city's growing network of docks and waterfront attractions between the Hudson River (on Manhattan's west side) and the East River (on its east side), including stops in Lower Manhattan (for access to the 9/11 Memorial & Museum) and the South Street Seaport and Governors Island, as well as multiple locations in Brooklyn and Queens. NYC Ferry tickets cost $4 per ride and are sold at dockside kiosks and on its app.

Also consider NY Waterway (🌐 *nywaterway.com*), which runs ferry service across the Hudson River between Manhattan and ports in New Jersey and upstate New York.

Car

If you plan to drive into Manhattan, try to avoid the morning and evening rush hours and lunch hour. Tune in to traffic reports online or on the radio (1010 WINS on the AM radio dial) before you set off, and don't be surprised if a bridge is partially closed or entirely blocked with traffic.

Driving within Manhattan can be a nightmare of gridlocked streets, obnoxious drivers, and seemingly suicidal jaywalkers and bicyclists. Narrow and one-way streets are common, particularly downtown, and can make driving even more difficult. The most congested streets of the city generally lie between 14th and 59th Streets and 3rd and 8th Avenues. In addition, sections of Broadway near Times Square (from 42nd to 47th Street) and Herald Square (33rd to 35th) are closed to motorized traffic. This can create gridlock and confusion on nearby streets.

CAR RENTALS

When you reserve a car, ask about cancellation penalties, taxes, drop-off charges (if you're planning to pick up the car in one destination and leave it in another), and surcharges (for being under or over a certain age, additional drivers, or driving across state or country borders or beyond a specific distance from your point of rental). All these things can add substantially to your costs. Request car seats and extras such as GPS or E-ZPass toll tags when you book.

Rates are sometimes—but not always—better if you book in advance or reserve through a rental agency's website, or if you pick up or drop off at an airport. There are other reasons to book ahead, though: for popular destinations (like NYC), during busy times of the year, or to ensure that you get certain types of cars (vans, SUVs, exotic sports cars). ■TIP→ **Make sure that a confirmed reservation guarantees you a car. Agencies sometimes overbook, particularly for busy weekends and holiday periods.**

Rates in New York City average \$80–\$120 a day and \$350–\$500 a week (plus tax) for an economy car with air-conditioning, automatic transmission, and unlimited mileage. Rental costs are lower outside New York City, specifically in such places as Hoboken, New Jersey, and Yonkers, New York. If you already have a membership with a short-term car-rental service like Zipcar, it's likely more convenient and cost-effective for your car needs in the city.

CAR-RENTAL INSURANCE

If you own a car and carry comprehensive car insurance for both collision and liability, your personal auto insurance probably covers a rental, but read your policy's fine print to be sure. If you don't have auto insurance, you should probably buy the collision- or loss-damage waiver (CDW or LDW) from the rental company. This eliminates your liability for damage to the car. Some credit cards offer CDW coverage, but it's usually supplemental to your own insurance and might not cover special vehicles (SUVs, minivans, luxury models, and the like). If your coverage is secondary, you might still be liable for loss-of-use costs from the car-rental company (again, read the fine print). If you're planning on using credit-card insurance, use that card for *all* transactions, from reserving to paying the final bill.

You might also be offered supplemental liability coverage. The car-rental company is required to carry a minimal level of liability coverage insuring all renters, but it might not be enough to cover claims in a

Getting Here and Around

really serious accident if you're at fault. Your own auto-insurance policy should also protect you if you own a car; if you don't, you have to decide whether you are willing to take the risk.

U.S. rental companies sell CDWs and LDWs for $9–$15 per day based on the car's value; supplemental liability is usually about $10.95 per day. The car-rental company might offer you all sorts of other policies, but they're rarely worth the cost. Personal accident insurance, which is basic hospitalization coverage, is an especially egregious rip-off if you already have health insurance.

You can decline insurance from the rental company and purchase it through a third-party provider such as AIG's Travel Guard (🌐 *travelguard.com*).

GASOLINE

Gas stations are few and far between in Manhattan. If you can, fill up at stations outside Manhattan, where prices are generally cheaper (at this writing, the price of regular gas was $3.35 and up in Manhattan). In Manhattan, you can refuel at stations along 10th and 11th Avenues south of West 57th Street and in other locations scattered throughout the island. Some gas stations in New York require you to pump your own gas; others provide attendants (which is always the case in New Jersey).

PARKING

Free parking is virtually impossible to find in Manhattan south of Central Park. If you find a spot on the street, check parking signs carefully, and scour the curb for a faded yellow line indicating a no-parking zone, the bane of every driver's existence. Violators might be towed away or ticketed within minutes. If you do drive, use your car sparingly in Manhattan. If you can't find public parking, pull into a guarded parking garage; note that hourly rates (which can be $40 or more for just two hours) decrease somewhat if a car is left for a significant amount of time. SpotHero (🌐 *spothero.com*) helps you find the cheapest parking-lot options for your visit; search by neighborhood, address, or attraction.

ROAD CONDITIONS

New York City streets are generally in good condition, although there are enough potholes and bad patch jobs to make driving a little rough in some areas, as on sections of 2nd and 3rd Avenues and along Broadway. In neighborhoods like TriBeCa, you may also find extra-bumpy cobblestone roads. Road and bridge repairs seem never-ending, so you might encounter the occasional detour or a bottleneck where a three-lane street narrows to one lane. Many drivers don't slow down for yellow lights here—they (foolishly) speed up to make it through the intersection, sometimes unaware of mounted police cameras that capture their license plates. Heavy rains can cause street flooding in some areas, most notoriously on the Franklin D. Roosevelt Drive (known as the FDR Drive and sometimes as East River Drive), where the heavy traffic can grind to a halt when little lakes suddenly appear on the road.

RULES OF THE ROAD

On city streets, the speed limit is 25 mph, unless otherwise posted. No right turns during red lights are allowed within city limits, unless otherwise posted. Be alert for one-way streets and "no left turn" intersections.

The law requires that front-seat passengers wear seat belts at all times. Children under 16 must wear seat belts in both the front and back seats. Always strap children under age four into approved child-safety seats. It is illegal to use a handheld cell phone while driving in New York State. Police have the right to seize the car of anyone arrested for DWI (driving while intoxicated) in New York City.

Metro/Public Transport

When it comes to getting around New York, you have your pick of transportation in almost any neighborhood you're likely to visit. The subway and bus networks are extensive, especially in Manhattan, although getting across town can take some extra maneuvering. If you're not pressed for time, consider taking a public bus; they are generally slower than subways, but you can also see the city as you travel, and you'll avoid stairs.

Yellow cabs are abundant, except during the evening rush hour, when many drivers' shifts change, and in bad weather, when they get snapped up quickly. If it's late at night or you're outside Manhattan, using a ride-sharing service such as Lyft or Uber may be a good idea. Like a taxi ride, the subway is a true New York City experience; it's also often the quickest way to get around.

Getting Here and Around

However, New York (especially Manhattan) is really a walking town, and depending on the time of day, the weather, and your destination, hoofing it could be the easiest and most enjoyable option.

During the height of weekday rush hours (especially from 7:30 to 9:30 am and 5 to 7 pm), avoid Midtown if you can—subways and streets are jammed, and travel time on buses and taxis can easily double.

Subway and bus fares are $2.90 per ride, payable by tapping on with a contactless device or swiping a MetroCard, a plastic card with a magnetic strip sold mostly at entrance kiosks; buses also accept fares in coins. A Single Ride Ticket (sold only at MetroCard vending machines) is $3.25. Reduced fares are available for senior citizens and people with disabilities, but require an application be submitted for approval for such discounts. Kids under 44 inches ride free with a paying adult.

In 2021, the MTA installed the "OMNY" contactless-payment card readers at all stations and on all buses, enabling riders to pay for a ride by tapping a credit card, smartphone, wearable device, or OMNY card at a subway turnstile or bus entrance. A single OMNY ride costs the same as using a MetroCard, $2.90; and OMNY offers a "weekly fare cap," so once you tap the same card or device for 12 rides within seven days, each subsequent ride is free. (It's the equivalent of buying a $34 seven-day-unlimited MetroCard.) Just use the same card or device for an OMNY-tap transfer between subway and bus, or from one bus to another (free transfers are valid for two hours from your first payment).

The MTA has announced plans to phase MetroCards out altogether in 2024. As of this writing, plenty of New Yorkers still use a refillable one. There is a $1 fee for any new MetroCard purchase, so keep yours to reload as needed—especially if you're taking the subway for your airport transportation; MetroCards can be used for the JFK AirTrain, too. As you swipe the card through a subway turnstile or insert it in a bus's card reader, the cost of the fare is automatically deducted. Free transfers with a MetroCard also work between subway and bus, and from bus to bus (within two hours of first swipe).

MetroCards are sold at most (but not all) subway stations and some stores—look for an "Authorized Sales Agent" sign. The MTA sells two kinds of MetroCards: unlimited-ride and pay-per-ride. Seven-day unlimited-ride MetroCards ($34) allow bus and subway travel for a week; for 30 days it'll cost $132. If you expect to ride more than 12 times in one week, get the seven-day. Unlike in most other cities, there are no single-day unlimited MetroCards.

Unlike unlimited-ride cards, pay-per-ride MetroCards can be shared between riders. (Unlimited-ride MetroCards can be used only once at the same station or bus route in an 18-minute period.)

You can buy or add money to an existing MetroCard at a MetroCard vending machine, available at most subway station entrances (usually near the station booth). The machines accept major credit cards and ATM or debit cards. Many also accept cash, but the maximum amount of change they return is $6, which is doled out in dollar coins.

Subway stations do have cellular access underground.

TIP→ You can download the "MYmta" app for real-time train and bus arrivals, service changes for individual stations and routes, maps, and lots of other transit details—or just visit 🌐 *new.mta.info.*

ACCESSIBILITY

Although the city is working to retrofit subway stations to comply with the ADA, many stations, including major ones, are not yet fully accessible, or have out-of-service elevators. Accessible stations are clearly marked on subway and rail maps; but always check 🌐 *new.mta.info/elevator-escalator-status* before your ride.

For ADA accessibility, most mass-transit riders have better success with public buses, all of which have wheelchair lifts and "kneelers" at the front to facilitate getting on and off. Bus drivers will gladly assist riders with special needs.

BUS

Most city buses in Manhattan follow easy-to-understand routes along the island's street grid. Routes go north and south on the avenues and east and west on the major two-way crosstown streets: 96th, 86th, 79th, 72nd, 66th, 57th, 42nd, 34th, 23rd, and 14th. Bus routes usually operate 24 hours a day, but service is

Getting Here and Around

infrequent late at night. Traffic jams can make rides maddeningly slow, especially along 5th Avenue in Midtown and on the Upper East Side.

Certain bus routes provide express or "limited-stop service" during weekday rush hours, which saves travel time by stopping only at major cross streets and transfer points. A sign posted at the front of the bus indicates limited service; ask the driver whether the bus stops near where you want to go before boarding.

To find a bus stop, look for a light-blue sign (green for a "limited" bus, which skips more stops) on a green pole; bus numbers and routes are listed, with the stop's name underneath.

Bus fare is the same as subway fare: $2.90. Tap to pay when you board, insert your MetroCard into the reader, or use exact change in coins (no pennies, no dollar bills, and no change is given).

MetroCards allow you one free transfer between buses or from bus to subway; when using coins on the bus, you can ask the driver for a free transfer coupon, good for one change to an intersecting bus route. Legal transfer points are listed on the back of the slip. Transfers generally have time limits of two hours.

Several routes in the city now have so-called Select Bus Service (SBS) rather than limited-stop service. These routes include those along 1st and 2nd Avenues and 34th Street in Manhattan, as well as the M60, which travels between LaGuardia Airport and 125th Street in Harlem. The buses, which are distinguished from normal city buses by signs identifying the bus as SBS on the front, make fewer stops.

In addition, SBS riders must pay the fare before boarding with either a MetroCard or coins (but not pennies) at a machine mounted on the street. The machine prints out a receipt. This receipt is the only proof of payment, so be sure to hold on to it for your entire trip, or risk a fine for fare evasion. Some buses have OMNY readers on board, allowing you to just tap on the reader instead.

Bus route maps and schedules are posted at many bus stops in Manhattan, major stops throughout the other boroughs, and at 🌐 *new.mta.info*. Each of the five boroughs of New York has a separate bus map; they're available from some subway-station booths, but rarely on buses. The best places to obtain them are the information kiosks in Grand Central Terminal and Penn Station, and on the MTA website.

Most buses that travel outside the city depart from the Port Authority Bus Terminal, on 8th Avenue between 40th and 42nd Streets. You must purchase your ticket at each individual company's website or ticket counter, not from the bus driver, so give yourself enough time to wait in line if buying in person. The terminal is connected to the subway (A, C, E, N, Q, R, S, W, 1, 2, 3, and 7 lines), which offers direct travel on to Penn Station, Grand Central Terminal, and more. Several bus lines serving northern New Jersey and Rockland County, New York, make daily stops at the George Washington Bridge Bus Station from 5 am to 1 am. The station is connected to the 175th Street station on the A line of the subway, which travels down the west side of Manhattan.

A variety of discount bus services, including FlixBus and Megabus, run direct routes to and from cities including Philadelphia, Boston, and Washington, D.C., with the majority of destinations along the East Coast. These budget options, priced from as little as $10 one-way (sometimes even less, if you book well in advance), depart from locations throughout the city and can be more convenient than traditional bus services.

SUBWAY

The subway system operates on more than 840 miles of track 24 hours a day and serves nearly all the places you're likely to visit. It's cheaper than a cab, and, during the workweek, it's often faster than either taxis or buses. The trains are well lighted and air-conditioned. Still, the New York subway is hardly problem-free. Many trains are crowded, the older ones are noisy, the air-conditioning can break, and platforms can be dingy and smelly. Panhandlers and buskers head there for a captive audience and people without homes sometimes take refuge by riding the trains. Police presence has recently stepped up, especially at major stations; should you need to report an incident, look for NYPD officers patrolling the platform or stationed near turnstiles. Although trains usually run frequently, especially during rush hours, you never know when an incident somewhere on the line will stall traffic. In addition, subway construction sometimes causes delays or limitation of service, especially on weekends and after 10 pm on weekdays.

Getting Here and Around

You can transfer between subway lines an unlimited number of times at any of the numerous stations where lines intersect. You also can transfer to intersecting MTA bus routes for free (within two hours) with your MetroCard or with the OMNY contactless system—just tap with the same card or device.

Most subway entrances are at street corners and marked by lampposts with an illuminated Metropolitan Transportation Authority (MTA) logo or globe-shape green or red lights—green means the station is open 24 hours and red means the station closes at night (though the colors don't always correspond to reality). Subway lines are designated by numbers and letters, such as the 3 line or the A line. Some lines run "express" and skip stops, and others are "local" and make all stops. Each station entrance has a sign indicating the lines that run through the station. Some entrances are also marked "uptown only" or "downtown only." Before entering subway stations, read the signs carefully. One of the easiest mistakes to make is taking the right train in the wrong direction.

Maps of the full subway system are posted in the middle of every train car and usually on the subway platform; and at 🌐 *map.mta.info*. You can usually pick up free paper maps at station booths. In the 2010s, the MTA installed new electronics in stations, including countdown clocks (usually on platforms), digital maps, and, of course, video advertisements. On some platforms, you might even find interactive touchscreen maps and service kiosks. Since 2017, subway stations have cellular service.

For the most up-to-date information on subway lines, call the MTA's Travel Information line (dial ☎ *511* and say "service status") or visit its website (🌐 *new.mta.info*). Alternatively, ask a station agent or a local commuter.

 Ride-Sharing

Rideshare apps like Lyft and Uber are booming in NYC. These services tend to be more convenient and sometimes cheaper than a yellow taxi, but not always. Most of the services offer a carpool or walk-to-pickup option that allows passengers to share rides at a discounted fare. But when "surge pricing" is in effect (during rush hour, when it's raining, or at other high-demand times), rideshare rates can skyrocket. At least the apps share your set rate before you book.

Payment and tipping (if applicable) are also done via the apps. Unlike in some other cities, only licensed livery drivers are allowed to work for the rideshare companies in New York City (hence the sometimes higher rates). Thanks to a partnership that debuted in 2022, riders can also use the Uber app to "e-hail" a yellow taxi, with standard app prices; the taxi option appears at the bottom of results, under "More."

Taxi

Yellow taxis are almost everywhere in Manhattan, cruising the streets looking for fares. You'll know a cab is available when its rooftop lights are lit, meaning the driver is ready to take passengers. They are usually easy to hail on the street or from a cabstand in front of major hotels and transit hubs, though finding one at rush hour or in the rain can take some time (and assertiveness).

Riders can also "e-hail" and pay for a yellow taxi using the Curb taxi app or Uber (after agreeing to standard Uber rates and policies, including surge prices). Of course, there are other rideshare apps like Lyft to choose from; just avoid accepting a ride from an unmarked taxicab (these are unlicensed), which could put you (or at least your wallet) at risk.

Official NYC yellow taxis always have numbered aluminum medallions bolted to their hoods. By law, NYC cabs are required to take passengers to any location in the five boroughs as well as Newark Airport and two adjoining counties, although only NYC and Newark locations are metered. Once the meter is engaged (off-meter rates are prohibited; even JFK and out-of-town "flat" fares must be recorded by the meter for the passenger's protection), the fare is $3 just for entering the vehicle, which includes the first 1/5 mile, and 70¢ for each unit thereafter.

A unit is defined as either 1/5 mile when the cab's cruising at 12 mph or faster or as 60 seconds when the cab is either not moving or moving at less than 12 mph. New York State

Getting Here and Around

adds 50¢ to each cab ride. There's also a $1 night surcharge added between 8 pm and 6 am, a $2.50 rush-hour surcharge tacked on between 4 pm and 8 pm on weekdays, and a congestion surcharge of $2.50 for rides below 96th Street in Manhattan. Lastly, there is also a $1 "improvement surcharge" for all rides.

All taxi drivers are required to accept credit cards as payment. Fares can be paid directly through the Curb app by tapping the "Pair & Pay" button once inside the cab and entering the 7-digit code that appears on the screen in the backseat. On rare occasions, some who prefer cash claim their machines are broken when that isn't actually the case. If a driver waits until the end of the ride to mention a broken machine and you want to pay by credit card, you can ask the driver to *turn off the meter* and drive you to an ATM to see if the meter is truly broken.

One taxi can hold a maximum of four passengers (an additional passenger under the age of seven is allowed if the child sits on someone's lap). You must pay any bridge or tunnel tolls incurred during your trip (they are automatically added to the meter). In order to keep things moving quickly, all taxi drivers are required to use an E-ZPass in their cabs to automatically pay tolls, and they must pass the discounted toll rate along to the passenger; the total toll amount is added to the final fare. Taxi drivers expect a 10%–20% tip, which should be awarded for safe driving and good service.

Before you hail a cab, it's best to know where you want to go and generally how to get there; or at least be able to share the cross streets of your destination (for instance, "5th Avenue and 42nd Street").

Also, speak simply and clearly to make sure the driver has heard you correctly—few are native English speakers, so try to confirm that your destination was understood. If headed for a far-flung location in Brooklyn or Queens, consider pulling up the location on a smartphone app to track your route.

When you leave the cab, always take your receipt. It includes the cab's medallion number, which can help you find the cabbie if you forget something in the cab (or to share a taxi complaint or compliment with the city's 311 service). Your receipt also will itemize charges (for tolls, etc.), letting you double-check your ride total.

Yellow taxis can be difficult to find in parts of Brooklyn, Queens, the Bronx, and Staten Island. To help with this issue, in 2013 the city of New York created a new class of taxi service: apple-green Boro Taxis, which act like yellow taxis. They charge the same metered rates, accept credit cards, and must take you to any location within the city of New York. The difference is that green taxis are only allowed to pick up fares in non-Manhattan boroughs and in Manhattan locations above 96th Street.

If you're outside Manhattan and can't find a yellow or green taxi, and don't wish to use Curb or Uber apps for e-hailing NYC taxis, it might be more convenient and less expensive to call a car service. Locals and staff at restaurants and other public places can often recommend a reliable company that's headquartered in a particular neighborhood or borough. For example, Arecibo Car Service offers low rates from Brooklyn to any of NYC's airports. Most services offer flat-rate fares, but always confirm the fee when calling for the ride; a 10%–20% tip is customary.

Train

⇨ *For information about the subway, see Metro/Public Transport.*

Metro-North Railroad trains take passengers from Grand Central Station to points north of New York City, both in New York State and Connecticut. Amtrak trains mainly use spacious Moynihan Train Hall, the 2021 extension of the labyrinthine Penn Station. The Long Island Rail Road (LIRR) connects New York City with points in Long Island from Penn Station and Grand Central Station. To reach most parts of New Jersey, board New Jersey Transit (NJT) trains from Penn Station. Alternatively, New Jersey commuter PATH trains offer service to Newark, Jersey City, Harrison, and Hoboken; the main Manhattan PATH stations are located at 33rd Street and the World Trade Center. Each individual train line provides its own information; for Metro-North and LIRR visit 🌐 *new.mta.info.*

Essentials

Activities

BASEBALL

New York City is a baseball town, and many travelers will want to see a game if they come during the season. You can usually get seats for any game except a major draw (a match-up between the Yankees and Mets, for instance) or a major playoff game if you are willing to sit in the cheap seats. Public transit gets you directly to the stadiums of both New York–area major-league teams, as well as to the city's minor-league stadiums.

Brooklyn Cyclones
BASEBALL & SOFTBALL | FAMILY
The Mets-affiliated minor-league Brooklyn Cyclones are named for Coney Island's famous wooden roller coaster. They play 38 home games at Maimonides Park, next to the boardwalk, with views of the Atlantic Ocean over the right-field wall and Luna Park amusement park over the left-field wall. Most people make a day of it, with time at the beach and amusement rides before an evening game. Take the D, F, N, or Q subway to the Coney Island–Stillwell Avenue Station, and walk one block to the right of the original Nathan's Famous hot dog stand. ✉ *Maimonides Park, 1904 Surf Ave., at 19th St., Coney Island* ☎ *718/372–5596* 🌐 *www.milb.com/brooklyn* Ⓜ *D, F, N, Q to Coney Island–Stillwell Ave.*

New York Mets
BASEBALL & SOFTBALL | FAMILY
The New York Mets play at Citi Field, at the next-to-last stop on the 7 train in Queens. ✉ *Citi Field, 123–01 Roosevelt Ave., at 126th St. and Roosevelt Ave., Flushing* ☎ *718/507–8499* 🌐 *www.mlb.com/mets* Ⓜ *7 to Mets–Willets Point.*

New York Yankees
BASEBALL & SOFTBALL | FAMILY
The Yankees defend their turf at Yankee Stadium in the Bronx, accessible via the B, D, and 4 trains. ✉ *Yankee Stadium, 1 E. 161st St., at River Ave., Bronx* ☎ *718/293–6000* 🌐 *www.mlb.com/yankees* Ⓜ *4, B, D to 161st St.–Yankee Stadium.*

Staten Island FerryHawks
BASEBALL & SOFTBALL | FAMILY
For a fun, family-oriented experience, check out the Staten Island FerryHawks. The stadium, a five-minute walk from the Staten Island Ferry terminal, has magnificent views of Lower Manhattan and the Statue of Liberty. ✉ *Richmond County Bank Ballpark, 75 Richmond Terr., St. George* ☎ *929/594–2957* 🌐 *www.ferryhawks.com* Ⓜ *Staten Island Ferry.*

BASKETBALL

The men's basketball season runs from late October through April. New York City has two NBA teams, the Brooklyn Nets and the New York Knicks, as well as a WNBA team, the New York Liberty.

Brooklyn Nets

BASKETBALL | FAMILY | The Brooklyn Nets play just across the East River from Manhattan, in Brooklyn's Barclays Center. The stadium is easily reachable by numerous subway lines (there are nine at the center itself) and the LIRR. ✉ *Barclays Center, 620 Atlantic Ave., at Flatbush Ave., Prospect Heights* ☏ *917/618–6700 for box office* 🌐 *www.nba.com/nets* Ⓜ *2, 3, 4, 5, B, D, N, Q, R to Atlantic Ave.–Barclays Center.*

New York Knicks

BASKETBALL | FAMILY | The New York Knicks arouse intense hometown passions, which means tickets for home games at Madison Square Garden are hard to come by even when the team is not playing as well as it should. **■ TIP→ Try Stub-Hub to score tickets.** ✉ *Madison Square Garden, 4 Pennsylvania Plaza, between 31st and 33rd Sts. and between 7th and 8th Aves., Midtown West* ☏ *212/465–5867* 🌐 *www.nba.com/knicks* Ⓜ *1, 2, 3, A, C, E to 34th St.–Penn Station.*

New York Liberty

BASKETBALL | FAMILY | The team, a member of the WNBA (Women's National Basketball Association), had its first season in 1997. The season runs from May through September, with home games played at Barclays Center in Brooklyn. ✉ *Barclays Center, 620 Atlantic Ave., at Flatbush Ave., Prospect Heights* ☏ *212/564–9266 for tickets* 🌐 *liberty.wnba.com* Ⓜ *2, 3, 4, 5, B, D, N, Q, R to Atlantic Ave.–Barclays Center.*

BICYCLING

Bicycling the streets of Manhattan and the outer boroughs skyrocketed in popularity in recent years. City government and biking organizations have helped make it safer, and drivers and pedestrians are more alert to cyclists sharing NYC streets, whether in bike lanes or sharing pavement. Still, vehicular traffic volumes are sky-high on weekdays, and drivers can be pushy or downright threatening—so it's best to take to a bike only if you're a seasoned big-city cyclist. Check the NYC Department of Transportation's website for a cycling map that shows the best routes and roads with designated bike lanes, as well as local road rules, including for taking a bike on public transit (🌐 *www.nyc.gov/bikes*). Google Maps offers a bike-route navigation option for New York, too, using bike lanes as much as possible.

For biking under more controlled conditions, head to New York's major parks. Central Park has a 6-mile circular drive with a couple of climbs. The park's roadways are closed to most car traffic, making cycling here particularly appealing.

Beware of renting a bike from the many illegal vendors that hang out on the streets near Central Park, especially by Columbus Circle. It's usually better to rent from a business with an actual storefront; there are a number of reputable bike shops within a few blocks of the park. Most bike-rental stores have copies of the very handy official NYC Bike Map, which is published annually and shows traffic flow and bike lanes for all of New York City.

The busy bike lane along the Hudson River Park's esplanade parallels the waterfront from West 59th Street south to the esplanade of Battery Park City. Rentals are available within the linear park. The lane also heads north, connecting with the bike path in Riverside Park and the esplanade between West 72nd and West 100th Streets, continuing all the way to the George Washington Bridge. From Battery Park it's a quick ride up to the Wall Street area, which is relatively deserted on weekends, and over to the bike lane along the East River.

The 3.3-mile circular drive in Brooklyn's Prospect Park is closed to cars year-round. It has a long, gradual hill that tops off near the Grand Army Plaza entrance.

Toga Bike Shop

BIKING | This established bike shop also offers rentals near Lincoln Center. ✉ *110 West End Ave., at 64th St., Upper West Side* ☎ *212/799–9625* 🌐 *www.togabikes.com* Ⓜ *1 to 66th St.–Lincoln Center.*

Unlimited Biking

BIKING | The company rents bikes (pedal and electric) and in-line skates and offers biking and walking tours. ✉ *Multiple locations, New York* ☎ *212/749–4444* 🌐 *www.unlimitedbiking.com/new-york.*

CITI BIKE BICYCLE SHARE

New York's bike-sharing program debuted in 2013 with hundreds of stations, the majority in Manhattan south of Central Park and northern Brooklyn; hundreds more have rolled out since then, with expansions covering most of Manhattan, much of Brooklyn, Long Island City and Astoria in Queens, and even Jersey City. The three-speed, 40-pound, bright-blue bikes are outfitted with automatic lights, plus a front rack and bungee cord to secure small items. When they're available, you'll find electric bikes at docks, too; they gently motor-assist your pedaling, and come with a nominal surcharge. Citi Bikes don't come with helmets—they're recommended but not mandatory.

A single ride costs $4.79 for a regular bike (an e-bike costs 30¢ more per minute), paid via either the Citi Bike or Lyft rideshare app, or with a credit card at the bike-dock kiosk; you can keep the bike out for 30 minutes, after which you'll be charged 30¢ per minute. Alternately, you can pay $19 for a 24-hour, unlimited-ride pass, or $205 for an annual Citi Bike membership. Both limit your time to 30 and 45 minutes, respectively; additional per-minute charges are added to your credit card for keeping a bike out longer. Another option is simply docking one bike, then unlocking another (even from the same dock). A lost bike costs $1,200 (plus tax), so never leave it parked anywhere but a dock.

Before you pull a bike from one of the bays and start the 30-minute clock, spend a little time planning your route. Citi Bike's website (🌐 *www.citibikenyc.com*) and app are helpful, because they show the best routes to destinations, which of the computerized outdoor stations have bikes or e-bikes available, and—just as important—which have empty docks available for your returned bike.

Citi Bike

BIKING | The Citi Bike website and app help locate nearby bike stations and availability, as well as the best routes to reach destinations. ✉ *New York* ☎ *855/245–3311 for customer service* 🌐 *www.citibikenyc.com.*

BOATING, KAYAKING, AND PADDLEBOARDING

Central Park Boathouse

BOATING | **FAMILY** | Central Park has rowboats on the 22-acre Central Park Lake. Rent your own, which holds up to four people, at the Boathouse, near East 74th Street, from April through November ($25 an hour, paid with card or Apple Pay.) Children must be at least 3 feet tall. ✉ *East side of Central Park between 74th and 75th Sts., Central Park* ☎ *212/517–2233* 🌐 *www.thecentralparkboathouse.com/boats.php* Ⓜ *6 to 77th St.; Q to 72nd St.*

Downtown Boathouse

BOATING | The Downtown Boathouse, at Pier 26 in TriBeCa, offers free kayaks with instruction and all necessary equipment. The season runs from late May to early October, but it's strictly first-come, first-served. ✉ *Pier 26 Boathouse, near N. Moore St. at the Hudson River, TriBeCa* 🌐 *www.downtownboathouse.org* Ⓜ *1 to Franklin St.; A, C, E to Canal St.*

Manhattan Community Boathouse

BOATING | **FAMILY** | Operated by Manhattan Community Boathouse, the Pier 96 Boathouse in Midtown West is where you can take a sturdy kayak out for a free paddle from June through early October. The kayaking program is suitable for people of all ages and abilities; kayaks, paddles, life jackets, and basic instruction are provided. All participants must sign a liability waiver and know how to swim; make your free reservation online in advance. ✉ *56th St. at the Hudson River, Midtown West* 🌐 *www.manhattancommunityboathouse.org* Ⓜ *1, A, B, C, D to 59th St.–Columbus Circle.*

Manhattan Kayak + SUP

BOATING | The company gives kayak and stand-up paddleboarding (SUP) lessons for all levels and runs trips on the Hudson River between May and October, including a fun Night Kayak Tour. ✉ *Pier 84, 555 12th Ave., at 44th St., Midtown West* ☎ *212/924–1788* 🌐 *www.manhattankayak.com* Ⓜ *A, C, E to 42nd St.–Port Authority.*

ICE-SKATING

There are many opportunities for ice-skating during the season (and year-round at Chelsea Piers). Among many public and private rinks across NYC, Central Park has two, both open from late October through early April, including the beautifully situated Wollman Rink, which has skating until long after dark beneath the lights of the city. Skate rentals are available at all rinks.

Lasker Rink

ICE-SKATING | **FAMILY** | The Lasker Rink, at the north end of Central Park, is usually less crowded than Wollman. (As of this writing, the rink is closed for renovation until winter 2024 and will become part of a new complex called Harlem Meer Center, along with Lasker Pool.) ✉ *Midpark near 106th St., Upper West Side* ☎ *212/310–6600* 🌐 *www.centralpark.com* Ⓜ *B, C to Cathedral Pkwy.–110th St.; 2, 3 to Central Park North–110th St.*

LeFrak Center at Lakeside Prospect Park

ICE-SKATING | **FAMILY** | In Brooklyn, the beautiful LeFrak Center at Lakeside Prospect Park offers seasonal skating, though it's a bit of a hike from the nearest subway stations. ✉ *171 East Dr., southeast corner of Prospect Park, Prospect Park* ☎ *718/462–0010*

⊕ lakesidebrooklyn.com Ⓜ Q to Parkside Ave.; B, S to Prospect Park.

The Rink at Rockefeller Center

ICE-SKATING | FAMILY | The outdoor rink in Rockefeller Center, open from early November to late March, is much smaller in real life than it appears on TV and in movies—though it is as beautiful, especially when Rock Center's enormous Christmas tree towers above it. Timed tickets can be booked via the website and are recommended—especially around the holidays. *⇨ Find more rink and pricing details in the Midtown West chapter. ✉ 30 Rockefeller Plaza, between 49th and 50th Sts., lower plaza, Midtown West ☎ 212/771–7200 ⊕ www.rockefellercenter.com Ⓜ B, D, F, M to 47th–50th Sts./Rockefeller Center.*

The Rink at Winter Village at Bryant Park

ICE-SKATING | The rink at the Winter Village in Bryant Park has "free" skating, although there are rental fees for skates and lockers. *⇨ Find more rink info in the Midtown West chapter. ✉ 476 5th Ave., between 40th and 42nd Sts. (closer to 6th Ave.), Midtown West ☎ 917/438–5174 ⊕ bryantpark.org Ⓜ B, D, F, M to 42nd St.–Bryant Park.*

Sky Rink at Chelsea Piers

ICE-SKATING | FAMILY | The Chelsea Piers Sky Rink has two year-round indoor rinks overlooking the Hudson River. *✉ Pier 61, W. 21st St., at the Hudson River, Chelsea ☎ 212/336–6100 ⊕ www.chelseapiers.com Ⓜ C, E to 23rd St.*

Wollman Skating Rink

ICE-SKATING | FAMILY | One of two ice-skating rinks in Central Park, Wollman is more easily accessible at the southeast corner of the park. Be prepared for daytime crowds, especially on weekends. *✉ North of 6th Ave. and Central Park S entrance, between 62nd and 63rd Sts., Central Park ☎ 833/615–3500 ⊕ www.wollmanrinknyc.com Ⓜ 1, A, B, C, D to 59th St.–Columbus Circle; N, R, W to 5th Ave./59th St.; F to 57th St.*

Dining

Ready to take a bite out of New York? Bring your appetite. In a city where creativity is expressed in innumerable ways, the food scene takes center stage, with literally thousands of chances to taste the countless flavors of Gotham. Whether lining up at street stands, gobbling down legendary deli and diner grub, or chasing a coveted

Essentials

reservation at the latest celebrity-chef venue, New Yorkers are a demanding yet appreciative audience.

Every neighborhood offers temptations high, low, and in between, meaning there's truly something for every taste, whim, and budget. No matter how you approach dining out here, it's hard to go wrong. Planning a day of shopping among the glittering flagship boutiques along 5th and Madison Avenues? Stop into one of the Upper East Side's storied restaurants for a repast among the "ladies who lunch." Clubbing in the Meatpacking District? Tuck into a meal at eateries as trendy as their patrons. Craving authentic global fare? From food trucks to hidden joints, there are almost more choices than there are appetites. Recent years have also seen entire food categories, from ramen to meatballs to doughnuts, riffed upon and fetishized, and at many restaurants you find an almost religious reverence for seasonal, locally sourced cuisine.

And don't forget—New York is still home to more celebrity chefs than any other city. Your chances of running into your favorite cookbook author, Food Network celeb, or paparazzi-friendly chef are high, adding even more star wattage to a restaurant scene with an already through-the-roof glamour quotient. The pandemic also introduced outdoor dining—a trend that appears here to stay. Newfound economic realities, however, have revived appreciation for value, meaning you can tap into wallet-friendly choices at every level of the food chain. Rest assured, this city does its part to satisfy your cravings and curiosity.

CHECK BEFORE YOU GO

The nature of the restaurant industry means that places open and close in a New York minute. It's always a good idea to phone ahead and make sure your restaurant is still turning tables.

CHILDREN

Although it's unusual to see children in the dining rooms of Manhattan's most elite restaurants, dining with youngsters in New York does not have to mean culinary exile. Many of the restaurants reviewed here are excellent choices for families and are marked as such.

HOURS

New Yorkers seem ready to eat at any hour. Many restaurants stay open between lunch and dinner, some have late-night seating, and still others serve around the clock. Restaurants that serve breakfast often do so until noon or later. Restaurants in the East Village, Lower East Side, SoHo, TriBeCa, and Greenwich Village are likely to remain open late, whereas Midtown spots and those in the Theater and Financial districts and uptown generally close earlier. Unless otherwise noted, the restaurants listed are open daily for lunch and dinner.

PRICES

⇨ *Restaurant reviews have been shortened. For full information, see Fodors.com. Restaurant prices are the average cost of a main course at dinner or, if dinner is not served, at lunch.*

What It Costs in U.S. Dollars

$	$$	$$$	$$$$
RESTAURANTS			
under $15	$15–$29	$30–$40	over $40

Be sure to ask the price of the daily specials recited by the waiter; the charge for specials at some restaurants is noticeably out of line with the other prices on the menu. Beware of the $10 bottle of water; ask for tap water instead (NYC has high-quality tap water), and always review your bill.

If you eat early or late, you might be able to take advantage of a prix-fixe (fixed-price) deal not offered at peak hours. Most upscale restaurants have great lunch deals.

Credit cards are widely accepted, but many restaurants (particularly smaller ones downtown) accept only cash. If you plan to use a credit card, it's a good idea to confirm that it is acceptable when making reservations or before sitting down to eat.

RESERVATIONS

It's always a good idea to plan ahead, and to make a reservation if you can. Some renowned restaurants are booked weeks or even months in advance. If that's the case, you can get lucky at the last minute if you're flexible—and friendly. Most restaurants keep a few tables open for walk-ins and VIPs. Show up for dinner early (5:30) or late (after 10), and politely inquire about any last-minute vacancies or cancellations.

Occasionally, an eatery may take your credit-card number and ask you to call the day before your scheduled meal to reconfirm: don't forget or you could lose out, or possibly be charged for your oversight.

SMOKING

Smoking is prohibited in all enclosed public spaces in New York City, including restaurants and bars; some bars do have small dedicated outdoor smoking areas. (And a small handful of long-standing cigar and smoking lounges still remain.)

TIPPING AND TAXES

In most restaurants, tip the server at least 15%–20%. (To figure out a 20% tip quickly, just move the decimal point one place to the left on your total and double that amount.) Tip at least $1 per drink at the bar, and $1 for each coat checked. Never tip the maître d' unless you're out to impress your guests or expect to pay another visit soon. Your restaurant bill will include a charge for a meal tax of 8.875%. You'll win your server's gratitude by tipping in cash, even if you pay the bill by card.

WHAT TO WEAR

New Yorkers like to dress up, and so should you. Whatever your style, dial it up a notch. Have some fun while you're at it. Pull out the clothes you've been saving for a special occasion and get glamorous. Unfair as it is, the way you look can influence how you're treated—and where you're seated. Generally speaking, jeans and a button-down shirt suffice at most table-service restaurants in the $ to $$ range. Few places require a jacket or jacket and tie, or ban sneakers and jeans, but if you have doubts, call the restaurant and ask.

Disabilities and Accessibility

New York has come a long way in making life easier for people with disabilities. Around the city, New Yorkers welcome visitors with special needs with improvements from audio-amplified crosswalks and braille provided in more locations to larger yellow cabs with easier doors and American sign-language interpreters at some events and performances. At most street corners, curb cuts allow wheelchairs to roll along unimpeded. Many restaurants, shops, and movie theaters with step-up entrances have wheelchair ramps. Though some New Yorkers might rush past those in need of assistance, you'll find plenty of people who are more than happy to help you get around.

New York City Tourism + Conventions' website (🌐 *nyctourism.com*) has information on the accessibility of many landmarks and attractions in a free downloadable guide. The NYC Mayor's Office for People with Disabilities is another great resource outlining accessibility throughout the city. If you need to rent a wheelchair or scooter while in New York, Scootaround will deliver it to your hotel (or wherever you're staying); reservations can be made up to a year in advance.

SIGHTS AND ATTRACTIONS

Most public facilities in New York City, whether museums, parks, or theaters, are wheelchair-accessible. Some attractions have special programs for people with mobility, visual, hearing, or cognitive disabilities.

TRANSPORTATION

Although the city is working to retrofit transport stations to comply with the ADA, not all stations, including many major ones, are accessible, and they are unlikely to be so in the near future. Accessible stations are clearly marked on subway and rail maps; just be aware that elevator and escalator outages can happen without any posted notices (see 🌐 *new.mta.info/elevator-escalator-status* for current outages). Visitors in wheelchairs have better success with public buses, all of which have wheelchair lifts and "kneelers" at the front to facilitate getting on and off. Bus drivers provide assistance.

Reduced fares are available to passengers with disabilities, but you'll need to apply for a Reduced-Fare MetroCard in advance of your visit. Visitors to the city are also eligible for the same Access-a-Ride program benefits as New York City residents (🌐 *new.mta.info*). Drivers with disabilities can use windshield cards from their own state or Canadian province to park in designated handicapped spaces.

Health and Safety

In 2024, the only real reminder of COVID-19 in New York is the occasional sight of someone wearing a mask on the subway, while shopping, or at the theater. You won't be asked for proof of vaccination anywhere. Even so, anyone can still get COVID: if you feel you might be coming down with it, most pharmacies still sell tests and many local libraries give them out for free in flu season, no questions asked. In case your travel is curtailed abruptly, consider buying trip insurance. Just be sure to read the fine print: many travel-insurance policies don't cover COVID-related cancellations these days.

NYC has statistically been one of the safer big U.S. cities over the years. A spike in crime in 2021 prompted an increased police presence and foot patrols on subways, streets, and landmarks. While incidents have subsequently decreased, unsuspecting tourists remain particularly easy marks for pickpockets and hustlers.

Essentials

Ignore the panhandlers on the streets and subways, along with people who offer to hail you a cab (like outside Penn Station, the Port Authority, and Grand Central), and limousine and "gypsy-cab" drivers who (illegally) offer you a ride.

Keep jewelry out of sight on the street; better yet, lock valuables and your passport in your hotel safe. Don't carry wallets, smartphones, or other gadgets in your back pockets and make sure bags and purses stay closed and close by.

Avoid deserted blocks in unfamiliar neighborhoods. A brisk, purposeful pace helps deter trouble wherever you go. Don't wear headphones on the street.

The subway runs around the clock and is generally well trafficked until midnight (and until at least 2 am on Friday and Saturday night). Watch out for shady characters lurking around the inside or outside of stations and bus shelters. As crime and homelessness have become more prominent on the MTA, NYPD police have been stationed either on the platform, near the entrance, or both. Take care when you ride and splurge for a taxi or rideshare late at night.

When waiting for a train, stand far away from its edge, especially when trains are entering or leaving the station. Once the train pulls into the station, avoid empty cars. While on the train, don't engage in verbal exchanges with aggressive riders. If a fellow passenger makes you nervous while on the train, trust your instincts and change cars. When disembarking, stick with the crowd until you reach the street.

Some NYPD security measures implemented following the September 11, 2001, terrorist attacks are still in place. Never leave any bags unattended, and expect to have yourself and your possessions inspected thoroughly in such places as airports, sports stadiums, commercial buildings, transit entrances, and museums.

Travelers Aid International helps stranded travelers, airport passengers, and unaccompanied children, and works closely with the police and other social service agencies.

■ TIP→ **Distribute your cash, credit cards, IDs, and other valuables between a deep front pocket, an inside jacket or vest pocket, and a hidden money pouch.**

LGBTQ+

The City of New York is among the world's most diverse and welcoming communities. It's also home to the Stonewall National Monument in Greenwich Village, America's sole national monument commemorating the gay, lesbian, bisexual, transgender, and queer civil-rights movements. LGBTQ+ visitors can feel right at home in Manhattan and across the city. Hell's Kitchen, Chelsea, and the East Village are some of the most prominently out-and-proud neighborhoods, but Brooklyn and Queens (along with a few spots in the Bronx and Staten Island) all have their own LGBTQ+ communities and gathering places. In fact, Brooklyn neighborhoods like Park Slope, Williamsburg, and Bushwick, and Queens's Astoria and Jackson Heights, are go-to "gayborhoods" for queer New Yorkers.

NYC Pride is the world's oldest and among the largest LGBTQ+ pride celebrations, with a long lead-up of activities that culminate in the march, held the last Sunday in June. Over the prior weekends, each of the four outer boroughs holds its own pride parade and festival.

The Center (🌐 *gaycenter.org*) is New York's LGBTQ+ community center, located on West 13th Street in Greenwich Village and open to visitors 365 days a year. The always-active Center offers educational programs as well as health and support services and hosts art and social events for the LGBTQ+ community (in addition to its own prized art collection). Other cultural stops include the feminist, queer-friendly bookstore and community space Bluestockings Cooperative on Suffolk Street in the Lower East Side, which hosts diverse readings and performances. In addition to Manhattan's merry sing-along piano bars and drag showcases, Joe's Pub at the Public hosts fabulous cabarets with an array of LGBTQ+ luminaries. In SoHo, the Leslie-Lohman Museum of Art exhibits one of the world's best collections of fine (and often risqué) genre art in its spacious galleries.

PUBLICATIONS

New York is strong on LGBTQ+ culture and nightlife—some say it's the best in the world. For current listings of LGBT goings-on, pick up a copy of the weekly *Time Out New York* magazine, monthly lesbian-centric *GO* magazine, and biweekly newspaper *Gay City News*, or check out each one's latest updates online.

Essentials

 Lodging

There are more hotel rooms than ever in New York City, not only in Manhattan but also in Brooklyn (especially downtown and Williamsburg), Queens (especially Long Island City), and more distant outer-borough neighborhoods. But does that mean that New York is cheap? Not really, but you can still find sweet deals, especially if you're not set on a specific property or neighborhood, and if you don't mind a few extra minutes of commuting time.

Hotels continue to slash rates based on market sensitivity—especially if you and all of those other Internet-savvy shoppers are willing to either plan far in advance or wait until the last minute. But if you want to stay in a specific place, and the rate seems reasonable, book it—it's just as likely to go up, especially during peak seasons (spring and fall).

How to choose? The first thing to consider is location.

Many New York City visitors focus on staying in the hectic Midtown area—and bargains can be had there—but other neighborhoods are often just as convenient. Less touristy areas, such as Gramercy, the Lower East Side, the Upper West Side, and Brooklyn, invite genuine local perspectives of New York life, too.

Also consider timing: the least expensive months to book rooms in the city are January and February. If you're flexible on dates, compare room rates during your preferred traveling month (and even call the hotel directly)—that way you can avoid peak dates, like Fashion Week and the New York City Marathon. Be sure to ask about possible weekend packages that could include a third night free. (The Financial District in particular can be a discount gold mine on weekends.)

Another source of bargains? Chain hotels. Many have moved into the city and charge reasonable room rates. In addition to favorites like the Marriott, Hilton, and Hyatt brands, there are Best Westerns, Days Inns, and Comfort Inns. The rates for such properties aren't as low as you find outside Manhattan, but they're certainly getting closer.

ACCESSIBILITY

Despite the Americans with Disabilities Act (ADA), the level of accessibility seems to differ from hotel to hotel. Some properties might be accessible by ADA standards for people with mobility disabilities, but not for people with hearing or vision impairments, for example.

If you have a hearing impairment, check whether the hotel has devices to alert you visually to the ring of the telephone, a knock at the door, and a fire/emergency alarm.

If you're bringing a service dog, you're not required to let the hotel staff know ahead of time (they must accommodate your service animal regardless); however, you might wish to notify them in advance as a courtesy and to square away any necessary details.

DOES SIZE MATTER?

If room size is important to you, ask how many square feet a room has, not just if it's big. A hotel room in New York is considered large if it's 500 square feet. Very large rooms are 600 square feet. To stay anywhere larger, book a multiroom suite. Small rooms are a tight 150–200 square feet, sometimes less.

FAMILY TRAVEL

New York has gone to great lengths to attract family vacationers, and hotels have followed the family-friendly trend. Some properties provide such diversions as in-room video games. Most full-service Manhattan hotels provide babysitting and stroller rental, but be sure to make these arrangements when booking, not when you arrive.

New York City hotel rooms are smaller than average, and some might not accommodate roll-away beds even though many hotels offer them. Most hotel rooms in New York City have a maximum number of legal occupants, so check with the hotel instead of making assumptions.

NEED A RESERVATION?

Hotel reservations are a necessity when planning your trip to New York. Competition for clients also means properties must undergo frequent improvements, so when booking, ask about any current or upcoming renovations, lest you get a room within earshot of noisy construction, or end up temporarily (and inconveniently) without amenities such as room service or gym access.

PRICES

⇨ *Hotel reviews have been shortened. For full information, see Fodors.com. Prices are for a standard double room in high season, excluding 14.75% city and state taxes and daily flat fee.*

What It Costs in U.S. Dollars

	$	$$	$$$	$$$$
HOTELS	under $300	$300–$449	$450–$600	over $600

Essentials

There's no denying that New York City hotels are expensive, but rates run the full range. For high-end luxury hotels, prices may start at over $1,000 a night for a standard room in high season, which runs from September through December. At the lower end of the spending spectrum, a bunk at the Jane starts at $199 for a single. But don't be put off by the prices printed here—many hotels slash their rates significantly for promotions and online-only deals.

SERVICES

Unless otherwise noted, all hotels listed have private baths, central heating, air-conditioning, and wireless Internet (Wi-Fi) available, though it's not always free. Most large hotels have video or high-speed check-in/check-out capability, and many can arrange lots of services like tours and babysitting. Pools are a rarity, but most properties have fitness centers and, sometimes, full-scale spas; hotels without facilities usually have arrangements for guests at nearby gyms, sometimes for a fee.

WHAT ABOUT AN APARTMENT RENTAL?

Many people looking to save money on accommodations look for apartments to rent on a short-term basis. Whether you use VRBO, Airbnb, or some other platform, understand that apartment rentals of nonowner-occupied units for less than 30 days are illegal in New York City (and often prohibited by residential-building regulations). In 2023, a new city law restricted short-term rentals even further by requiring hosts to register with the city, live in the place they're renting out, and actually be there at the same time as their guest. Scams are common, so if you do rent an apartment, take special care to rent in a way that you are fully covered if something goes wrong. Always pay with a credit card, and never wire money. Ever. Most listed apartments in New York City are illegal. You can legally rent a *room* in an occupied apartment or house, but generally not the full unit for your own private use.

Nightlife

New Yorkers are fond of the "work hard, play hard" maxim, but the truth is, Gothamites don't need much of an excuse to hit the town. Any day of the week could easily be mistaken for a Friday or Saturday; the bottom line is that when the mood strikes, there are always plenty of choices in this 24-hour city. It isn't hard for visitors to get a piece of the action, whether this means raising a glass in a historic saloon, a dimly lit cocktail den, or a swanky rooftop lounge; checking out the latest band; or laughing it up at a comedy show.

The nightlife scene still resides largely downtown—in the dives and speakeasies of the East Village and Lower East Side, the classic jazz joints and piano bars of Greenwich Village, and the Meatpacking District's and SoHo's "see-and-be-seen" clubs. Midtown, especially around Hell's Kitchen, has developed a vibrant scene, too, and plenty of upscale hangouts dot the Upper East and Upper West Sides. Brooklyn and Harlem are go-to destinations for in-the-know locals.

Keep in mind that *when* you go is just as important as *where* you go. A club that is packed at 11 pm might empty out by midnight, and a bar that raged last night may be completely empty tonight. *Time Out New York* magazine has a good list of roving parties (🌐 *www.timeout.com/newyork*), as does *Thrillist* (🌐 *www.thrillist.com/newyork*). Scour industry-centric websites, too, like *Eater* and *Grub Street,* which catalog the comings and goings of many a nightlife impresario. *New York* magazine, its entertainment publication *Vulture*, and the *New York Times* list a variety of shows, too. Bear in mind that a venue's life span is often measured in months, not years. Phone ahead or check online to make sure your target hasn't closed or turned into a polka hall (although, you never know—that could be fun, too).

Performing Arts

The streets of New York alone are stageworthy. With so many people faking it 'til they make it, daily life can take on the feeling of performance—to exhausting, and inspiring, effect. No wonder that the city draws a constant influx of actors, singers, dancers, and musicians from around the globe, all striving for their big break and infusing the city with a crackling creative energy. This fiercely competitive scene produces an unrivaled wealth of culture and art that many New Yorkers cite as the reason they're here, and for which millions more are determined to travel to the city.

Although costly ticket prices can make attending a Broadway show a less common outing for even the most devout theater-loving New Yorkers, that's not true of many other kinds of more affordable performances. Whether the audiences are primarily local or not, it's their discernment that helps drive the arts scene, whether they are flocking to a concert hall to hear a world-class soprano deliver a flawless performance or crowding into a cramped café to support fledgling writers reading from their own work.

New York has upward of 200 "legitimate" theaters (meaning those with theatrical performances, not movies) and many more ad-hoc venues—parks, churches, lofts, galleries, rooftops, even parking lots. The city is also a revolving door of special events: summer jazz, one-act-play marathons, film festivals, and music and dance celebrations from the classical to the avant-garde, to name just a few.

Shopping

The Big Apple is one of the best shopping destinations in the world, rivaled perhaps only by London, Paris, and Tokyo. Manhattan's compact size, convenient subway system, and plentiful cabs (or Lyft or Uber rides) make the island easy to navigate with plenty of bags in tow. But what it really comes down to is the staggering number and variety of stores. If you can't find it in New York, it probably doesn't exist.

If you like elegant flagships and money is no object, head to Midtown, where you'll find international megabrands like Louis Vuitton, Yves Saint Laurent, and Gucci, as well as famed department stores Bergdorf Goodman and Bloomingdale's. Nearby Madison Avenue has couture from Carolina Herrera and Vera Wang, and 5th Avenue is lined with famous jewelry stores such as Tiffany, Van Cleef & Arpels, and Harry Winston. This is also the neighborhood to indulge in bespoke goods, such as handmade shoes from John Lobb. If you like designer pieces but can't afford them, don't despair—there are plenty of upscale consignment shops around the city where you can find last season's Chanel suit or a vintage YSL jacket.

The small, independent shops that once filled SoHo have largely been displaced by the likes of Banana Republic and UNIQLO, but if you want to hit the chains, this is a great place to do it, because the neighborhood also provides high-quality people-watching and superb lunches. Poke around on the side streets and in nearby NoLIta for outposts of smaller local and foreign designers, and, if you're craving some of old SoHo's artistic spirit, don't discount the street vendors' stalls, which sell handmade jewelry and simple cotton dresses.

The East Village and Lower East Side are hotbeds of creativity and quirky coolness, with little boutiques selling everything from retro furniture to industrial-inspired jewelry. They're tucked among bars and old tenement buildings. The Meatpacking District is another great shopping destination to find chic designer stores like Diane von Furstenberg and rag & bone along with independently owned boutiques. And if you jaunt over to Brooklyn, you'll discover that some of the city's hippest designers are hanging out at boutiques just across the East River.

Taxes

A sales tax of 8.875% applies to almost everything you can buy retail, including restaurant meals. However, prescription drugs and nonprepared food bought in grocery stores are exempt. Clothing and footwear costing less than $110 (per item) also are exempt.

Tipping

The customary tipping rate for taxi drivers is 10%–20%; bellhops are usually given $5 per bag in luxury hotels, $1 per bag for the least expensive hotels. Hotel housekeepers should be tipped $3–$5 per day of your stay. A doorman who hails or helps you into a cab can be tipped $1–$2. You should also tip your hotel concierge for services rendered; the size of the tip depends on the difficulty of your request, as well as the quality of the concierge's work. Tour guides should be tipped 15%–20% if you enjoyed the tour (or about $10–$20 per person on gratuity-only tours). Waiters should also be tipped 15%–20%, though at higher-end restaurants, a solid 20% is more the norm. Tip $1 or $2 per drink you order at the bar, or possibly more if you're ordering something especially time-consuming to make. Remember to bring at least a little cash with you everywhere in New York City, since cash tips are always appreciated more than credit-card add-on gratuities.

Visitor Information

The Grand Central Partnership staffs a number of information kiosks in and around Grand Central Terminal and also offers free tours of the neighborhood.

New York City Tourism + Conventions is the city's

Essentials

Tipping Guides for New York City

Bartender	$1–$5 per round of drinks, depending on the number of drinks
Bellhop	$1–$5 per bag, depending on the level of the hotel
Coat check	$1–$2 per coat
Hotel concierge	$5 or more, depending on the service
Hotel doorstaff	$1–$5 for help with bags or hailing a cab
Hotel housekeeper	$3–$5 a day (in cash, preferably daily since cleaning staff may be different each day you stay)
Hotel room service waiter	$1–$2 per delivery, even if a service charge has been added
Porter at airport or train station	$1 per bag
Restroom attendants	$1 or small change
Skycap at airport	$1–$3 per bag checked
Spa personnel	15%–20% of the cost of your service
Taxi driver	15%–20%
Tour guide	10%–15% of the cost of the tour, per person
Valet parking attendant	$2–$5, each time your car is brought to you
Restaurant server	15%–20%, with 20% being the norm at high-end restaurants; nothing additional if a service charge is added to the bill

official tourism and visitor information resource. Check out its comprehensive website (🌐 *www.nyctourism.com*) and official NYC Information Center, located in Midtown's Herald Square.

The Downtown Alliance has information on the area encompassing City Hall south to Battery Park, and from the East River to West Street; the Times Square Alliance covers much of Midtown West.

The Perfect Long Weekend in NYC

Three days in New York is just enough time to experience the city's culture and top sights, along with a few culinary highlights. As befits the City That Never Sleeps, it'll be a jam-packed itinerary, full of historic landmarks, gobsmacking art, staggering skyline views, and memorable nights out.

You'll definitely earn your steps, so bring good walking shoes. But when you need a break, you can always take the subway (make sure your credit card or smartphone is set up to tap and go.) You should also purchase an NYC CityPASS (🌐 *www.citypass.com*) for discounted admission at up to five city attractions; it's valid for nine days and quickly pays for itself.

DAY 1

Building on four centuries of history, Lower Manhattan is a prime starting point for your trip. So grab New York's breakfast of champions—coffee and a bagel—and prepare yourself for the morning rush hour on a subway to Battery Park. From this southernmost tip of the island, you'll be able to see the Statue of Liberty and Ellis Island in the distance. If time permits, take the free Staten Island Ferry to get a closer look (trips take 25 minutes each way).

Head up Broadway past Bowling Green and the famous *Charging Bull* statue on your way to Wall Street. Turn right at the 1846 Gothic Revival–style Trinity Church to view the giant George Washington statue at Federal Hall, across from the New York Stock Exchange. Stroll north, then take a left on Liberty Street to the World Trade Center site, home to the National 9/11 Memorial & Museum and the 104-story One World Trade Center. If your budget allows, make your way to the top of the latter for a bird's-eye view of Manhattan (tickets are pricey; book ahead for discounted rates.)

Afterward, drift north of Canal Street to discover SoHo and its unique cast-iron architecture and trendy shops. Stop for a seafood lunch at posh Lure Fishbar. Continue walking up to Washington Square Park to see its famous marble arch and central fountain, hear buskers playing their hearts out, and watch NYU students hanging out between classes.

Head northwest to Christopher Street, where the Stonewall National Monument marks where the LGBTQ+ civil rights movement began. From here, it's just a few blocks to the Gansevoort and Washington Street entrance of the High

The Perfect Long Weekend in NYC

Line. Take a sunset stroll on the elevated greenway to Chelsea, where, depending on your timing, you can pop into some of the neighborhood's megawatt contemporary art galleries before dropping by City Winery for small plates and live music. Then, if you're big on nightlife, explore the nearby Meatpacking District's bars and clubs well into the wee hours.

DAY 2

Start at Grand Central Terminal, one of NYC's most majestic spaces, where you can gaze up at the ceiling's sparkling constellations and down at the throngs of commuters whizzing through. There's lots to eat here to start the day: many local eateries maintain food kiosks here to fuel the morning rush.

Head north on 5th Avenue to check out Rockefeller Center (if it's winter, that'll include the ice-skating rink), and pop into the NBC Experience Store. On a clear day, visit the Top of the Rock observation deck for a perfect view of the Empire State Building and beyond (or head south to 34th Street to enjoy the Empire State Building's fantastic visitor experience and observation decks for yourself).

Continue walking uptown to the Museum of Modern Art (MoMA) to check out one of the world's great modern art museums; must-see exhibits include Andy Warhol's soup cans and *The Starry Night* by Vincent van Gogh. Grab lunch at one of the museum's excellent cafés before heading a few blocks north to explore Central Park, where meandering paths lead to many picturesque points of interest, including the glorious Bethesda Fountain.

Exit the park at East 79th Street to reach the Metropolitan Museum of Art, with its astonishing collection of works spanning 5,000 years of history. The Egyptian collection, including the Temple of Dendur, is reason enough to visit, but don't miss the superb Manhattan skyline views from the rooftop garden before you go (open seasonally from late-April to late-October).

After you get your art fill, take the subway down to Times Square to join travelers (and some locals) who converge on the "crossroads of the world" to bask in Broadway's bright lights, best experienced after dark. Grab a classic New York hot dog from a streetside stand while you take it all in. If you time it right, you might even be able to catch a Broadway show (look for half-price tickets at the TKTS booth in Duffy Square at 47th Street and Broadway in advance).

DAY 3

Take the subway or NYC Ferry over to DUMBO in Brooklyn, where Brooklyn Bridge Park delivers jaw-dropping views of its namesake bridge as well as miles of Lower Manhattan skyline. Explore the photogenic area's cobblestone streets and refurbished 19th-century warehouses before walking across the Brooklyn Bridge back to Manhattan (the stroll takes about 40 minutes). Head north to reach Chinatown, with plenty of tasty eateries to try for a late lunch.

Afterward, cross Canal Street and walk east past the regal Manhattan Bridge Arch into the Lower East Side. The Tenement Museum is among the city's most interesting historical experiences, so plan for an hour or two there touring the preserved apartments of several generations of immigrants who lived in the building (reserve your tickets in advance). Then, walk up buzzy Orchard Street to discover the neighborhood's best mix of galleries, shops, and restaurants. Stop to nosh on classic Jewish fare at Russ & Daughters Cafe.

Then continue north through the East Village and Alphabet City, with a break in Tompkins Square Park for eclectic downtown people-watching. Grab a craft cocktail at one of the neighborhood's many innovative bars, like PDT, with its "secret" entrance behind an unassuming hot dog restaurant.

Then, if you're still going strong, walk west on idiosyncratic St. Mark's Place—once the edgy hub of the neighborhood—to cap off your trip at The Public Theater, where many of Broadway's top productions, including *Hamilton,* regularly get their start. Enjoy one last evening performance or head up to the mezzanine, where The Library restaurant and bar is an elegant spot for a meal or drink, whether or not you're attending a show.

On the Calendar

Spring

Cherry Blossom Season. New Yorkers come out of hibernation en masse at the end of April (check online for dates) to witness the extremely popular annual cherry-blossom blooms at the Brooklyn Botanic Garden. In addition to the cherry trees, you may find special concerts and performances, exhibits, and more. 🌐 *www.bbg.org.*

Museum Mile Festival. For one day every June, thousands of locals and visitors celebrate the Museum Mile Festival when museums along 5th Avenue from 82nd Street to 105th Street open their doors for free from 6 to 9 pm. 🌐 *www.nyctourism.com.*

Tribeca Film Festival. Founded by Robert De Niro and Jane Rosenthal to contribute to the recovery of Lower Manhattan after 9/11, this has become one of the world's most prominent film festivals. It typically takes place in early June (check the website for dates and screenings). 🌐 *www.tribecafilm.com.*

Summer

Celebrate Brooklyn! This free outdoor performing arts festival is the place to catch excellent live music in the great Brooklyn outdoors. The artists and ensembles reflect the borough's diversity, ranging from internationally acclaimed performers to up-and-coming musicians. 🌐 *www.bricartsmedia.org/bric-celebrate-brooklyn-festival.*

Midsummer Night Swing. If you're in town, don't miss the Midsummer Night Swing festival, an outdoor music and dance party in Lincoln Center Plaza that occurs from late June to mid-July. Take lessons with pros, or just strut your natural moves on the dance floor. 🌐 *www.lincolncenter.org.*

Summer Streets. Over the first three Saturdays in August, you can join hundreds of thousands of locals to let loose on nearly 20 miles of pedestrianized arterials across all five boroughs. 🌐 *www.nyc.gov/summerstreets.*

Fall

Brooklyn Book Festival. The festival is a huge, (mostly) free public event with an array of established and emerging authors, readings, panels, discussions, parties, games, and signings—all held in clubs, parks, theaters, and libraries across Brooklyn in late September. 🌐 *www.brooklynbookfestival.org.*

Feast of San Gennaro. Every fall, thousands of locals and visitors flock to Little Italy for the multiday Feast of San Gennaro in mid-September. This festival is a mix of religion, food, colorful parades, and live entertainment. Don't miss the cannoli-eating competition at the beginning of the festival. 🌐 *sangennaronyc.org.*

New York City Marathon. Even if you're not joining the more than 50,000 runners taking a 26.2-mile tour through New York's five boroughs on the first Sunday in November, you'll want to experience the electric atmosphere and the very best of New York with the 2 million spectators who come out to watch and cheer. 🌐 *www.tcsnycmarathon.org.*

Winter

Lunar New Year. To ring in the Lunar New Year in January or February (the date varies), the streets of Chinatown give way to food vendors hawking traditional eats, colorful costumes and decorations, and a major parade of elaborate floats, marching bands, and dragon troupes running from Little Italy through Chinatown and Lower Manhattan. 🌐 *www.betterchinatown.com.*

New York Botanical Holiday Train Show. This is one of the city's top seasonal attractions. You'll find electric trains, more than 150 miniature replicas of city landmarks (made out of twigs and bark), and magical landscapes—all housed in a conservatory, so winter weather can't dampen your spirits. 🌐 *www.nybg.org.*

For five days each January, **Winter Jazzfest NYC** happens at venues around the city. From mid-January to early-February, **Broadway Week** offers two-for-one tickets to select musicals and plays. You can also sign up for a local event like the **Coney Island Polar Bear Plunge** each New Year's Day (and every Sunday at 1 pm, November–April).

Best Tours in New York City

BOAT TOURS

Circle Line Sightseeing Cruise. In good weather, a Circle Line Sightseeing Cruise around Manhattan Island is one of the best ways not only to get oriented but also to take outstanding skyline pictures. Popular options include the Best of NYC, Harbor Lights, and Landmarks cruises; prices vary by tour and date. ✉ *Pier 83, W. 42nd St., Midtown West* ☎ *212/563–3200* 🌐 *www.circleline.com* 🎫 *From $24* Ⓜ *A, C, E to 42nd St.–Port Authority; 1, 2, 3, 7, N, Q, R, S, W to Times Sq.–42nd St.*

Classic Harbor Line. Offering more than just sightseeing, this cruise line takes passengers around New York Harbor and along both rivers on its historic luxury yachts and schooners, all with on-board bars. Its unique, fairly priced experiences include cruises with live jazz, champagne brunches and sunset tours, wine tastings, and in-depth architecture tours. **TIP→ The company also offers full-day cruises up the Hudson River to Kingston and Bear Mountain; its fall-foliage cruise is especially lovely.** ✉ *Pier 62 at Chelsea Piers, at 22nd St., Chelsea* ☎ *212/627–1825* 🌐 *www.sail-nyc.com* 🎫 *From $64* Ⓜ *C to 23rd St.*

BUS TOURS

A Slice of Brooklyn. If you're interested in experiencing a more local holiday light tradition far from Rockefeller Center, take A Slice of Brooklyn's bus tour to the festive (and blinding) neighborhood light scene that is Brooklyn's Dyker Heights. The Christmas Lights tour, offered in December, introduces you to some of Brooklyn's less touristed neighborhoods. Other tours include the Original Brooklyn Pizza Tour, a bus tour of famous Brooklyn pizza joints, and tours of quintessential Brooklyn neighborhoods. ✉ *Brooklyn* ☎ *212/913–9917* 🌐 *www.asliceofbrooklyn.com* 🎫 *From $65.*

Big Bus New York. Like its double-decker competitors, Big Bus offers various hop-on, hop-off open-top tours of the city, but its most popular ticket is a two-day pass that includes loops that cover downtown, uptown, and Brooklyn, as well as a night tour or a sightseeing cruise, plus several city attractions. ✉ *Midtown West* ☎ *212/685–8687* 🌐 *www.bigbustours.com* 🎫 *From $60* Ⓜ *A, C, E to 42nd St.–Port Authority; 1, 2, 3, 7, N, Q, R, S, W to Times Sq.–42nd St.*

Gray Line New York Sightseeing. The company runs various hop-on, hop-off double-decker bus tours, including a downtown Manhattan loop, an upper Manhattan loop, a Brooklyn loop, and evening tours of the city. Packages include 48-hour and 72-hour options plus entrance fees to attractions. ✉ *777 8th Ave., between 46th and 47th Sts., Midtown West* ☎ *800/669–0051* 🌐 *www.newyorksightseeing.com* 🎫 *From $60* Ⓜ *A, C, E to 42nd St.–Port Authority; 1, 2, 3, 7, N, Q, R, S, W to Times Sq.–42nd St.*

WALKING TOURS

Big Onion Walking Tours. The wisecracking PhD candidates of Big Onion Walking Tours lead theme tours—such as Upper East Side: A Clash of Titans, Immigrant New York, and Gangs of New York—as well as renowned global-cuisine eating tours and guided walks through a variety of neighborhoods, including Harlem, the Financial District, and Brooklyn. Tours run daily. ✉ *New York* ☎ *212/439–1090* 🌐 *www.bigonion.com* 🎫 *From $30.*

Central Park Conservancy. The Central Park Conservancy offers free self-guided tours that provide an introduction to the different areas of Central Park—its woodlands, romantic vistas, Conservatory Garden, Seneca Village, statues and monuments, and off-the-beaten-path walks. Guided tours (from $25) meet at different points in the park and vary in price, so check the website for details and book in advance. ✉ *Central Park* ☎ *212/794–6564* 🌐 *www.centralparknyc.org* 🎫 *Free.*

Like a Local Tours. Walk like a local, talk like a local, and—best of all—eat like a local with a highly curated tour from Like a Local. Options include the Flatiron Food, History, and Architecture tour, which is a lovely walk from the Flatiron District to Union Square with a lot of tasty stops, photo ops, local history, and private kitchen visits along the way. If you're looking to feel like a hip local in Brooklyn, try the Sustainable Brooklyn Food and Fashion Tour. ✉ *New York* ☎ *917/417–0378* 🌐 *www.likealocaltours.com* 🎫 *From $68.*

New York Food Tours. Walking tour choices from this fun outfit focus on international foods, especially in and around downtown, including the Freakiest and Funniest Food, Tastes of Chinatown, Ultimate New York Food & Culture Tour, Everything Chocolate, and an East Village food and culture tour. Bring an appetite; you'll be sampling food. ✉ *New York* ☎ *347/559–0111* 🌐 *www.foodtoursofny.com* 🎫 *From $70.*

Contacts

 Air

AIRLINE SECURITY ISSUES Transportation Security Administration (TSA). *www.tsa.gov.*

AIRPORT INFORMATION JFK International Airport (JFK). *Queens* *718/244–4444* *www.jfkairport.com.* **LaGuardia Airport (LGA).** *718/533–3400* *www.laguardiaairport.com.* **Newark Liberty International Airport (EWR).** *Newark* *973/961–6000* *www.newarkairport.com.*

SHUTTLE SERVICE GO Airlink NYC. *212/812–9000* *www.goairlinkshuttle.com.* **SuperShuttle.** *800/258–3826* *www.supershuttle.com.*

JFK TRANSFER INFORMATION AirTrain JFK. *877/535–2478* *jfkairport.com/to-from-airport/air-train.* **Long Island Rail Road (LIRR).** *511* *www.mta.info/lirr.*

NEWARK AIRPORT TRANSFER INFORMATION AirTrain Newark. *888/397–4636* *www.airtrainnewark.com.* **Coach USA—Newark Airport Express.** *908/354–3330, 877/894–9155* *newarkairportexpress.com.*

Boat

FERRIES NY Waterway. *New York* *800/533–3779* *www.nywaterway.com.* **NYC Ferry.** *New York* *844/469–3377* *www.ferry.nyc.* **Staten Island Ferry.** *311, 212/839–3061 839–3061* *www.siferry.com.* **Statue City Cruises.** *877/523–9849* *www.statuecruises.com.*

Bus

BUSES IN NEW YORK Metropolitan Transportation Authority (MTA) Information. *511* *new.mta.info.*

BUSES TO NEW YORK Coach USA. *New York* *866/912–6224* *www.coachusa.com.* **FlixBus.** *New York* *855/626–8585* *www.flixbus.com.* **Go Buses (by Academy Bus).** *855/888–7160* *www.gobuses.com.* **Greyhound.** *New York* *800/231–2222* *www.greyhound.com.* **Megabus.** *New York* *877/462–6342* *us.megabus.com.* **New Jersey Transit.** *973/275–5555* *www.njtransit.com.* **Trailways.** *800/858–8555* *www.trailways.com.*

BUS STATIONS George Washington Bridge Bus Station. *4211 Broadway, between 178th and 179th Sts., Washington Heights* *800/221–9903*

🌐 *www.panynj.gov*. **Port Authority Bus Terminal.** ✉ *625 8th Ave., at 42nd St., Midtown West* ☎ *212/564–8484* 🌐 *www.panynj.gov*.

Metro/Public Transport

SCHEDULE AND ROUTE INFORMATION Metropolitan Transportation Authority (MTA) Information. ✉ *New York* ☎ *511* 🌐 *new.mta.info*.

SUBWAY INFORMATION Citymapper. ✉ *New York* 🌐 *www.citymapper.com*.

Taxi

CAR-SERVICE COMPANIES Arecibo Car Service. ✉ *Brooklyn* ☎ *718/783–6465* 🌐 *www.arecibocc.com*. **Carey.** ✉ *New York* ☎ *800/336–4646* 🌐 *www.carey.com*. **London Towncars.** ☎ *800/221–4009, 212/988–9700* 🌐 *www.londontowncars.com*.

RIDE-SHARE AND APP-BASED CAR SERVICES Curb. 🌐 *www.gocurb.com*. **Lyft.** 🌐 *www.lyft.com*. **Uber.** 🌐 *www.uber.com*.

Train

INFORMATION Amtrak. ✉ *Penn Station, Midtown West* ☎ *800/872–7245* 🌐 *www.amtrak.com*. **Long Island Rail Road.** ✉ *Penn Station/Grand Central, New York* ☎ *511* 🌐 *new.mta.info*. **Metro-North Railroad.** ✉ *Grand Central Terminal, Midtown East* ☎ *511, 212/532–4900* 🌐 *new.mta.info*. **New Jersey Transit.** ✉ *Penn Station, Midtown West* ☎ *973/275–5555* 🌐 *www.njtransit.com*. **PATH.** ✉ *New York* ☎ *800/234–7284* 🌐 *www.panynj.gov/path*.

TRAIN STATIONS Grand Central Terminal. ✉ *89 E. 42nd St., at Park Ave., Midtown East* ☎ *511* 🌐 *www.grandcentralterminal.com*. **Moynihan Train Hall.** ✉ *421 8th Ave., from 31st to 33rd Sts., Midtown West* 🌐 *www.moynihantrainhall.nyc*. **Penn Station.** ✉ *From 31st to 33rd St., between 7th and 8th Aves., Midtown West* ☎ *511*.

Visitor Information

ACTIVITIES NYC Department of Parks & Recreation. ✉ *New York* ☎ *311* 🌐 *www.nycgovparks.org*.

CITY INFORMATION Downtown Alliance. ✉ *New York* ☎ *212/566–6700* 🌐 *www.downtownny.com*.

Contacts

Grand Central Partnership. ✉ *New York* ☎ *212/883–2420* 🌐 *www.grandcentralpartnership.nyc.* **New York City Tourism + Conventions.** ✉ *New York* 🌐 *www.nyctourism.com.* **Times Square Alliance.** ☎ *212/768–1560* 🌐 *www.timessquarenyc.org.*

HEALTH/SAFETY Travelers Aid International (EWR). ✉ *Newark Liberty International Airport, Newark* ☎ *973/623–5052* 🌐 *www.travelersaid.org/newark.* **Travelers Aid International (JFK).** ✉ *JFK International Airport, Terminal 4, Queens* ☎ *718/656–4870* 🌐 *www.travelersaid.org/jfk.*

LGBTQ+ The Center (Lesbian, Gay, Bisexual & Transgender Community Center). ✉ *208 W. 13th St., between 7th and 8th Aves., Greenwich Village* ☎ *212/620–7310* 🌐 *www.gaycenter.org.* **Gay City News.** ✉ *New York* 🌐 *gaycitynews.com.* ***GO* magazine.** ✉ *New York* 🌐 *gomag.com.* **Time Out NY LGBT.** ✉ *New York* 🌐 *timeout.com/newyork/lgbt.*

LOCAL RESOURCES MTA Accessibility. ✉ *New York* ☎ *511* 🌐 *new.mta.info/accessibility.* **NYC Mayor's Office for People with Disabilities (MOPD).** ✉ *New York* ☎ *311* 🌐 *www.nyc.gov/mopd.* **Scootaround.** ✉ *New York* ☎ *888/441–7575* 🌐 *www.scootaround.com/en/new-york.*

STATEWIDE INFORMATION New York State Division of Tourism. ✉ *New York* ☎ *800/225–5697* 🌐 *www.iloveny.com.*

Chapter 3

LOWER MANHATTAN

Updated by
Arabella Bowen

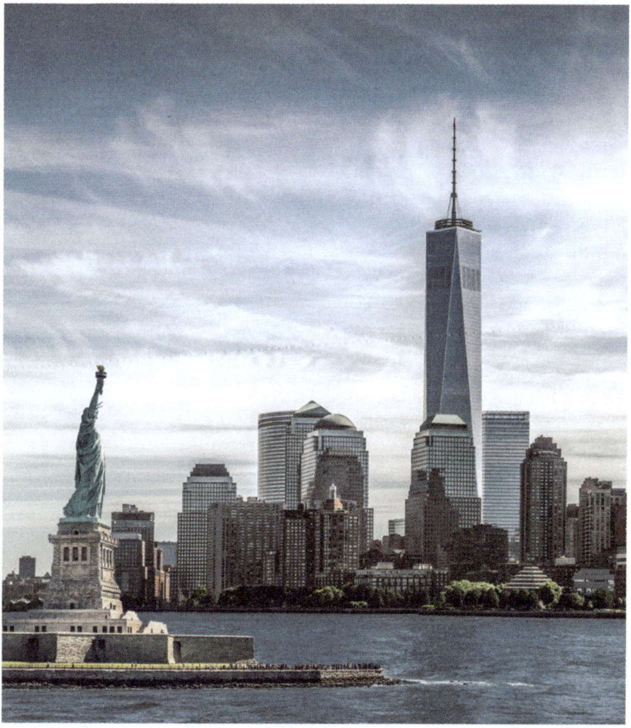

Sights	Restaurants	Hotels	Shopping	Nightlife
★★★★★	★★★★★	★★★★☆	★★★☆☆	★★★☆☆

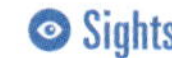

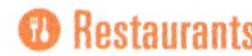

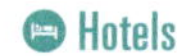

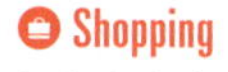

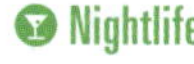

The Seaport Walking Tour

The Seaport has recently undergone a thorough makeover to become a culinary and shopping destination. But behind the gloss, centuries of history reveal themselves in this historic district pressed against the East River below the Brooklyn Bridge.

1 From the Fulton Street subway, walk east on Fulton Street to the corner of Pearl Street. You'll know you've arrived at the Seaport's gateway when you spot the *Titanic* Memorial Lighthouse, a small white lighthouse that commemorates the sinking of the RMS *Titanic* in 1912. Behind it, from 207 to 211 Water Street, three landmarked brick Greek Revival–style stores built around 1835 still feature classic period details: granite steps, cornices, and lintels. No. 211 is now Bowne & Co., a stationery store.

2 Turn left and walk along Water Street with the on-ramp to the Brooklyn Bridge in the distance. Pass the western end of Peck Slip and continue onto the next block. Many of the mixed-use buildings on the east side feature intact (or at least restored) details, starting with the former 19th-century mercantile factory at No. 265, adorned with striking green metal window shutters.

Walking Tour 101

HIGHLIGHTS

Notorious taverns, historic architectural details, cobblestone streets, Brooklyn Bridge and New York Harbor views

WHERE TO START

The *Titanic* Memorial Lighthouse at Fulton and Pearl Streets

LENGTH

45 minutes to one hour

WHERE TO END

Schermerhorn Row on Fulton Street

BEST TIME TO GO

Weekday afternoons when it's quieter

WORST TIME TO GO

January, when the weather can be quite raw; Saturday and Sunday evenings in summer, when it's extremely crowded

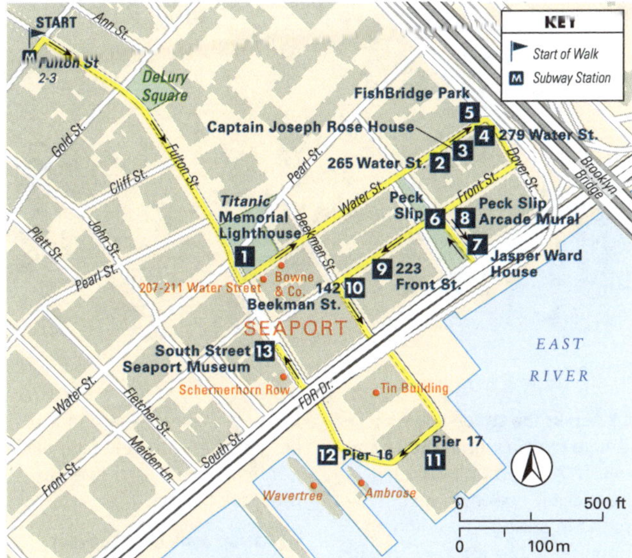

3 **Nearby, the four-story Captain Joseph Rose House at No. 273, is the area's oldest building**—and the third oldest in Manhattan, following the Morris-Jumel Mansion and St. Paul's Chapel. Built in 1773 for mahogany trader Captain Rose, the East River ran right behind it and he moored his rig outside. Subsequent owner Christopher "Kit" Burns really put the Georgian building on the map, however: he ran a scruffy tavern here in the 1860s, renowned for offering dog and rat fights as entertainment. (It's now a collection of genteel luxury condos.)

4 **The red wood-framed house at No. 279, on the corner of Dover Street, has an equally ribald past.** It officially dates to 1801, but may have been built earlier. It's held everything from a brothel to taverns in its time, but its most notorious tenant was "One-Armed Charley" Monell, whose Hole-in-the-Wall tavern employed two women, Kate Flannery and Gallus Mag, in the 1850s as "bouncers" to manage the riff raff. (It looks likely to become a bar again; an alcohol permit is pending.)

Pier 16

5 Across the street, tiny Fish-Bridge Park is worth a quick stop, too. This community garden bursts with peonies and spray roses in spring, providing an unusual frame for the Brooklyn Bridge lumbering above and a rare greenspace in Lower Manhattan.

6 Exit the park and head southeast one block on Dover Street to reach Front Street, one of the Seaport's most historic arteries. Turn right and walk on to re-enter Peck Slip. In its heyday, this urban parkette was a thriving fish market, boat slip, and ferry terminal. George Washington and his troops even used it as a temporary hideout when they fled the Battle of Long Island in August 1776.

7 One building of the era that remains is 45 Peck Slip, at the corner of South Street. Built for merchant Jasper Ward in the early 1800s you can still make out his name on the five-story red-brick facade.

8 As you walk back to Front Street, Richard Haas's large-scale trompe l'oeil *The Peck Slip Arcade* mural (1978) dominates the north side. Depicting a 19th-century Seaport scene and a view of the Brooklyn Bridge, it deceptively hides the entire wall of a Con Edison substation. Look up for a smashing view of Lower Manhattan's new architecture—including Frank Gehry's undulating 76-story residential skyscraper completed in 2010—rising above.

9 Turn left onto Front Street. The red-brick warehouses and new buildings here combine to create the neighborhood's most atmospheric commercial block, with taverns left and right.

Look for starfish in the facades to identify the originals from the new: the details aren't purely decorative, but anchor the tie rods that hold the buildings together. A plaque above the doorway of No. 223 is inscribed with a passage from *Moby Dick*, a reminder of the area's rich maritime history.

10 When Front meets Beekman Street, cross to the southwest corner to admire the facade of No. 142 Beekman on the northeast. Designed in 1885 by George B. Post, the same architect who designed the New York Stock Exchange in 1903, the Romanesque Revival building's unique cockleshell cornice and fantastic terra-cotta fish details reflect the Seaport's past as a major fish market.

11 Take Beekman toward the East River and cross FDR Drive to reach Pier 17. This wraparound public wharf, open year-round, offers seating and stunning views of the harbor and the Brooklyn Bridge. The pier was previously anchored by the Fulton Fish Market, reopened in 2022 by Jean-Georges as the Tin Building, a high-end food emporium. Walk left of it for the best vistas, then cut through the multilevel complex behind it to reach neighboring Pier 16 on the right.

Fulton Street

12 As the departure point for various seasonal cruises, there's always a hubbub on Pier 16. But it's also the docking point for five restored 19th- and 20th-century tall ships, including the 1907 lightship *Ambrose* and the 1885 ship *Wavertree* (admission to the South Street Seaport Museum at 12 Fulton Street includes tours of both).

13 Cross back over FDR Drive to reach Fulton Street, now a cobblestone pedestrian mall. On the south side is the Seaport's architectural centerpiece, Schermerhorn Row, a redbrick terrace of Georgian- and Federal-style warehouses and counting houses built from 1810 to 1812. While many of them now hold 21st-century retail shops (including a lovely McNally Jackson branch at No. 4), finish your walk at the unique South Street Seaport Museum at No. 12 to fully understand the area's vital role in making New York the ultimate commercial harbor of early America.

NEIGHBORHOOD SNAPSHOT

TOP EXPERIENCES

- Visiting the National 9/11 Memorial and Museum
- Riding the Staten Island Ferry
- Touring Ellis Island and the Statue of Liberty
- Browsing boutiques and people-watching in SoHo and NoLIta
- Ogling the out-of-the-ordinary produce and seafood in Chinatown

GETTING HERE

The Financial District's Fulton Center is serviced by many subway lines (2, 3, 4, 5, A, C, J, R, W, Z) and is within walking distance of the World Trade Center site and the Seaport. For the Brooklyn Bridge, take the 4, 5, or 6 to Brooklyn Bridge–City Hall.

For sights around New York Harbor, take the R or W to Whitehall Street or the 4 or 5 to Bowling Green. (Note that you can also reach the harbor area via the 1 train to South Ferry; it stops in the heart of TriBeCa, at Franklin Street, too.)

SoHo (**So**uth of **Ho**uston) is largely bounded by Houston Street, Canal Street, 6th Avenue, and Lafayette Street, with some parts west to the river. To the east, NoLIta (**No**rth of **L**ittle **Ita**ly) is contained by Houston, the Bowery, Kenmare, and Lafayette. Take the 6, C, or E to Spring Street; the N, R, or W to Prince Street; or the B, D, F, or M to Broadway–Lafayette Street. For Chinatown take the 6, J, N, Q, R, W, or Z to Canal Street or the B or D to Grand Street.

PAUSE HERE

- **Elizabeth Street Garden.** This tiny 1-acre garden between Prince and Spring Streets is one of NYC's prettiest community gardens, planted with flowers and dotted with sculptures. ✉ *Elizabeth St.* 🌐 *www.elizabethstreetgarden.com* 🚊 *6 to Spring St.*
- **Pier 17.** Walk down the pier, past the historic tall ships, where you can sit on benches and swings and gaze up at the Brooklyn Bridge and across the harbor. Then stop into the Tin Building market and food hall for a snack. ✉ *89 South St.* 🌐 *www.theseaport.nyc* 🚊 *2, 3, 4, 5, A, C, J, R, W, Z to Fulton St.*

Lower Manhattan, or "all the way downtown" in the parlance of New Yorkers, has long been where the action—and transaction—is. Originally the Dutch trading post called New Amsterdam (1626–47), this neighborhood is home to historic cobblestone streets beside soaring skyscrapers.

The whirl of Wall Street, concentration of city landmarks, buzz of The Seaport, and quintessential views of the Statue of Liberty and Ellis Island out in the harbor make the southern tip of Manhattan essential to any NYC visit.

Picturesque TriBeCa (the **Tri**angle **Be**low **Ca**nal Street) to the northwest feels a world apart, with its hushed streets lined by Federal row houses and grand cast-iron facades. Walk these uniquely New York blocks and you'll understand why celebrities and other moneyed New Yorkers own apartments here. (The two-block-long Staple Street, with its connecting overhead walkway, is a favorite of urban cinematographers).

To the northeast, Chinatown bustles with family-run shops and Instagram-worthy food shops and stalls, while SoHo and NoLIta are destinations for trendy boutiques, popular chains, and chic restaurants. These jam-packed areas offer prime people-watching as you shop, nibble, and wander. Don't forget to look up as you go: SoHo has one of the world's greatest concentration of cast-iron buildings, created in response to the fires that wiped out much of Lower Manhattan in the mid-18th century.

Sights

★ Brooklyn Bridge (Entrance)

BRIDGE | "A drive-through cathedral" is how the journalist James Wolcott once described the Brooklyn Bridge—one of New York's noblest and most recognizable landmarks—perhaps rivaling Walt Whitman's comment that it was "the best, most effective medicine my soul has yet partaken." The bridge stretches over the East River, connecting Manhattan and Brooklyn. A walk across its promenade—a boardwalk elevated above the roadway, shared by pedestrians and cyclists—is a quintessential New York

Lower Manhattan
Leroy St.
Clarkson St.
Houston St 1-2
W. Houston St.
Broadway-Lafayette St B-D-F-M
King St.
Hudson St.
Prince St.
Prince St N-Q-R-W
Spring St A-C-E
Charlton St.
Varick St.
Ave. of the Americas (6th Ave.)
Sullivan St.
Thompson St.
West Broadway
Greene St.
Spring St.
Spring St 4-6
Vandam St.
Greenwich St.
Spring St.
Dominick St.
SOHO
Wooster St.
Crosby St.
Lafayette St.
Holland Tunnel Entrance
Broome St.
Broome St.
Pier 34
Canal St.
Canal St 1-2
Grand St.
Mercer St.
Broadway
Centre St.
Holland Tunnel
Holland Tunnel
West Street
Watts St.
Desbrosses St.
Vestry St.
Holland Tunnel Exit
Canal St-Holland Tunnel A-C-E
Canal St R-W
4-6
N-Q
J-Z
Washington St.
Laight St.
Hubert St.
Lispenard St.
Walker St.
6th Ave.
Beach St.
White St.
9A
N. Moore St.
Franklin St 1-2
Franklin St.
Pier 26
Franklin St.
Church St.
Leonard St.
TRIBECA
Pier 25
Harrison St.
Jay St.
Hudson St.
Worth St.
Thomas St.
Thomas Paine Park
Duane St.
Duane St.
Reade St.
Chambers St.
Chambers St 1-2-3
Chambers St J-Z
Brooklyn Bridge - City Hall 4-5-6
Rockefeller Park
River Terrace
Warren St.
Chambers St A-C
City Hall R-W
City Hall Park
North End Ave.
Murray St.
Greenwich St.
Park Pl.
Park Pl 2-3
Park Row
Spruce St.
Barclay St.
Beekman St.
Vesey St.
Vesey St.
BATTERY PARK
World Trade Center
Ann St.
A-C
Fulton St.
Fulton St
PATH
E
Dey St.
J-Z
Fulton St 4-5
2-3
Cortlandt St N-R-W
Maiden Ln.
William St.
South End Ave.
Liberty St.
Nassau St.
Cedar St.
HUDSON RIVER
Albany St.
Carlisle St.
Pine St.
Wall St 2-3
Wall St 4-5
R-W
Wall St.
Rector Pl.
Rector St.
Rector St 1
New St.
Broad St J-Z
Exchange St.
W. Thames St.
FINANCIAL DISTRICT
Beaver St.
3rd Pl.
Broad St.
2nd Pl.
Bowling Green 4-5
0
1,000 ft
0
200 m
Battery Pl.
Bridge St.
Pearl St.
Water St.
Robert F. Wagner Park
The Battery
Whitehall St R-W
Whitehall St.
South Ferry 1
KEY
Sights
Restaurants
Hotels
Statue of Liberty Ferry
Ellis Island Ferry
Brooklyn-Battery Tunnel

Lower East Side-
2nd Ave
F
Stanton St.
Mott St.
Elizabeth St.
Bowery
Chrystie St.
Forsyth St.
Allen St.
Essex St.
Norfolk St.
Suffolk St.
Rivington St.
Ridge St.
Pitt St.
Columbia St.
NOLITA
Delancey St-
Essex St
F
J-M-Z
Williamsburg Bridge
Mulberry St.
Kenmare St.
Bowery
J-Z
Eldridge St.
Delancey St.
Clinton St.
Willett St.
Broome St.
Grand St.
Sara D. Roosevelt Park
Orchard St.
Ludlow St.
LOWER
EAST SIDE
Grand St
B-D
Grand St.
LITTLE
ITALY
Jackson St.
Hester St.
Elizabeth St.
Hester St.
Seward
Park
East
Broadway
F
East Broadway
Gouverneur St.
Montgomery St.
Baxter St.
Mott St.
Canal St.
CHINATOWN
Bayard St.
Henry St.
Rutgers St.
Madison St.
Clinton St.
FDR Drive
Columbus
Park
Division St.
Pike St.
Cherry St.
Pier 36
Park Row
Henry St.
Catherine St.
Monroe St.
Market St.
EAST RIVER
Pearl St.
Madison St.
Water St.
Manhattan Bridge
R.F. Wagner Pl.
John St.
Plymouth St.
Jay St.
Gold St.
Pearl St.
Water St.
Front St.
South St.
Brooklyn Bridge
DUMBO
Water St.
Front St.
Washington St.
Fulton St.
Beekman St.
John St.
Pier 17
Furman St.
Poplar St.
278
Fletcher St.
Maiden Ln.
Pier 16
Middagh St.
High St
A-C
Pearl St.
Front St.
Water St.
FDR Drive
Pier 15
Cranberry St.
Henry St.
Old Slip
Pier 11
Heli Port
Pier
Governors
Island
Ferry
Staten
Island
Ferry
Sights
Brooklyn Bridge (Entrance), 4
Ellis Island, 8
9/11 Memorial, 2
9/11 Museum, 3
One World Observatory, 1
The Seaport, 6
Staten Island Ferry, 5
Statue of Liberty, 7
Restaurants
Delmonico's, 9
Jing Fong, 6
Locanda Verde, 7
Lure Fishbar, 4
Metropolis by Marcus Samuelsson, 8
Raoul's, 2
Roscioli, 1
Sadelle's, 3
Torrisi, 5
Hotels
Arlo SoHo, 2
The Beekman, 6
Crosby Street Hotel, 1
Four Seasons New York Downtown, 5
The Greenwich Hotel, 3
Hotel 50 Bowery, 4
The Wall Street Hotel, 7

experience, and the roughly 40-minute stroll delivers exhilarating views. (Cyclists mainly use a lane on the vehicular level below.) If you start from Lower Manhattan near City Hall, you'll end up in the heart of Brooklyn Heights, but you can also take the subway to the Brooklyn side and walk back to Manhattan. From late morning through early evening, the narrow path gets very congested, especially when the weather is nice. Head here early in the morning to find the magical quiet hours. ✉ *East River Dr., Financial District* 🌐 *www.nyc.gov/html/dot/html/infrastructure/brooklyn-bridge.shtml* Ⓜ *4, 5, 6 to Brooklyn Bridge–City Hall; J, Z to Chambers St.*

★ Ellis Island

HISTORY MUSEUM | **FAMILY** | Between 1892 and 1924, millions of people first entered the United States at the Ellis Island federal immigration facility. When the complex closed in 1954, it had processed ancestors of more than 40% of Americans living today. The island's main building, now a national monument, is known as the Ellis Island National Museum of Immigration, and it tells the story not just of Ellis Island but of immigration from the Colonial era to the present day, through numerous galleries containing artifacts, photographs, and taped oral histories. The museum's centerpiece is the cavernous, white-tile Registry Room (also known as the Great Hall). There's much to take in, so make use of the museum's interpretive tools. Check at the visitor desk for free film tickets, a good audio tour, ranger-led tour times, and special programs.

There is no admission fee for the Statue of Liberty or Ellis Island, but an adult ferry ride (from Battery Park to Liberty Island to Ellis Island) costs $25 round-trip. Ferries leave from Battery Park (and from Liberty State Park in New Jersey) every 25–30 minutes depending on the time of year (buy your tickets online at 🌐 *www.statuecruises.com*). There are often long security lines, so arrive early, especially if you have a timed-entry ticket. There is an indoor-outdoor café on Ellis Island. ✉ *Financial District* ☎ *212/561–4588 Ellis Island, 212/561–4500 Wall of Honor information for names of immigrants, 877/523–9849 Statue Cruises* 🌐 *www.statueofliberty.org/ellis-island* 🎫 *Free; ferry $25 round-trip (includes Liberty Island)*

★ 9/11 Memorial

HISTORIC SIGHT | Opened in 2011 to mark the 10th anniversary of 9/11, the somber memorial occupies a large swath of the 16-acre World Trade Center complex, forming the Memorial Plaza (part of the National 9/11 Memorial & Museum). It comprises two recessed, 30-foot-tall waterfalls that occupy the giant,

The names of those lost on September 11th are commemorated on Memorial Plaza, at the former site of the Twin Towers.

square footprints where the Twin Towers once stood. Edging the memorial pools are bronze panels inscribed with the names of the nearly 3,000 people who were killed in the 1993 and 2001 terrorist attacks. Across the plaza are benches, grassy strips, and more than 400 swamp white oak trees harvested from within a 500-mile radius of the site, as well as from Pennsylvania and near Washington, D.C. The 9/11 Memorial is an open-access, free public plaza.

Along Liberty Street on the south side of the site is the elevated Liberty Park, home to Fritz Koenig's *The Sphere,* which for three decades stood on the plaza at the World Trade Center as a symbol of peace. Damaged in the 2001 attack, the sculpture was installed in the park in 2017. On the park's east end stands St. Nicholas Greek Orthodox Church and National Shrine (🌐 *stnicholaswtc.org*), erected to replace the church that was destroyed on 9/11. Unlike an average church, this house of worship cost $85 million, took 21 years to design and construct, and among its splendid features, was built with white marble sourced from the same Greek quarry as the Parthenon's stone. Visitors are welcome daily (except Tuesday), 10–3; and on Sunday 9–2. ✉ *180 Greenwich St., between Fulton and Liberty Sts., Financial District* ☎ *212/266–5211* 🌐 *www.911memorial.org* Ⓜ *1, R, W to Cortlandt St.; 2, 3, 4, 5, A, C, J, Z to Fulton St.; E to World Trade Center.*

9/11 Museum

HISTORY MUSEUM | Beside the twin pools that form the 9/11 Memorial Plaza is the glass pavilion of the 9/11 Memorial Museum (part of the complex known as the National 9/11 Memorial & Museum). The museum descends some seven stories down to the bedrock the Twin Towers were built on, and the vast space displays a poignant, powerful collection of artifacts, memorabilia, photographs, and multimedia exhibits, as well as a gallery that takes visitors through the history of events surrounding both the 1993 and 2001 attacks. You might appreciate the tissue boxes around the museum when experiencing the memorial wall with portraits and personal stories of those who perished. There's also a panoramic media installation about the site's "rebirth," as well as World Trade Center–related art and history exhibits that change throughout the year. Giant pieces of the towers' structural steel and foundations are displayed, along with the partially destroyed Ladder Company 3 fire truck. You can also see the remnants of the Survivors Stairs, which allowed hundreds of people to escape the buildings that fateful September day. (Check the website for current ticket packages and other discounts.) ✉ *180 Greenwich St., between Fulton St. and Liberty St. Walkway, Financial District* ☎ *212/312–8800* 🌐 *www.911memorial.org/museum* 🎫 *$33 (free Mon. 5:30–7 pm with same-day advance reservations)* ⏲ *Closed Tues.* Ⓜ *1, R, W to Cortlandt St.; 2, 3, 4, 5, A, C, J, Z to Fulton Center; E to World Trade Center.*

One World Observatory

VIEWPOINT | FAMILY | There are several thrills involved in visiting One World Trade Center, the tallest building in the Western Hemisphere, not the least of which are the spectacular views of Manhattan, Brooklyn, and New Jersey. If you time your visit around dusk, you'll get daytime views as well as sunset and sparkling evening lights. The observatory occupies the 100th, 101st, and 102nd floors of One WTC, and the experience includes an exhilarating trip up in the world's fastest elevators, during which a journey through history is projected on the elevator walls. After you step out at the top, there's also a two-minute video of time-lapse images of Lower Manhattan. The ground floor has exhibits and personal stories about the building of the tower. Admission prices rise for "priority" entrance and other combo tickets (best bought online with timed entry); the box office, security checkpoint, and observatory entrance are on the West Street side of the tower. **TIP→ With some reservations, you can purchase prix-fixe dining or bar packages for ONE Dine restaurant on 101st floor, which include observatory tickets.** ✉ *One World Trade Center, 285 Fulton St., between West and Greenwich Sts., Financial District* ☎ *844/696–1776, 212/602–4000* 🌐 *oneworldobservatory.com* 🎫 *$44* Ⓜ *1, R, W to Cortlandt; E to World Trade Center; 2, 3, 4, 5, A, C, J, Z to Fulton St.*

★ The Seaport

HISTORIC DISTRICT | Had this charming cobblestone neighborhood not been declared a historic district in 1977, the city's largest concentration of early 19th-century commercial buildings would have been destroyed. Thankfully they survived, and in recent years have come to enjoy new life. The landmarked "South Street Seaport Historic District" has undergone a thorough makeover as a diverse shopping and dining destination, with seasonal markets, art installations, IPIC Theater (a luxury cinema with dining), and live entertainment—plus a simplified moniker as the Seaport.

At the intersection of Fulton and Water Streets, the main Seaport gateway, is the *Titanic* Memorial Lighthouse, a small white lighthouse that commemorates the sinking of the RMS *Titanic* in 1912. Beyond the lighthouse, Fulton Street turns into a cobblestone pedestrian mall. On the south side of Fulton is the Seaport's architectural centerpiece, Schermerhorn Row, a redbrick terrace of Georgian- and Federal-style warehouses and countinghouses built from 1810 to 1812. Cross South Street to Pier 16, where historic 19th- and 20th-century ships are docked. Pier 16 also is the departure point for various seasonal cruises. (Ship tours are included in the admission to the South Street Seaport Museum).

Across South Street along the East River are Pier 17 and the renovated Tin Building. Previously the longtime site of the Fulton Fish Market, in 2022, the latter reopened as the Tin Building by renowned chef Jean-Georges Vongerichten, a high-end dining destination and specialty food market (🌐 *tinbuilding.com*). In 2018, the Pier 17 building became a multilevel office complex with several restaurants and bars at street level, and a 60,000-square-foot rooftop that's programmed with live summer concerts (🌐 *rooftopatpier17.com*). But the real highlight is the wraparound public wharf that's open year-round, with seating and stunning views of the harbor and Brooklyn Bridge. ✉ *The Seaport, Financial District* ☎ *212/732–8257* 🌐 *www.seaportdistrict.nyc* Ⓜ *2, 3, 4, 5, A, C, J, Z to Fulton St.*

★ Staten Island Ferry

NAUTICAL SIGHT | Some 70,000 people ride the free ferry daily to Staten Island, one of the city's five boroughs, and you, too, can join them for the city's most scenic commute. Without paying a cent, you get phenomenal views of the Lower Manhattan skyline, the Statue of Liberty, Ellis Island, and Governors Island during the 25-minute cruise across New York Harbor. You also pass tugboats, freighters, and cruise ships—a reminder that this is very much still a working harbor. The ferry sails every 15–30 minutes (24 hours a day, 365 days a year) from Whitehall Terminal

On a typical weekday, five ferries make roughly 110 trips back and forth between Staten Island and Manhattan, transporting thousands of passengers.

at Whitehall and South Streets, on the east side of Battery Park. You must disembark once you reach the opposite terminal, but you can loop around and reboard if you don't plan to stay. A small concession stand on each ferry sells a few snacks and beverages (including beer). If you're sightseeing, avoid the packed morning and afternoon rush hours. ✉ *4 Whitehall St., Financial District* ☎ *212/639–9675* 🌐 *www.siferry.com* 🎫 *Free* Ⓜ *1 to South Ferry; R, W to Whitehall St.; 4, 5 to Bowling Green.*

★ Statue of Liberty

ISLAND | Though you must endure a long wait and onerous security, it's worth the trouble to see one of the quintessential images of New York. Access to the crown is strictly limited, and tickets must be booked months in advance; otherwise, it's possible to view the museum in the pedestal, but even those tickets often sell out. Much more interesting—and well worth exploring—is the Ellis Island museum, which traces the story of immigration in New York City with moving exhibits throughout the restored processing building. Go early if you want to see everything, and allow plenty of time for security and lines. The ferry stops first at the statue and then continues to Ellis Island. ✉ *Liberty Island, Financial District* ☎ *212/363–3200, 877/523–9849 ticket reservations* 🌐 *www.statueofliberty.org* 🎫 *Free; ferry $24.50 round-trip (includes Ellis Island)* Ⓜ *4, 5 to Bowling Green; 1 to South Ferry; R, W to Whitehall St.*

Restaurants

Delmonico's

$$$$ | STEAK HOUSE | One of the city's oldest restaurants (open since 1837), elegant Delmonico's is steeped in history. It was Manhattan's first fine-dining establishment, with an inventive 19th-century chef de cuisine whose most famous dishes, including eggs Benedict, lobster Newberg, and baked Alaska, are still served. **Known for:** outstanding steak and seafood selection; classic ambience and decor; good brunch/lunch deals. *$ Average main: $49 ✉ 56 Beaver St., at William St., Financial District ☎ 212/381–1237 ⊕ www.theoriginaldelmonicos.com M 2, 3 to Wall St.; R to Whitehall St.; 4, 5 to Bowling Green; J, Z to Broad St.*

Jing Fong

$$ | CHINESE | FAMILY | The legendary Jing Fong restaurant, which could seat 800, moved into a (relatively) smaller space after the pandemic (it now seats about 125) but the dim sum and other favorite dishes still draw legions of fans, especially for weekend brunch. The dim sum carts still rove between the tables, with goodies that range from the familiar (barbecue pork buns and rice rolls) to more adventurous items like chicken feet, tripe, and snails. **Known for:** casual but classy decor; dim sum; crowds on weekends. *$ Average main: $18 ✉ 202 Centre St., at Howard St., Chinatown ☎ 212/964–5256 ⊕ www.jingfongny.com M 6, J, N, Q, R, W, Z to Canal St.; B, D to Grand St.*

Locanda Verde

$$$ | ITALIAN | Run by one of Manhattan's top chefs, Andrew Carmellini, this is a consistently fine option for satisfying, sophisticated TriBeCa dining. Occupying the ground floor corner of the Greenwich Hotel (and affiliated with Robert De Niro), Locanda Verde is warm and welcoming, with accents of brick and wood, and large windows that open to the street, weather permitting. **Known for:** exquisite handmade pasta; seasonally inspired dishes; occasional celebrity sightings. *$ Average main: $39 ✉ 377 Greenwich St., at N. Moore St., TriBeCa ☎ 212/925–3797 ⊕ www.locandaverdenyc.com M 1 to Franklin St.*

Lure Fishbar

$$$ | SEAFOOD | Decorated like the clubby interior of a sleek luxury liner, Lure has been serving oceanic fare in multiple culinary styles since 2004 and is still on-trend and serving the highest caliber seafood. From the sushi bar, try the Lure House Roll—a shrimp tempura roll crowned with spicy tuna—or opt for well-executed dishes from the kitchen, like steamed red snapper with bok choy

Some of the storefronts and signage in Chinatown are bilingual—but some are just in Chinese.

in a red curry or a classic lobster roll. **Known for:** clubby atmosphere; cool bar scene; popular brunch. $ *Average main: $37* ✉ *142 Mercer St., at Prince St., SoHo* ☎ *212/431–7676* 🌐 *www.lurefishbar.com* Ⓜ *B, D, F, M to Broadway–Lafayette St.; N, R, W to Prince St.*

Metropolis by Marcus Samuelsson

$$$$ | **MODERN AMERICAN** | Adding to downtown's destination-dining scene is this contemporary-American restaurant helmed by celebrity chef Marcus Samuelsson, located on the lobby level of the new Perelman Performing Arts Center at the World Trade Center. Its creative menu reinvents, and in some cases, perfects, classic dishes with touches from Italy, Mexico, Japan, and the Caribbean—such as short rib with potato churro, smoked hamachi taco, angel hair vongole with salsa verde, and aged Long Island duck with mole and braised sweet potatoes. **Known for:** globally influenced, farm-fresh dishes; daring cocktails; unique design befitting modern PAC architecture. $ *Average main: $42* ✉ *251 Fulton St., at Greenwich St., Financial District* ☎ *212/266–3018* 🌐 *www.metropolisbymarcus.com* ⏲ *Closed Mon.* Ⓜ *1 to WTC Cortlandt; E to WTC; 2, 3, 4, 5, A, C, J, Z to Fulton St.*

★ **Raoul's**

$$$$ | **FRENCH** | One of the first trendy spots in SoHo, this arty French restaurant with closely packed tables and booths has yet to lose its touch, either in the kitchen or with the atmosphere. Expect a chic bar scene and bistro-inspired dishes, with oysters and salads to start and pastas, fish, and meat options for mains.

Known for: legendary burgers; walls covered with paintings and photos; narrow stairs to the upper room are a bit treacherous in heels. *Average main: $42* *180 Prince St., between Sullivan and Thompson Sts., SoHo* *212/966–3518* *www.raouls.com* *No lunch weekdays* *C, E to Spring St.*

Roscioli

$$ | **ITALIAN** | Does New York City *really* need another Italian restaurant? When it's a long-time beloved favorite eatery from Rome, the answer is a resounding *sì*! **Known for:** legendary restaurant from Rome; excellent takes on Roman pasta staples; rustic atmsophere. *Average main: $27* *43 MacDougal St., at King St., SoHo* *rosciolinyc.com* *1 to Houston.*

Sadelle's

$$ | **AMERICAN** | Brunch staples like smoked fish, bagels, pancakes, and French toast don't get more refined than they do at this airy, sophisticated spot in the heart of the SoHo action. Come during the week for a more leisurely experience, because who said brunch has to be relegated to weekends? **Known for:** elevated NY delicatessen scene; one of the few spots in town that takes reservations for brunch; to-die-for cinnamon sticky buns. *Average main: $21* *463 W. Broadway, near W. Houston St., SoHo* *212/776–4926* *www.sadelles.com* *No dinner* *B, D, F, M to Broadway–Lafayette St.*

★ Torrisi

$$$ | **ITALIAN** | The high ceiling with green pillars sculpted into the walls and deep circular leather booths on the periphery of the dining room, opulent Torrisi is a quintessential New York dining experience. Technically, Torrisi is Italian cuisine, but the menu is an homage to old immigration patterns to Little Italy, Chinatown, and the Lower East Side, as dishes' ingredients often make references to various demographics: the chopped chicken liver with Manischewitz, octopus Nha Trang, stir-fried lobster with ginger... you get the idea. **Known for:** difficult to nab a table without a reservation; professional service; excellent martinis. *Average main: $30* *275 Mulberry St., at Jersey St., NoLIta* *212/254–3000* *torrisinyc.com* *Closed Sun. No lunch Mon.* *B, D, F, M to Broadway–Lafayette St.*

Hotels

Arlo SoHo

$ | **HOTEL** | Affordable rates, a prime location, a popular restaurant and bar, and a funky vibe make up for the tiny rooms at this sleek microhotel. **Pros:** supersleek design; reasonable prices for prime

SoHo location; upgraded rooms are a bit larger, some with balconies. **Cons:** small rooms; glass-enclosed bathrooms lack privacy; no in-room minibar. *Rooms from: $290* *231 Hudson St., near Canal St., SoHo* *212/806–7000* *www.arlohotels.com* *325 rooms* *No Meals* *1 to Canal St.; C, E to Spring St.*

★ The Beekman

$$$ | **HOTEL** | After sitting abandoned for many years, a historic, late-19th-century office building was transformed into a chic hotel that channels old New York, home to the gorgeous lobby's Bar Room and atmospheric Temple Court restaurant, by award-winning chef Tom Colicchio; and Le Gratin, helmed by chef Daniel Boulud. **Pros:** gorgeous design with notable atrium and lots of character; romantic, refined restaurant; fantastic concierge team. **Cons:** service can be inconsistent; buzzy lobby bar can be overcrowded; pricey for the location. *Rooms from: $450* *123 Nassau St., at Beekman St., Financial District* *212/233–2300* *www.thebeekman.com* *287 rooms* *No Meals* *2, 3, 4, 5, A, C, J, Z to Fulton St.*

★ Crosby Street Hotel

$$$$ | **HOTEL** | This whimsically designed boutique hotel has an eclectic aesthetic, with colorful furnishings and large, sun-filled rooms that have floor-to-ceiling windows. **Pros:** fabulous, fun design; solicitous service; great bar. **Cons:** small gym; comes at a very high price; no pool or spa. *Rooms from: $995* *79 Crosby St., between Prince and Spring Sts., SoHo* *212/226–6400* *www.firmdalehotels.com* *86 rooms* *No Meals* *6 to Spring St.; N, R, W to Prince St.; B, D, F, M to Broadway–Lafayette St.*

Four Seasons New York Downtown

$$$$ | **HOTEL** | This superluxurious property by the Four Seasons is a posh haven near the World Trade Center, with a modern residential-inspired design, a 75-foot indoor pool, an indulgent spa, and CUT restaurant by celebrity chef Wolfgang Puck. **Pros:** sleek design; excellent pool, spa, and gym; high-rise views. **Cons:** expensive for the location; limited dining and nightlife options nearby; far from uptown sites and museums. *Rooms from: $890* *27 Barclay St., at Church St., TriBeCa* *646/880–1999* *www.fourseasons.com/newyorkdowntown* *161 rooms* *No Meals* *A, C to Chambers St.; 2, 3 to Park Pl*

★ The Greenwich Hotel

$$$$ | **HOTEL** | Understated and inviting, this award-winning boutique hotel manages to fly under the radar even though Robert De Niro is an owner and its rustic Italian restaurant, Locanda Verde, is widely acclaimed. **Pros:** fabulous restaurant (also available for room service); gorgeous indoor pool; excellent service. **Cons:** some plumbing noise; high prices; the location is far from most subways. *$ Rooms from: $955 ✉ 377 Greenwich St., between N. Moore and Franklin Sts., TriBeCa ☎ 212/941–8900 🌐 www.thegreenwichhotel.com 88 rooms No Meals M 1 to Franklin St.*

Hotel 50 Bowery

$$ | HOTEL | With a design aesthetic and food offerings inspired by the neighborhood's multifaceted heritage, this thoroughly modern hotel from Hyatt's Joie de Vivre group takes full advantage of its downtown location. **Pros:** rooms on higher floors have great views; double-paned windows mean no street noise; great rooftop bar. **Cons:** $30 "resort" tax nightly add-on fee; busy streets outside; a subway ride from most uptown tourist sites. *$ Rooms from: $399 ✉ 50 Bowery, near Canal St., Chinatown ☎ 212/508–8000 🌐 www.jdvhotels.com 229 rooms No Meals M B, D to Grand St.*

The Wall Street Hotel

$$$$ | HOTEL | Notable for its elegance, service, and history, this sophisticated hotel is a rival to Midtown's upscale lodging—large rooms are outfitted with soft textures and tones inspired by pearls—alluding to the building's commercial heritage—including velvet furnishings and Frette linens. **Pros:** spacious, inviting guest rooms; outstanding hospitality; fantastic on-site restaurant. **Cons:** neighborhood nightlife is minimal; peak hotel rates are high for area; narrow streets make noise echo upward. *$ Rooms from: $585 ✉ 88 Wall St., between Water and Pearl Sts., Financial District ☎ 212/688–9255 🌐 www.thewallsthotel.com 180 rooms No Meals M 2, 3 to Wall St.*

★ The Dead Rabbit

COCKTAIL BARS | For exquisite cocktails in a quintessentially old–New York locale, venture to the tip of Manhattan for a night of Irish hospitality in a 19th-century-inspired saloon. The ground-floor taproom serves craft beers and whiskeys of the world, while a warren of upstairs parlor spaces shakes and stirs craft cocktails, many putting Irish whiskey to excellent use. If the drink menu isn't doing the trick, challenge one of the ace bartenders to mix up something special for your palate. The Dead Rabbit is always lively and unpretentious, and isn't hung up on dress codes or door policies typical of some New York cocktail dens—though it's still a good idea to reserve a table. There's also a solid food menu built on Irish faves, Monday oyster and Guinness specials, guest chefs, and occasional live music. ✉ *30 Water St., between Broad St. and Coenties Slip, Financial District* 🌐 *www.deadrabbitnyc.com* Ⓜ *1 to South Ferry; R, W to Whitehall St.*

★ Overstory

COCKTAIL BARS | High up on Floor 64 of the historic 70 Pine tower is this suave cocktail lounge, where guests come as much for the spectacular views and polished service as they do for the high-end, deliciously creative libations. Pass through the fine dining room that is Saga on your way up a flight of stairs, into oval-shape Overstory, which occupies the former A.I.G. board room and whose art deco design befits this 1930s-era skyscraper. The wrap-around balcony has seating, though lofty winds may limit outdoor time to just long enough for a few marvelous skyline photos. Reservations are highly recommended. ✉ *70 Pine St., 64th fl., between William and Pearl Sts., Financial District* ☎ *212/339–3963* 🌐 *overstory-nyc.com* Ⓜ *2, 3, 4, 5 to Wall St.; 2, 3, 4, 5, A, C, J, Z to Fulton St.*

Performing Arts

Perelman Performing Arts Center

PERFORMANCE VENUES | The World Trade Center site's final public element opened to much fanfare in 2023, adding a major cultural attraction to Lower Manhattan. The Perelman Performing Arts Center, or PAC, is a striking architectural vision wedged between the WTC's skyscrapers and the 9/11 Memorial & Museum. It's built like a patterned stone cube rising 10 stories, its entry stairs and elevator tucked modestly below on Fulton Street, with innovative lighting making the facade's 5,000 half-inch-thick marble tiles appear to glow at night. Its 90,000 square feet encompass the Lobby Stage with free shows (usually Thursday–Sunday); the lobby's modern, elegant restaurant and bar, Metropolis by Marcus Samuelsson; and three principal theaters within. What makes the PAC uncommon, however, is that each venue can be used independently or by combining them. The auditoria can transform into more than 60 stage-audience arrangements, with capacities ranging from 90 to 950 seats, and with audience circulation and lobby areas varying to match. Artistic programming is intended to be as daring as the architecture, with a wide array of works, including feature commissions, world premieres, co-productions, and collaborative work across theater, dance, music, opera, film, and more. Tickets are pleasantly priced for all budgets. ✉ *251 Fulton St., at Greenwich St., Financial District* ☎ *212/266–3000* 🌐 *pacnyc.org* Ⓜ *1 to WTC Cortlandt; E to WTC; 2, 3, 4, 5, A, C, J, Z to Fulton St.*

Chapter 4

THE VILLAGE AND LOWER EAST SIDE

Updated by
Arabella Bowen

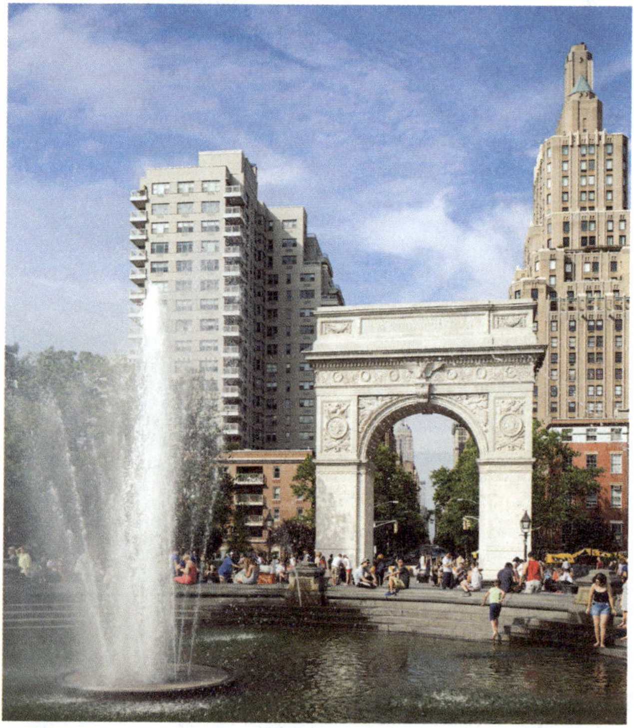

Sights	Restaurants	Hotels	Shopping	Nightlife
★★★☆☆	★★★★★	★★★☆☆	★★★☆☆	★★★☆☆

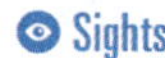

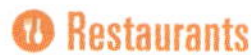

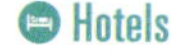

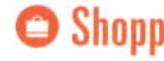

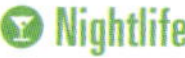

The Village Walking Tour

Curving streets, pretty alleys, and historic townhouses—many with artsy and literary pasts—put the tree-lined streets of Greenwich Village and the West Village in high demand. These charming areas are often grouped together as "the Village."

1 Start at Washington Square Park's classic, circular greystone fountain, arguably the beating heart of downtown, a magnet for all kinds of walks of life. You'll see everyone from New York University students to buskers and protesters to skateboarders hanging around it day and night. The triumphal Washington Arch looming above was designed by celebrated New York architect Stanford White to mark the centennial of George Washington's 1789 inauguration as president of the United States.

2 Head through the Washington Arch to reach the foot of 5th Avenue, the very start of the grand avenue that stretches all the way to West 143rd Street in Harlem. Turn right and walk along Washington Square North to admire its Greek Revival and Federal row houses built between 1833 and 1937. Known as The Row, they belonged to merchants and bankers, then artists and writers. Edward Hopper, the artist best known for *Nighthawks*, lived and painted at No. 3 from 1913 until his death in 1967.

Walking Tour 101

HIGHLIGHTS
Literary haunts, LGBTQ+ monuments, and picturesque, tree-lined blocks where getting lost is part of the charm

WHERE TO START
Washington Square Park

LENGTH
1½ hours

WHERE TO END
West 3rd Street (just south of Washington Square Park)

BEST TIME TO GO
Weekday afternoons and the weeks before Halloween, when locals go all out to decorate their stoops for the holiday

WORST TIME TO GO
Weekends at brunch hour

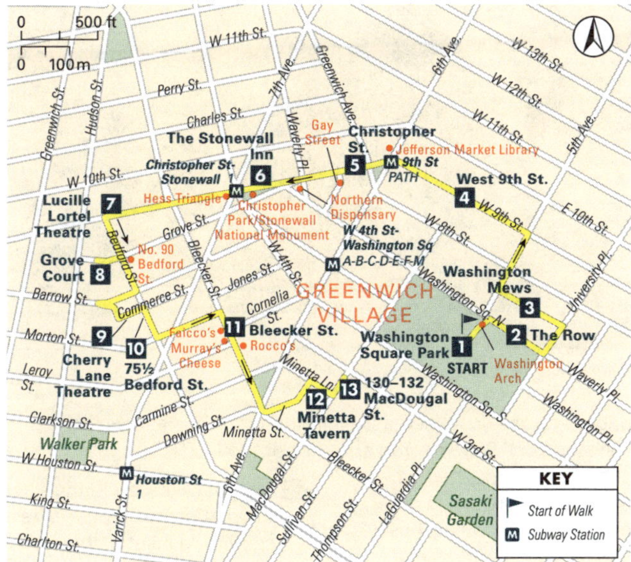

3 Turn left onto University Place and walk a few steps north until you see a gated brick-wall alley on the left. A rarity in Manhattan, Washington Mews is a pretty, pedestrian-only cobblestone street lined with former mews (carriage houses). Stroll through it to 5th Avenue and turn right.

4 Walk a block and a half north to West 9th Street, and turn left. With its handsome brownstones, eclectic ornamental details, and stately Ginkgo trees ("Greenwich" came from the Dutch *Groenwijck*, for "Green District"), one-block-long West 9th Street captures the essence of Greenwich Village. At the corner of 6th Avenue, look to the right to admire Jefferson Market Library at 425 6th Avenue. The striking redbrick Victorian Gothic building was originally built as part of a courthouse and jail for women prisoners; its clock tower still works and the gated garden out front is the area's loveliest greenspace.

5 Cross 6th and Greenwich avenues to reach the start of Christopher Street, the symbolic heart of New York's LGBTQ+ community. As you head west, look out for Gay Street on your left, a tiny thoroughfare that became famous in the 1930s, when Ruth McKenney began

Cherry Lane Theatre

publishing zany autobiographical stories in *The New Yorker* about what happened when she and her sister moved to No. 14 from Ohio. Those stories went on to inspire the 1953 Broadway musical *Wonderful Town*. (In 2022, the landmarked building was declared condemned and was torn down the following year.)

6 Stay to the right of the redbrick Northern Dispensary. It's located at the intersection of Waverly Place—built in 1831 on what was then the northernmost part of the city—to reach The Stonewall Inn at No. 53, site of the famous Stonewall riots of 1969, which became one of the biggest catalysts of the gay civil rights movement. The inn—which is still a bar today—along with the triangular Christopher Park across the street, now comprise the Stonewall National Monument, the first U.S. national monument to LGBTQ+ rights.

7 Cross 7th Avenue. On the southwest corner, look for the Hess Triangle inset in the pavement. The city's tiniest piece of private property, its mosaic tiles spell out: PROPERTY OF THE HESS ESTATE WHICH HAS NEVER BEEN DEDICATED FOR PUBLIC PURPOSES. Two blocks west, on the north side of Christopher Street facing the top of Bedford Street, the Lucille Lortel Theatre at No. 121 is an acclaimed Off-Broadway theater. Look for stars honoring legendary playwrights like David Mamet in the sidewalk.

8 Turn left onto Bedford Street, an attractive artery that runs diagonally southeast to 7th Avenue, with maze-like streets offside. One block down, jag right on Grove Street to peep through the gate to magical Grove Court, whose red row houses with white window shutters were built in 1848 to house local workers. Back at the corner of Grove and Bedford, fans of *Friends* will recognize the six-story tan building at No. 90 as the location of Monica's and Joey's apartments.

9 At Barrow Street, loop around to the right, then left along Commerce. This street is an atmospheric elbow that connects back to Bedford, passing by the Cherry Lane Theatre at 38 Commerce Street (Barbra Streisand worked here as an assistant manager before making it big on Broadway).

10 Just south of Commerce, 75½ Bedford Street on the right has the distinction of being New York City's narrowest house. Measuring just 9½ feet wide by 32 feet deep, past residents include the actor John Barrymore and poet Edna St. Vincent Millay.

Grove Court

11 Continue one block to Morton Street, turn left, and walk two blocks north on 7th Avenue to reach Bleecker Street. Cross 7th Avenue to the right to reach a stretch of Bleecker Street with speciality purveyors beloved by foodies. Pop into the old-world Faicco's (No. 260) for Italian specialties, sniff out stinky cheeses at Murray's Cheese (No. 254), or try cannolis at Rocco's (No. 243).

12 When you reach 6th Avenue, cross the street and make a hard left onto Minetta Street. Then turn right again when it curves into Minetta Lane to hit MacDougal Street, where a vintage neon sign advertises the Minetta Tavern on the corner, at No. 113. Originally a Prohibition speakeasy, it became the Minetta Tavern in 1937, attracting the likes of Ernest Hemingway and Dylan Thomas. (It's still a restaurant and drinking hole, with many original details still intact.)

13 Cross the street and head north to reach the last stop on this walk, just below West 3rd Street. Here, two adjoining brick row houses (Nos. 130–132) are notable for their delicate cast-iron double porch. Author Louisa May Alcott lived here from 1867 to 1870 and likely finished *Little Women* here in 1868 before returning to New England. From here, you're just a block south from where you started, at Washington Square Park.

NEIGHBORHOOD SNAPSHOT

TOP EXPERIENCES

- People-watching in Washington Square Park
- Strolling and window-shopping along the picturesque streets of the West Village
- Taking a tour at the Lower East Side Tenement Museum
- Checking out the art galleries on the Lower East Side and, increasingly, in the East Village, too
- Eating at some of the city's most varied and delicious restaurants

GETTING HERE

The West 4th Street subway stop—serviced by the A, B, C, D, E, F, and M lines—puts you on the west side of Greenwich Village. Farther west, the 1 train has stops at Houston Street and at Christopher Street–Sheridan Square. The L stops at 8th Avenue, and the A, C, and E trains stop at 14th Street, which is the northern boundary of the West Village.

For the East Village, take the N, R, or W subway line to 8th Street–New York University (NYU), the 6 to Astor Place, the L to 3rd Avenue or 1st Avenue, or the F to 2nd Avenue. For the Lower East Side, go to the 2nd Avenue stop on the F and then walk southeast, or take the F, M, J, or Z to the Delancey Street–Essex Street stop.

PAUSE HERE

- **64 Perry Street.** This brownstone, just west of West 4th Street, was the home of Carrie Bradshaw, the fictional writer on *Sex and the City*. On the show, she actually lived in the East 60s but the building's steps made for many memorable scenes. ✉ *64 Perry St.* 🚆 *1 to Christopher St.*
- **The *Physical Graffiti* Buildings.** Fans of classic rock might recognize the twin five-story buildings at 96 and 98 St. Marks Place, just east of 1st Avenue. They are the cover models for Led Zeppelin's 1975 double album *Physical Graffiti*. ✉ *96–98 St. Marks Pl.* 🚆 *L to 1st Ave.*

The charming tree-lined streets of the Village are beloved by New Yorkers (whether they can afford to live here or not) for their cozy restaurants and cafés, chic cocktail bars, and inviting boutiques.

Long the home of writers, artists, bohemians, and bon vivants, "the Village" is made up of Greenwich Village proper (the area surrounding Washington Square Park) and the West Village, from around 7th Avenue to the Hudson River. Greenwich Village, in prime New York University (NYU) territory, has lots of young people, while the West Village's maze-like streets attract well-to-do couples and families and a substantial community of older gay men and some lesbians. Both residential areas are a joy to roam around, camera in hand; getting a little bit lost is part of the fun.

In contrast, the streets of the East Village and the Lower East Side are some of the most eclectic in New York City. These lively neighborhoods have a deep immigrant past and have evolved into vibrant destinations known for their experimental restaurants, ever-expanding contemporary art gallery scene, and gritty dive bars and sultry live-music venues where you can party until the wee hours any day of the week. But spend time wandering the side streets, and you'll be struck by the pastiche of ethnicities whose imprints are still visible in the neighborhoods' shops, eateries, and of course, people.

Sights

Bleecker Street

STREET | Walking the stretch of Bleecker Street between 7th Avenue and Broadway provides a smattering of just about everything synonymous with Greenwich Village these days: NYU buildings, record stores, Italian cafés and food shops, pizza and takeout joints, bars and nightclubs, and funky boutiques. A lazy afternoon here may consist of sampling some of the city's best pizza, grabbing an espresso, and soaking up the downtown fashion scene. Foodies love the blocks between 6th and 7th Avenues for the specialty purveyors like Murray's Cheese (No. 254). At the intersection of Bleecker and Carmine Streets is Our Lady of Pompeii Church, where Mother Cabrini, a naturalized Italian immigrant who became the first American citizen to be canonized, often prayed. West of 7th Avenue, the shops get more upscale,

The Village and Lower East Side
MEATPACKING DISTRICT
WEST VILLAGE
TRIBECA
Little Island
HUDSON RIVER
Pier 52
Pier 51
Pier 46
Pier 45
Pier 40
West Street
W. 18th St.
W. 17th St.
W. 16th St.
W. 15th St.
W. 13th St.
W. 12th St.
W. 11th St.
W. 8th St.
8th Avenue
7th Avenue
Avenue of the Americas (6th Ave.)
W. 14th St.
18th St 1-2
14th St 1-2-3
14th St A-C-E-L
14th St F-M
PATH
Little W. 12th St.
Gansevoort St.
Horatio St.
Jane St.
W. 12th St.
Bethune St.
Bank St.
Hudson St.
Greenwich St.
Washington St.
Perry St.
Charles St.
W. 10th St.
Christopher St.
W. 11th St.
W. 4th St.
Bleecker St.
Greenwich Ave.
Waverly Pl.
9th St PATH
Christopher St-Stonewall 1-2
W 4th St-Washington Sq A-C-E B-D-F-M
Christopher St PATH
Grove St.
7th Ave. South
Jones St.
Cornelia St.
MacDougal St.
Bedford St.
Carmine St.
Downing St.
Barrow St.
Morton St.
Leroy St.
Clarkson St.
Hudson St.
Houston St 1-2
W. Houston St.
King St.
Varick St.
Charlton St.
Vandam St.
Spring St.
Spring St A-C-E
Ave. of the Americas
Washington St.
Greenwich St.
Dominick St.
Broome St.
Watts St.
Holland Tunnel Entrance
Canal St 1-2
Holland Tunnel Exit
Vestry St.
Laight St.
Hubert St.
Beach St.
N. Moore St.
Franklin St.
Harrison St.
Greenwich St.
Jay St.
0 1,000ft
0 200m
Sights
Bleecker Street, 1
International Center of Photography, 6
Orchard Street, 7
St. Marks Place, 3
Tenement Museum, 5
Tompkins Square Park, 4
Washington Square Park, 2
Restaurants
Cauldron Chicken, 5
Don Angie, 1
Emily, 4
Fish Cheeks, 6
Katz's Delicatessen, 9
L'Antica Pizzeria Da Michele, 2
The Little Owl, 3
Momofuku Noodle Bar, 7
Russ & Daughters Cafe, 8
Hotels
The Bowery Hotel, 3
citizenM New York Bowery Hotel, 4
The Jane, 1
Nine Orchard, 5
Washington Square Hotel, 2

KEY
Sights
Restaurants
Hotels
GREENWICH VILLAGE
EAST VILLAGE
NOHO
NOLITA
SOHO
LITTLE ITALY
LOWER EAST SIDE
CHINATOWN
Union Square
Union Square Park
Stuyvesant Park
Tompkins Square Park
Washington Square Park
Sara D. Roosevelt Park
Columbus Park
Thomas Paine Park
Union Sq-14th St
4-5-6
N-Q-R-W
3rd Ave
1st Ave
8th St-NYU
Astor Pl
Bleecker St
Broadway-Lafayette St
B-D-F-M
Lower East Side-2nd Ave
Prince St
Spring St
Bowery
J-Z
Delancey St-Essex St
J-M-Z
Grand St
B-D
Canal St-Holland Tunnel
A-C-E
Canal St
R-W
N-Q
East Broadway
Franklin St
1-2
E. 18th St.
E. 17th St.
E. 16th St.
E. 15th St.
W. 15th St.
E. 14th St.
E. 13th St.
E. 12th St.
E. 11th St.
E. 10th St.
W. 10th St.
W. 9th St.
E. 9th St.
St. Marks Pl.
E. 7th St.
E. 6th St.
E. 5th St.
E. 4th St.
E. 3rd St.
E. 2nd St.
E. 1st St.
E. Houston St.
W. Houston St.
Washington Sq. N.
Washington Sq. S.
W. 4th St.
W. 3rd St.
Bleecker St.
Bond St.
Astor Pl.
Stuyvesant St.
Irving Pl.
Park Avenue
Union Sq. W.
University Pl.
Broadway
4th Avenue
3rd Avenue
2nd Avenue
1st Avenue
Avenue A
5th Avenue
Lafayette St.
Bowery
Sullivan St.
Thompson St.
Wooster St.
West Broadway
Greene St.
Mercer St.
Crosby St.
Mulberry St.
Mott St.
Elizabeth St.
Chrystie St.
Forsyth St.
Eldridge St.
Allen St.
Orchard St.
Essex St.
Norfolk St.
Ludlow St.
Stanton St.
Rivington St.
Prince St.
Spring St.
Kenmare St.
Delancey St.
Broome St.
Grand St.
Hester St.
Canal St.
Centre St.
Lispenard St.
Walker St.
White St.
Franklin St.
Leonard St.
Worth St.
Thomas St.
Church St.
W. Broadway
Baxter St.
Bayard St.
Park Row
Catherine St.
Henry St.
Madison St.
Market St.
E. Broadway
Manhattan Bridge

The East Village is predominantly residential and has mostly low-rise buildings.

with fashion and home-furnishings boutiques featuring antiques, eyeglasses, handbags, shoes, and designer clothing. ✉ *Greenwich Village* Ⓜ *A, B, C, D, E, F, M to W. 4th St.*

International Center of Photography

ART MUSEUM | Founded in 1974 by photojournalist Cornell Capa (photographer Robert Capa's brother), ICP continues to put on exhibitions that explore the timely social and political aspects of photojournalism. The institution, which has moved its collection of more than 150,000 original prints—spanning the history of photography, from daguerreotypes to large-scale pigment prints—several times, finally has a permanent home with both education and exhibition spaces. The new building's spacious, second- and third-floor galleries really allow the exhibits to shine. There's a gift shop and small café on the ground floor. **■ TIP→ It's pay-what-you-wish ($5 minimum) on Thursday night 6 pm–9 pm.** ✉ *79 Essex St., between E. Houston and Broome Sts., Lower East Side* ☎ *212/857–0000* 🌐 *www.icp.org* 🎟 *$18* 🕒 *Closed Tues.* Ⓜ *F, M, J, Z to Delancey–Essex St.; B, D to Grand St.*

Orchard Street

STREET | If you're looking for a good place to start your exploration of the Lower East Side, Orchard Street, from Houston all the way down to Canal Street, is probably the densest conglomeration of restaurants, cafés, boutiques, and art galleries. It's the perfect place to wander, checking out the art, browsing for clothes and knickknacks, stopping for a coffee or a glass of wine, and having a meal. Although no one gallery really stands out—you're best off visiting whatever catches your eye—look out for Perrotin (✉ *130 Orchard St.*) and Krause Gallery (✉ *149 Orchard St.*). ✉ *Orchard St., Lower East Side* Ⓜ *F to East Broadway or 2nd Ave.*

St. Marks Place

STREET | Once the hub of the edgy East Village, St. Marks Place is the name given to idiosyncratic East 8th Street between 3rd Avenue and Avenue A. During the 1950s, beatniks Allen Ginsberg and Jack Kerouac lived in the area; the 1960s brought Bill Graham's Fillmore East (✉ *105 2nd Avenue*) and the experimental Electric Circus nightclub (at Nos. 19–25 St. Marks), where the Velvet Underground and the Grateful Dead played. The shaved-head punk scene followed, and at No. 33, is where the punk store Manic Panic first foisted its lurid hair dyes on the world. At No. 57 stood the short-lived Club 57, which attracted such 1980s stalwarts as artist Keith Haring.

These days, there's not much cutting edge left. Some of the facades lead to luxury condos, and there are a number of global fast-food restaurants for ramen and dumplings. The block between 2nd and 3rd Avenues has turned into a bit of a global fast-food mecca, with boba tea shops and several Asian restaurants alongside stores selling cheap jewelry, smoking paraphernalia, and souvenir T-shirts. The cafés and bars from here over to Avenue A attract customers late into the night—thanks partly to lower drink prices. ✉ *8th St., between 3rd Ave. and Ave. A, East Village* Ⓜ *6 to Astor Pl.; N, R, W to 8th St.–NYU.*

★ Tenement Museum

HISTORIC SIGHT | For a step back to various points in time on the Lower East Side, book one of the experiences that revolve around the partially restored 19th-century buildings that comprise the Tenement Museum. Options include apartment tours, neighborhood walks (including "Reclaiming Black Lives" introduced in 2021), and informative talks. At 97 Orchard Street, theme tours take you through the preserved apartments of several generations of immigrants who lived in the building. The "Hard Times" tour visits the homes of Natalie Gumpertz, a German–Jewish dressmaker (dating from 1878), and Adolph and Rosaria Baldizzi, Catholic immigrants from Sicily (1935). "Sweatshop Workers" visits the Levine family's garment shop–apartment and the home of the Rogarshevsky family from Eastern Europe (1918), while "Irish Outsiders" explores the life of the Moores, an Irish American family living in the building in 1869. Nearby, at 103 Orchard Street, the *Under One Roof* exhibition explores the lives of immigrant families from Poland, China, and Puerto Rico who lived in the building after World War II. All the tours fill up fast so it's best to sign up

The Tenement Museum offers a fascinating glimpse into the lives of late-19th and early-20th-century immigrants.

in advance. ✉ *103 Orchard St., at Delancey St., Lower East Side* ☎ *877/975–3786* 🌐 *www.tenement.org* 🎟 *Most tours $30 (not all allow children under 5)* Ⓜ *B, D to Grand St.; F to Delancey St.; J, M, Z to Essex St.*

★ Tompkins Square Park

CITY PARK | **FAMILY** | This leafy park is a favorite spot, year-round, for the neighborhood locals who lunch on the benches, picnic in the central green spaces, and put on impromptu jazz concerts. There's a year-round farmers' market by the southwest corner on Sunday, and an annual Halloween dog-costume event. It wasn't always so rosy in the park, though: in 1988, police followed then-mayor Ed Koch's orders to evict the many homeless people who had set up makeshift shelters here, and homeless rights and anti-gentrification activists fought back with sticks and bottles. The park was reclaimed and reopened in 1992 with a midnight curfew, still in effect today. ✉ *From 7th to 10th St., between Aves. A and B, East Village* 🌐 *www.nycgovparks.org/parks/tompkinssquarepark* Ⓜ *6 to Astor Pl., L to 1st Ave.*

★ Washington Square Park

CITY PARK | **FAMILY** | NYU students, street musicians, skateboarders, chess players, and those just watching the grand opera of it all generate a maelstrom of activity in this physical and spiritual heart of Greenwich Village. The 9¾-acre park with its gorgeous central fountain had inauspicious beginnings as a cemetery, principally for yellow-fever victims—an estimated 10,000–22,000 bodies lie below (a headstone was even unearthed in 2009). In the early

1800s, the park was a parade ground and the site of public executions; the notorious Hanging Elm still stands at the northwest corner of the square.

The triumphal European-style **Washington Arch** at the square's northern flank marks the start of 5th Avenue. The original wood-and-papier-mâché arch, situated a half block north, was erected in 1889 to commemorate the 100th anniversary of George Washington's presidential inauguration. The arch was reproduced in Tuckahoe marble in 1892, and the statues—*Washington as General Accompanied by Fame and Valor* on one side, and *Washington as Statesman Accompanied by Wisdom and Justice* on the other—were added in 1916 and 1918, respectively. ✉ *5th Ave. between Waverly Pl. and 4th St., Greenwich Village* Ⓜ *A, B, C, D, E, F, M to W. 4th St.*

Restaurants

Cauldron Chicken

$ | CHINESE | FAMILY | This fast casual spot serves up possibly the best chicken on the planet. Servers hand you plastic gloves with your food because the chicken is so fall-off-the-bone tender and juicy that using anything but your hands to eat it is an exercise in futility. **Known for:** fall-off-the-bone chicken; very affordable combo deals; sometimes long lines to get in. Ⓢ *Average main: $14* ✉ *190 Bleecker St., between MacDougal St. and 6th Ave., Greenwich Village* ☎ *646/869–8888* 🌐 *cauldronchicken.dine.online* Ⓜ *A, B, C, D, E, F, M to W. 4th St.*

Don Angie

$$ | ITALIAN | If you have a hankering for red sauce Italian–American fare, steer clear of Little Italy, and book yourself into Don Angie, a restaurant that took a staid cuisine, updated it, and made it wholly edible again: quite a task. Sit in the retro front room—featuring checkerboard floors and arched doorways—and chow down on sopressini pasta paired with mussels, garganelli noodles with meatballs and *guanciale* (cured pork jowl), or the excellent (and hugely portioned) lasagna for two, a spiral-shape reimagining of the classic dish. **Known for:** hard table to nab; lasagna for two; creative takes on pasta dishes. Ⓢ *Average main: $26* ✉ *103 Greenwich Ave., at 12th St., West Village* ☎ *212/889–8884* 🌐 *www.donangie.com* 🕓 *No lunch* Ⓜ *1, 2, 3 to 14th St.; A, C, E to 14th St.; L to 8th Ave.*

Emily

$$ | PIZZA | The specialties at this beloved Brooklyn pizzeria and Italian-ish eatery, named for its proprietor and situated on a

Out and On Display: George Segal's sculptures of two gay couples in Christopher Park embody LGBTQ+ pride in the Village.

charming block, range from Detroit-style grandma pies (think square instead of round, thick instead of thin) to wood-fired pizzas with ingredients like clams, anchovies, and Calabrian chiles. One item that might convince you to forego pizza, though, is the signature burger, an American cheese and caramelized onion–topped beef patty on a pretzel bun. **Known for:** different kinds of pizza; great signature burger; Brooklyn favorite. *Average main: $23* *35 Downing St., at Bedford St., West Village* *917/935–6434* *www.pizzalovesemily.com* *A, B, C, D, E, F, M to W. 4th St.*

★ Fish Cheeks

$$$ | **THAI** | Seafood, spicy, and sharing plates are the key concepts at this convivial and colorful Thai restaurant, where the dishes aren't what you find on typical Thai restaurant menus. Order for the table and if you like spice, make sure to include the *zabb* (a Thai spice blend) wings to start and move on to the coconut crab curry, among other things. **Known for:** the prawn karee (yellow curry) is a luscious curry; delicious cocktails; things can get a little spicy. *Average main: $30* *55 Bond St., between Bowery and Lafayette St., East Village* *212/677–2223* *www.fishcheeksnyc.com* *6 to Bleecker St.; B, D, F, M to Broadway–Lafayette St.*

★ Katz's Delicatessen

$$ | **SANDWICHES** | Everything and nothing has changed at Katz's since it first opened in 1888, when the neighborhood was dominated by Jewish immigrants: lines still form for the giant, hand-carved corned beef and pastrami sandwiches, soul-warming soups, juicy hot dogs, and crisp half-sour pickles. You get a ticket when you walk in and then get it punched at the various stations where you pick up your food; don't lose it, or you'll have to pay the lost-ticket fee. **Known for:** pastrami sandwiches; Formica tables and vintage deli decor; weeknights are more laid-back. $ *Average main: $20* ✉ *205 E. Houston St., at Ludlow St., Lower East Side* ☎ *212/254–2246* 🌐 *www.katzsdelicatessen.com* Ⓜ *F to 2nd Ave.*

★ L'Antica Pizzeria Da Michele

$$ | **NEAPOLITAN** | The New York outpost of the 154-year-old pizzeria in Naples that the travel memoir *Eat, Pray, Love* single-handedly turned into a must-visit stop on the tourist trail, this West Village pizzeria opened in late 2022 and has managed to quickly become one of the best Neapolitan-style pizzerias in the city. The menu here is much more expansive than the original, treading into all-encompassing trattoria fare, such as pastas and salads, but stick to the classic Margherita pie and you'll walk out of here a very happy eater. **Known for:** one of the best pizzerias in the city; open early for Italian-style breakfast; "Eat, Pray, Love". $ *Average main: $25* ✉ *81 Greenwich Ave., at Bank St., West Village* ☎ *929/524–6682* 🌐 *damicheleusa.com/nyc* Ⓜ *1, 2, 3 to 14th St.*

The Little Owl

$$ | **MODERN AMERICAN** | This tiny neighborhood joint, with seating for 28 people, is exceptionally eager to please—and this attitude, plus the food, is a winning combination. The menu is just as small, which actually makes it easier to decide what you want; and what you want are the pork-veal-beef-pecorino-cheese meatball "sliders." **Known for:** perfect West Village neighborhood spot; pork loin chop; raspberry-filled beignets. $ *Average main: $27* ✉ *90 Bedford St., at Grove St., West Village* ☎ *212/741–4695* 🌐 *www.thelittleowlnyc.com* Ⓜ *1 to Christopher St.–Sheridan Sq.; A, B, C, D, E, F, M to W. 4th St.*

★ Momofuku Noodle Bar

$$ | **ASIAN FUSION** | David Chang's first restaurant, a riff on the Japanese ramen bar, opened back in 2004, and it's still a strong crowd favorite for the daily changing menu of ramen, steamed buns, and various other innovative options. The spare, bright space has plenty of counter seating and a few low tables that you might end up sharing communal-style. **Known for:** creative noodle options from a famous chef; lines out the door at meal times; pork buns. $ *Average main: $18* ✉ *171 1st Ave., between 10th and 11th Sts., East Village* ☎ *212/777–7773* 🌐 *www.momofuku.com* Ⓜ *L to 1st Ave.*

Russ & Daughters Cafe

$$ | **EASTERN EUROPEAN** | The sit-down location of the long-established (since 1914) family-owned Russ & Daughters "appetizing" shop on Houston Street offers the same smoked fish, caviar, bagels, and potato latkes as the original, along with egg dishes, salads, and cocktails in a bright, updated-deli atmosphere. The "boards" are individual (but shareable) platters of smoked fish, accompanied by your bagel, bialy, or bread of choice, so that you can assemble your own sandwich. **Known for:** classic Jewish deli food; expect lines for weekend brunch; original takeout location still at 179 East Houston Street. *Average main: $19 ✉ 127 Orchard St., between Rivington and Delancey Sts., Lower East Side ☎ 212/475–4880 🌐 www.russanddaughterscafe.com ⏲ No dinner Ⓜ F to 2nd Ave.; J, Z to Bowery.*

Hotels

★ The Bowery Hotel

$$$ | **HOTEL** | Warmed by rich tapestries and fireplaces, the Bowery Hotel is like an English hunting lodge in Manhattan, and the red-coated doormen, clubby bar, and trendy address makes this a hot property. **Pros:** fun downtown location; happening bar and lobby-lounge area; international crowd. **Cons:** service can be inconsistent; rooms lack luxe touches some might expect; lobby can get too sceney for some. *Rooms from: $565 ✉ 335 Bowery, at E. 3rd St., East Village ☎ 212/505–9100 🌐 www.theboweryhotel.com 135 rooms No Meals Ⓜ F to 2nd Ave.; 6 to Bleecker St.*

★ citizenM New York Bowery Hotel

$$ | **HOTEL** | Rising 21 floors into the sky, the citizenM makes an outsized statement that starts at ground level, with the fabulous lobby "living room," and reaches all the way to its rooftop bar and terrace. **Pros:** affordable stylish spot; especially appealing for solo travelers; enthusiastic service. **Cons:** quite small rooms; no upgrades, all rooms are the same; iPad-controlled room features can be frustrating. *Rooms from: $315 ✉ 189 Bowery, at Spring St., Lower East Side ☎ 212/372–7274 🌐 www.citizenm.com 300 rooms No Meals Ⓜ J to Bowery.*

The Jane

$ | **HOTEL** | To some, the Jane, with its appealing public spaces, is impossibly chic; to others, the tiny rooms with single beds and a shared unisex bathroom down the hall are reminiscent of Sing Sing. **Pros:** extraordinary value for the neighborhood; nice location for Meatpacking District fun; rooftop lounge. **Cons:** comically tiny standard rooms; some rooms have shared bathrooms; noise from the bar. *Rooms from: $135 ✉ 113 Jane St., at West St., West Village ☎ 212/924–6700 🌐 www.thejanenyc.com 171 rooms No Meals Ⓜ A, C, E to 14th St.; L to 8th Ave.*

★ Nine Orchard

$$$ | **HOTEL** | Housed in a 12-floor Neo-Renaissance former bank building from 1912, Nine Orchard is one of the chicest places in lower Manhattan to lay one's head for the night. **Pros:** friendly, professional service; in-house eatery from famed chef Ignacio Mattos; high-ceilinged cocktail bar for night caps. **Cons:** semi-transparent bathroom doors; slow breakfast service; in summer, expect a party in the neighborhood. *Rooms from: $525 ✉ 9 Orchard St., at Canal St., Lower East Side ☎ 212/804–9900 🌐 nineorchard.com 116 rooms Free Breakfast Ⓜ F to East Broadway.*

Washington Square Hotel

$ | **HOTEL** | Since 1902, this low-key hotel has hosted famous people (Ernest Hemingway, the Rolling Stones, and Bob Dylan all stayed here), and today it is popular with visiting New York University parents thanks to its location near Washington Square Park. **Pros:** parkside location; lots of historic character; great hotel bar. **Cons:** NYU students everywhere in the neighborhood; rooms are small; interior rooms don't get much light. *Rooms from: $250 ✉ 103 Waverly Pl., at MacDougal St., Greenwich Village ☎ 212/777–9515 🌐 www.washingtonsquarehotel.com 152 rooms Free Breakfast Ⓜ A, B, C, D, E, F, M to W. 4th St.*

Nightlife

★ Blue Note

LIVE MUSIC | Considered by many (not least its current owners) to be "the jazz capital of the world," the Blue Note was once the stomping ground for such legends as Dizzy Gillespie and still hosts a variety of acts, from Chris Botti to jazz to Latin orchestras to Maceo Parker. Expect a steep cover charge except for late shows on weekends, when the music goes from less jazzy to more funky. *✉ 131 W. 3rd St., near 6th Ave., Greenwich Village ☎ 212/475–8592 🌐 www.bluenotejazz.com Ⓜ A, B, C, D, E, F, M to W. 4th St.*

★ PDT

BARS | One of the first of the retro speakeasy bars in NYC, PDT ("Please Don't Tell") made a name for itself with top-line cocktails and it's "secret" entrance, and although it's not much of a secret anymore it's still a great spot for excellent drinks with a touch of cloak-and-dagger. Make a reservation online, then head to the unassuming Crif Dogs hot dog restaurant, where you'll be escorted through the phone booth's false back. The upscale cocktails are perfectly complemented by the hot dog specials from the neighboring shop that are also served here. ✉ *113 St. Marks Pl., between 1st Ave. and Ave. A, East Village* ☎ *212/614–0386* 🌐 *www.pdtnyc.com* Ⓜ *6 to Astor Pl.*

Performing Arts

★ The Public Theater

THEATER | Fresh, exciting theater keeps people talking about the Public Theater, which was founded in 1954 but has most recently seen such hits as Lin-Manuel Miranda's current Broadway sensation *Hamilton*, and David Byrne and Fatboy Slim's "poperetta" *Here Lies Love*, about Imelda Marcos. Many more noted productions that began here (*Hair* and *A Chorus Line*, among others) went on to Broadway and beyond. Tickets for the constantly changing roster of shows are available through the website; some "rush" tickets (day-of) are available on a first-come-first-served basis. This is also the company that puts on Shakespeare in the Park in Central Park in summer. On the mezzanine of the theater, The Library restaurant and bar is an elegant spot for a meal or a drink, whether or not you're attending a show. ✉ *425 Lafayette St., south of Astor Pl., East Village* ☎ *212/539–8500, 212/967–7555 for tickets* 🌐 *www.publictheater.org* Ⓜ *6 to Astor Pl.; N, R, W to 8th St.–NYU.*

Shopping

★ Murray's Cheese

FOOD | When you walk into this revered shop, the pungent, funky aromas will immediately announce to your olfactory glands that you've entered a cheese shop. Since 1962, Murray's has been making Bleecker Street the cheesiest spot in the city, stocking various cheddars, bries, chevres, goudas, gruyeres, manchegos, and stinky varieties. They also peddle artisanal cured meats, sausages, crackers, nuts, jams, and condiments. You can even take home a Murray's T-shirt or tote bag with "BIG CHEESE" scrawled across it. ✉ *254 Bleecker St., at Leroy St., Greenwich Village* ☎ *212/243–3200* 🌐 *murrayscheese.com* Ⓜ *A, B, C, D, E, F, M to W. 4th St.*

Chapter 5

5

UNION SQUARE AND CHELSEA

Updated by
Arabella Bowen

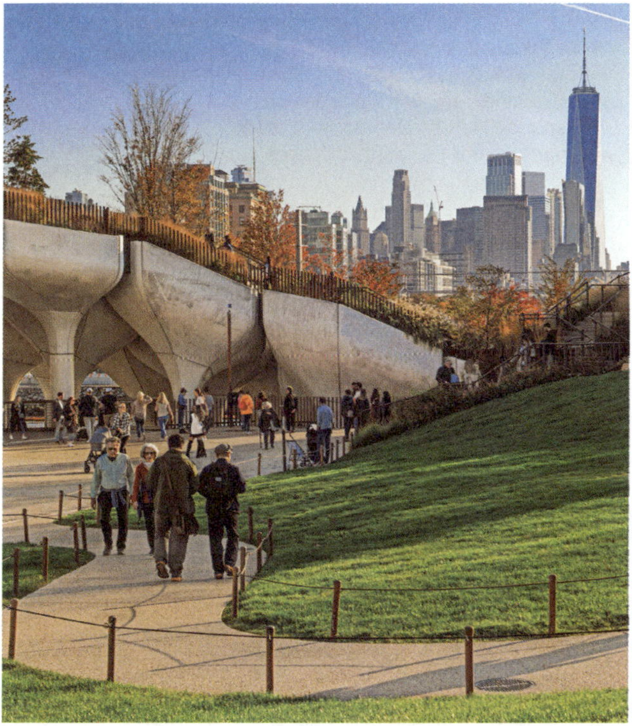

Sights ★★★★☆ | Restaurants ★★★★☆ | Hotels ★★★★☆ | Shopping ★★☆☆☆ | Nightlife ★★☆☆☆

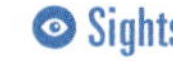

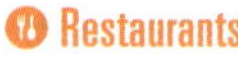

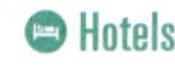

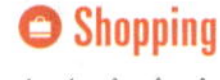

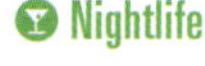

NEIGHBORHOOD SNAPSHOT

TOP EXPERIENCES

- Checking out the produce, flowers, and baked goods at the Union Square greenmarket
- Browsing the miles of books in Strand bookstore
- Gallery-hopping in Chelsea
- Walking along the High Line
- Exploring the Whitney Museum of American Art

GETTING HERE

Union Square is a major subway hub, with the 4, 5, 6, L, N, Q, R, and W lines all converging here. For Madison Square Park and the Flatiron District, take the N or R train to 23rd Street (this lets you out on Broadway). The 6 stops at 23rd and 28th Streets (on Park Avenue South).

The A, C, E, L, 1, 2, and 3 trains stop at 14th Street for both the Meatpacking District and Chelsea. The latter neighborhood is further served by the C, E, F, M, and 1 lines at 23rd Street and by the 1 train at 18th Street and 28th Street.

PAUSE HERE

- **10th Avenue Square and Overlook.** Located on the High Line at West 17th Street meet, this overlook has several rows of stadium-style seating leading down to four large picture windows that frame bustling 10th Avenue. ✉ *The High Line at 10th Ave. and 18th St.* 🌐 *www.thehighline.org* 🚇 *A, C, E to 14th St.*
- **Stuyvesant Square Park.** This lovely square, with its inviting benches and flower beds, is unknown even to many New Yorkers. It's named for Peter Stuyvesant, the last Dutch governor of New Amsterdam. ✉ *Rutherford Pl.* 🌐 *www.nycgovparks.org/parks/stuyvesant-square* 🚇 *4, 5, 6, N, Q, R, W to 14th St.–Union Sq.; L to 1st Ave.*

When a certain breed of New Yorker says they don't like to travel above 14th Street, they're usually thinking of Union Square.

This busy open space teems with skateboarders, artists, and protesters; shoppers browsing the city's largest farmers' market; and people just passing through on their way to somewhere else. The surrounding neighborhoods have their own distinct appeal: the Flatiron buzzes with hot eateries while stately Gramercy exudes small-village charm.

To the west, Chelsea, once the nexus of New York City's gay scene, is still home to plenty of gay New Yorkers, but is much more diverse today than it was in the 1990s. It's also the epicenter of the city's contemporary art galleries; there are literally hundreds along the streets here (often several in one building). The area has attracted art enthusiasts for years, but the 2009 opening of the High Line above 10th Avenue gave new life to this part of town.

Due north of the West Village, the compact Meatpacking District used to be the center of New York City's wholesale meat industry. While there are few meat markets left, the area's swanky restaurants and clubs are definitely figurative meat markets at night. The 2015 arrival of the Whitney Museum of American Art established the district's status as a major art destination. In 2021, the delightful Little Island in the Hudson River added yet another reason to visit.

Sights

★ Chelsea Market

MARKET | This former Nabisco plant—where the first Oreos were baked in 1912—now houses more than 50 shops, food vendors, and sit-down restaurants. Probably the biggest draw are the food kiosks (some with counter seating), including favorite taco spot Los Tacos No. 1, Israeli-based sandwich spot Miznon, Amy's Bread, Berlin Currywurst, Ninth Street Espresso, and so much more. Also look for an Anthropologie store, an outpost of Pearl River Mart, a wine bar, upscale groceries, teas, spices, gift baskets, kitchen supplies, and one of New York City's last independent bookstores (Posman Books). The market's funky industrial design—a tangle of glass and metal for an awning, a factory pipe converted into an indoor waterfall—complements the eclectic assortment of shops, but the narrow space can get very

34th St-
Penn Station
A-C-E
34th St-
Penn Station
1-2-3
34th St-
Herald Sq
B-D-F-M-
N-Q-R-W
W. 34th St.
34th St-
Hudson Yards
7
W. 33rd St.
33rd St
PATH
HUDSON
YARDS
7th Avenue
W. 31st St.
W. 30th St.
W. 29th St.
10th Avenue
8th Avenue
W. 28th St.
28th St
1-2
Chelsea Park
W. 27th St.
Highline
Park
11th Avenue
W. 26th St.
W. 25th St.
W. 24th St.
CHELSEA
W. 23rd St.
23rd St
A-C-E
23rd St
1-2
F-M
23rd St
PATH
9th Avenue
W. 22nd St.
W. 21st St.
W. 20th St.
W. 19th St.
W. 18th St.
18th St
1-2
CHELSEA
PIERS
11th Avenue
W. 17th St.
W. 16th St.
Avenue of the Americas (6th Ave.)
Highline
Park
W. 15th St.
Pier 57
14th St
1-2-3
F-M
14th St
W. 14th St.
14th St
A-C-E-L
PATH
MEATPACKING
DISTRICT
W. 13th St.
Little
Island
Little W. 12th St.
Greenwich Ave.
Hudson St.
Gansevoort St.
Horatio St.
Pier 52
Jane St.
Waverly Pl.
W. 4th St.
W. 12th St.
0
1,000ft
0
200m
Bethune St.
W. 11th St.
9th St
PATH
Sights
Chelsea Market, 3
Flatiron Building, 6
The High Line, 2
Little Island, 4
Pace Gallery, 1
Union Square Park and Greenmarket, 7
Whitney Museum of American Art, 5
Restaurants
Casa Mono, 8
Cosme, 6
Eataly NYC Flatiron, 5
Gramercy Tavern, 7
Loulou, 3
Market 57, 1
Pastis, 2
Skirt Steak, 4
Hotels
Ace Hotel New York, 5
The Fifth Avenue Hotel, 7
Freehand New York, 12
High Line Hotel, 1
Hotel Giraffe by Library Hotel Collection, 10
Hyatt Union Square New York, 13
The James New York – NoMad, 8
MADE Hotel, 3
The Ned, 6
The New York EDITION, 11
Park South Hotel, 9
The Ritz-Carlton Hotel, NoMad, 4
The Standard, High Line, 2

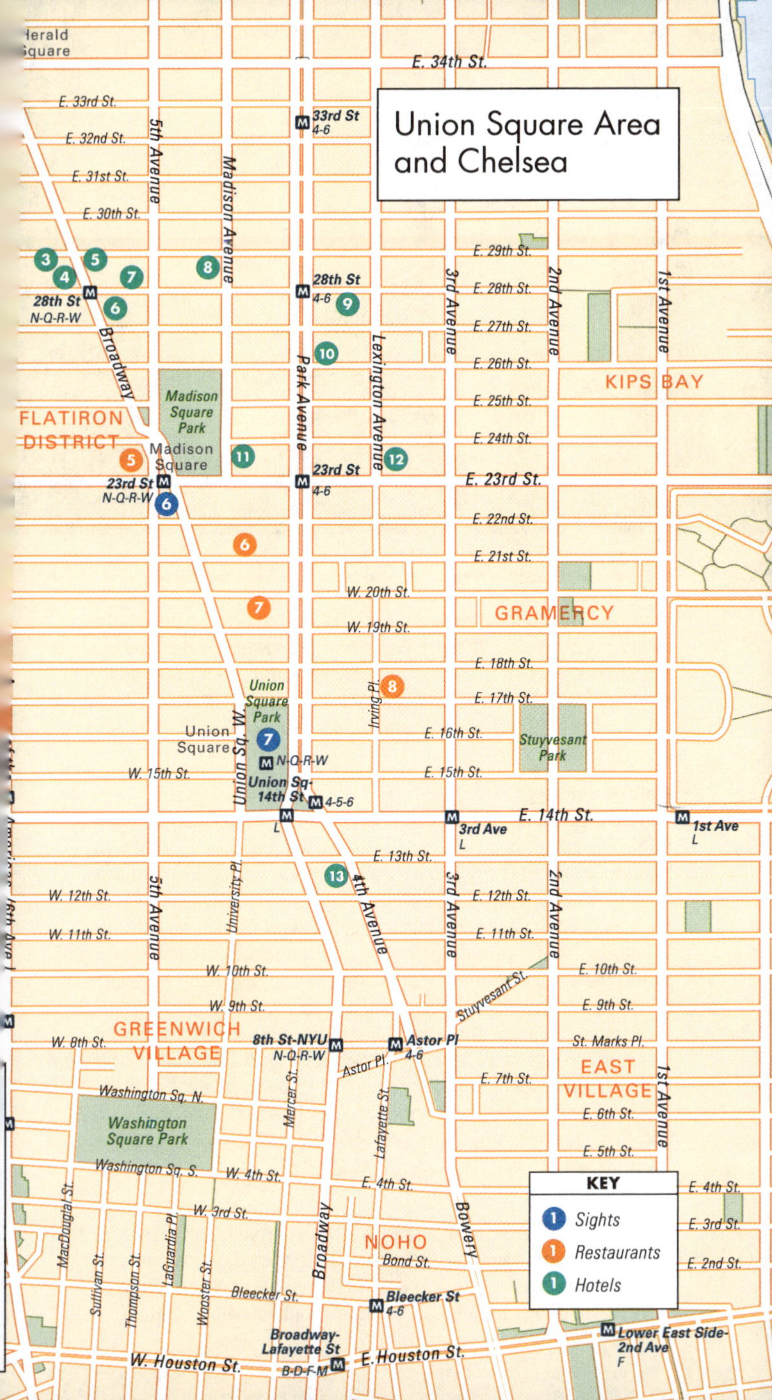

Union Square Area and Chelsea
KEY
Sights
Restaurants
Hotels
FLATIRON DISTRICT
KIPS BAY
GRAMERCY
GREENWICH VILLAGE
EAST VILLAGE
NOHO
Madison Square Park
Union Square Park
Washington Square Park
Stuyvesant Park
Madison Square
Union Square
Herald Square
5th Avenue
Madison Avenue
Park Avenue
Lexington Avenue
3rd Avenue
2nd Avenue
1st Avenue
4th Avenue
Broadway
Bowery
Union Sq. W.
University Pl.
Irving Pl.
Mercer St.
Lafayette St.
MacDougal St.
Sullivan St.
Thompson St.
LaGuardia Pl.
Wooster St.
Stuyvesant St.
Astor Pl.
E. 34th St.
E. 33rd St.
E. 32nd St.
E. 31st St.
E. 30th St.
E. 29th St.
E. 28th St.
E. 27th St.
E. 26th St.
E. 25th St.
E. 24th St.
E. 23rd St.
E. 22nd St.
E. 21st St.
W. 20th St.
W. 19th St.
E. 18th St.
E. 17th St.
E. 16th St.
E. 15th St.
W. 15th St.
E. 14th St.
E. 13th St.
W. 12th St.
E. 12th St.
W. 11th St.
E. 11th St.
W. 10th St.
E. 10th St.
W. 9th St.
E. 9th St.
W. 8th St.
St. Marks Pl.
E. 7th St.
E. 6th St.
E. 5th St.
Washington Sq. N.
Washington Sq. S.
W. 4th St.
E. 4th St.
W. 3rd St.
E. 3rd St.
E. 2nd St.
Bond St.
Bleecker St.
W. Houston St.
E. Houston St.
33rd St 4-6
28th St 4-6
28th St N-Q-R-W
23rd St N-Q-R-W
23rd St 4-6
Union Sq-14th St 4-5-6
N-Q-R-W
L
3rd Ave L
1st Ave L
8th St-NYU N-Q-R-W
Astor Pl 4-6
Bleecker St 4-6
Broadway-Lafayette St B-D-F-M
Lower East Side-2nd Ave F

The wedge-shaped Flatiron Building got its nickname because of its resemblance to the shape of a clothes iron. Its original name was the Fuller Building.

crowded. A downstairs level has a few additional food stands as well as bathrooms. **TIP→ There is some seating inside and outside along West 15th Street, but if the weather's nice, take your goodies to the High Line.** ✉ *75 9th Ave., between 15th and 16th Sts., Chelsea* ☎ *212/652–2117* 🌐 *www.chelseamarket.com* Ⓜ *A, C, E to 14th St.; L to 8th Ave.*

Flatiron Building

NOTABLE BUILDING | When completed in 1902, the wedge-shaped Fuller Building, as it was originally known, caused a sensation. Architect Daniel Burnham made ingenious use of the triangular wedge of land at 23rd Street, 5th Avenue, and Broadway, employing a revolutionary steel frame that allowed for the structure's 22-story, 286-foot height. Covered with a facade of limestone and white terra-cotta in the Italian Renaissance style, the building's shape resembled a clothing iron, hence its nickname. When it became apparent that the building generated strong winds, gawkers would loiter at 23rd Street hoping to catch sight of ladies' billowing skirts. Local traffic cops had to shoo away the male peepers—one purported origin of the phrase "23 skidoo." ✉ *175 5th Ave., bordered by 22nd and 23rd Sts., 5th Ave., and Broadway, Flatiron District* Ⓜ *N, R, W to 23rd St.*

★ The High Line

CITY PARK | **FAMILY** | Once a railroad track carrying freight trains, this elevated space has been transformed into one of the city's top attractions—a 1½-mile landscaped "walking park," with curving walkways, picnic tables and benches, public art installations, and views of the Hudson River and the Manhattan skyline. Running from Gansevoort Street in the Meatpacking District (at the Whitney Museum of American Art) to West 34th Street and Hudson Yards, the High Line somehow manages to host about 5 million visitors a year and still feel like a wonderful retreat. That said, the crowds can seem overwhelming when the weather is nice, so visit as early in the morning as possible and avoid the lunchtime and weekend mass of humanity.

One of the main draws of the High Line is the landscaping, which is both wild and cultivated at the same time, and dotted with public art. Chelsea Market Passage, between 15th and 16th Streets, is accented with Spencer Finch's stained-glass art and is home to public art displays, video programs, music performances, and sit-down events. A feature that illustrates the High Line's greatest achievement—the ability to see the city with fresh eyes—is the 10th Avenue Square (between 16th and 17th Streets). This viewing window with stadium seating and large picture windows frames the city below as art, encouraging viewers to linger.

To fully appreciate the High Line, walk a length in one direction (preferably from Gansevoort Street uptown so that you can end with panoramic city and river views) and then make the return journey at street level, taking in the Chelsea neighborhood below. ■ **TIP→ Nearby Chelsea Market and Gansevoort Market are convenient places to pick up fixings for a picnic lunch.** ✉ *10th Ave., from Gansevoort St. to 34th St., Chelsea* ☎ *212/206–9922* 🌐 *www.thehighline.org* 🎫 *Free* Ⓜ *A, C, E, 1, 2, 3 to 14th St.; L to 8th Ave.; 1 to 23rd St. or 28th St.; 7 to 34th St.–Hudson Yards.*

★ Little Island

CITY PARK | **FAMILY** | Much like the High Line when it opened, Little Island was an instant hit with locals and visitors when the gates to this man-made isle in the middle of the Hudson River first swung open in May 2021. The 2.4-acre park is elevated on 132 tulip-looking concrete stilts and connected to Manhattan by two footbridges. Funded mostly by Barry Diller and Diane von Fürstenberg, the island park and its rolling stair-clad hills make for a fun wander. It also provides stunning views of the Manhattan skyline. There's a small outdoor food court and an ambient amphitheater for free concerts. ✉ *Pier 55, Hudson River Park at W. 13th St., Meatpacking District* 🌐 *littleisland.org* 🎫 *Free* Ⓜ *A, C, E to 14th St.; L to 8th Ave.*

★ Pace Gallery

ART GALLERY | In September 2019, Pace moved into a new eight-story building at 540 West 25th Street, turning the gallery more into an art center than just a gallery. The impressive roster of talent represented here includes a variety of upper-echelon artists, sculptors, and photographers, such as Richard Avedon, Alexander Calder, Tara Donovan, Chuck Close, Sol LeWitt, and Robert Rauschenberg. Pace has two spaces in Chelsea, including 510 West 25th Street. ✉ *540 W. 25th St., between 10th and 11th Aves., Chelsea* ☎ *212/421–3292* 🌐 *www.thepacegallery.com* 🎫 *Free* 🕐 *Closed Sun. and Mon.* Ⓜ *C, E to 23rd St.*

★ Union Square Park and Greenmarket

CITY PARK | FAMILY | A park, farmers' market, meeting place, and the site of rallies and demonstrations, this pocket of green space and surrounding public square sit in the center of a bustling residential and commercial neighborhood. The name "Union" originally signified that two main roads—Broadway and 4th Avenue—crossed here. It took on a different meaning in the late 19th and early 20th centuries, when the square became a rallying spot for labor protests; many unions, as well as fringe political parties, moved their headquarters nearby.

Union Square is at its best on Monday, Wednesday, Friday, and Saturday (8–6), when the largest of the city's greenmarkets draws farmers and food purveyors from the tristate area selling fruit and vegetables, plants, fresh-baked pies and breads, cheeses, cider, fish, and meat. Between Thanksgiving and Christmas, artisans sell gift items and food at the large Union Square Holiday Market (🌐 *www.usqholiday.nyc*).

New York University dormitories, theaters, and cavernous commercial spaces occupy the restored 19th-century commercial buildings that surround the park, along with some chain stores and restaurants. Statues in the park include those of George Washington, Abraham Lincoln, Mahatma Gandhi (often wreathed in flowers), and the Marquis de Lafayette (sculpted by Frédéric-Auguste Bartholdi, designer of the Statue of Liberty). ✉ *From 14th to 17th St., between Broadway and Park Ave. S, Union Square* ☎ *212/788–7900* 🌐 *www.facebook.com/unionsquaregreenmarket* Ⓜ *4, 5, 6, L, N, Q, R, W to 14th St.–Union Sq.*

★ Whitney Museum of American Art

ART MUSEUM | The Renzo Piano–designed museum welcomes visitors with a lively plaza, bold works of contemporary and modern American art, plenty of terraced outdoor spaces, and expansive windows. There are eight floors (not all open to the public), with a lauded French bakery on the ground floor and a café on the eighth floor. The galleries house rotating exhibitions from the permanent collection of postwar and contemporary works by artists such as Jackson Pollock, Jim Dine, Jasper Johns, Mark Rothko, Chuck Close, Cindy Sherman, and Roy Lichtenstein. Notable pieces

Did You Know?

If you start by Piers 63 and 64 in Chelsea, you can walk through Hudson River Park all the way to TriBeCa, getting great views of One World Trade Center on the way.

often on view include Hopper's *Early Sunday Morning* (1930), Bellows's *Dempsey and Firpo* (1924), Calder's beloved *Circus*, and several of O'Keeffe's dazzling flower paintings.

The Whitney experience is as much about the setting as the incredible artwork. The outdoor terraces on floors six, seven, and eight are connected by exterior stairs that provide a welcome reprieve from crowded galleries as well as stunning skyline views. After 7 pm on Friday, the price of admission is pay-what-you-wish. **TIP→ Skip the long lines and buy tickets in advance, but note that you cannot buy same-day tickets online. They must be purchased the day before.** ✉ *99 Gansevoort St., between Washington St. and 10th Ave., Meatpacking District* ☎ *212/570–3600* 🌐 *www.whitney.org* 🎟 *$30* 🕒 *Closed Tues.* Ⓜ *A, C, E to 14th St.; L to 8th Ave.*

Restaurants

★ Casa Mono

$$ | TAPAS | Most of the delectable items on the menu at this Iberian, small-plates, corner restaurant are made for sharing, but of particular note are all things seared *à la plancha* (on a metal plate), including blistered peppers and garlic-kissed mushrooms. The atmosphere is always bustling but the best seats are those at the Casa Mono counter overlooking the chef's open kitchen. **Known for:** high-quality, authentic Spanish tapas; hard to get a table so reserve in advance; small Bar Jamón annex around the corner. 💲 *Average main: $24* ✉ *52 Irving Pl., at 17th St., Gramercy* ☎ *212/253–2773* 🌐 *www.casamononyc.com* Ⓜ *4, 5, 6, L, N, Q, R, W to 14th St.–Union Sq.*

★ Cosme

$$ | MODERN MEXICAN | When Enrique Olvera, the chef at Pujol, which many agree is Mexico City's best restaurant, announced he was coming north of the border, New York foodies went loco. Olvera's haute touch to his native cuisine is magic, and, coupled with the sleek design (soft lighting, minimalist decor), Cosme makes for a fine dining experience of sophisticated food, focused on small plates. **Known for:** creative Mexican fare; duck carnitas; corn tempura soft-shell crab. 💲 *Average main: $24* ✉ *35 E. 21st St., between Park Ave. S and Broadway, Flatiron District* ☎ *212/913–9659* 🌐 *www.cosmenyc.com* 🕒 *No lunch weekdays* Ⓜ *Q, N, R, W to 23rd St.*

Eataly NYC Flatiron

$$ | ITALIAN | FAMILY | Both a bustling food hall and a marketplace where you can shop for produce, baked goods, prepared foods, and kitchen staples, Eataly is a temple to all things gourmet

Italian. You can graze at individual stands, sit down for a meal at one of several restaurants that each specialize in different aspects of Italian cuisine, or head upstairs to Serra by Birreria, a covered rooftop space that's open year-round and serves Italian specialties and microbrews that change with the seasons. **Known for:** maddening crowds on the weekends; Italian foods from burrata to gelato; gourmet everything to eat in or take home, at a price. *Average main: $22* *200 5th Ave., at 23rd St., Flatiron District* *212/229–2560* *www.eataly.com* *6, N, R, W to 23rd St.*

★ Gramercy Tavern

$$$$ | AMERICAN | Danny Meyer's perennially popular restaurant tops many a New Yorker's list of favorite dining spots, as much for the exemplary food as for the clubby, art-filled space. In front, the first-come-first-served tavern has an à la carte menu (the burger is a standout) along with great craft beers and cocktails; the more formal dining room in back serves a four-course Greenmarket Lunch and a show-stopping five-course tasting menu for dinner. **Known for:** impeccable service; standout seasonal fare; good-value prix-fixe lunch in the tavern. *Average main: $168* *42 E. 20th St., between Broadway and Park Ave. S, Gramercy* *212/477–0777* *www.gramercytavern.com* *6, N, R, W to 23rd St.*

Loulou

$$$ | FRENCH | Your inner magpie might be first attracted to Loulou for its colorful floral bedecked exterior as well as the romantic, dimly lit interior, but the food at this classic French bistro is as dazzling on the taste buds as the decor is on the eyes. The Gallic-accented menu doesn't stray too far from tradition, and that's a good thing. **Known for:** over-the-top floral facade; classic French bistro fare; downstairs speakeasy cocktail lounge. *Average main: $32* *176 8th Ave., at W. 19th St., Chelsea* *212/337–9577* *loulounyc.com* *A, C, E to 14th St.; L to 8th Ave.*

★ Market 57

$$ | ECLECTIC | This innovative food hall opened in spring 2023 to great fanfare. Run by the James Beard Foundation and set on historic Pier 57, the market boasts a lineup of 15 food stalls from James Beard Award–winning chefs. **Known for:** Good to Go by JBF, a food incubator for female and BIPOC chefs; a diverse array of edible offerings; run by the James Beard Foundation. *Average main: $15* *25 11th Ave., at W. 14th St., Meatpacking District* *pier57nyc.com* *A, C, E to 14th St.; L to 8th Ave.*

★ Pastis

$$$ | BISTRO | Pastis looks like it's been here for decades—it moved into this space in 2019—and has all the signature Keith McNally elements: smoky mirrors, a long curving bar, floor-to-ceiling windows, and white subway tiles. French favorites are front and center, including toothsome steak frites with béarnaise, mussels steamed in Pernod, and a tasty apple tartlet with phyllo crust. **Known for:** steak frites; great people-watching; outdoor tables in summer. *Average main: $31 52 Gansevoort St., between Greenwich and Washington Sts., Meatpacking District 212/929–4844 www.pastisny.com A, C, E to 14th St.; L to 8th Ave.*

Skirt Steak

$$$$ | **STEAK HOUSE** | If you're a restaurant that only serves one main item, you better be good at it. Fortunately, for Skirt Steak, the namesake item is excellent at this casual, rustic spot from chef Laurent Tourondel. **Known for:** just serving skirt steak with unlimited fries; secret, off-menu items; long lines for a table. *Average main: $45 835 6th Ave., at W. 29th St., Chelsea 212/201–4069 www.skirtsteaknyc.com No lunch 1 to 28th St.*

Hotels

★ Ace Hotel New York

$ | **HOTEL** | The Ace is not your ordinary boutique hotel; the lively lobby melds the look of an Ivy League library with the concept of a curiosity cabinet—eclectic artwork, mosaic tile floors, wooden bookcases, antique sofas, a photo booth—and the vibe is laid-back, making it a popular hangout for freelancers and creatives. **Pros:** fun, unique decor; supercool but friendly vibe; lobby bar scene. **Cons:** small rooms; caters to a young crowd; may be too much of a scene for some. *Rooms from: $269 20 W. 29th St., at Broadway, Flatiron District 212/679–2222 www.acehotel.com/newyork 285 rooms No Meals N, R, W to 28th St.*

The Fifth Avenue Hotel

$$$$ | **HOTEL** | This discreet Nomad hotel exudes Gilded Age decadence from the moment you enter its discreet lobby—set in a former Fifth Avenue bank designed by lauded architects McKim, Mead & White in 1907, plus a sleek new tower next door, it's a jewel box wrapped up in lavish European wallpapers and fabrics and infused with a signature house scent. **Pros:** lavish Gilded Age atmosphere; great restaurant and bar on-site; complimentary soft drinks and snacks from in-room bars. **Cons:** no outdoor public space; smallest rooms lack bathtubs; no gym or spa. *Rooms from: $1025 1 W. 28th St., at 5th Ave., Flatiron District 212/231–9400 www.thefifthavenuehotel.com 153 rooms Free Breakfast R, W to 28 St.*

Freehand New York

$ | HOTEL | FAMILY | The New York location of this hip hotel combines chic-but-homey design, several restaurants and bars, and accommodations that range from single rooms to rooms with bunk beds to suites. **Pros:** destination dining and drinking; great value for NYC; fun, social vibe. **Cons:** rooms are on the small side; no bathtubs; could be too hip and busy for some. *Rooms from: $185 ✉ 23 Lexington Ave., between 23rd and 24th Sts., Gramercy ☎ 212/475–1920 🌐 www.freehandhotels.com 395 rooms No Meals Ⓜ 6 to 23rd St.*

★ **High Line Hotel**

$$ | HOTEL | A late-19th-century, redbrick, Gothic-style building on the landscaped grounds of a seminary was transformed into this lovely hotel that's full of original architectural details like stained-glass windows and pine floors. **Pros:** historic property with garden and lots of character; quality coffee bar in the lobby; close to the High Line. **Cons:** doesn't have the best subway access; outdoor restaurant only open May–October; no gym on-site. *Rooms from: $350 ✉ 180 10th Ave., at 20th St., Chelsea ☎ 212/929–3888 🌐 www.thehighlinehotel.com 60 rooms No Meals Ⓜ C, E to 23rd St.*

★ **Hotel Giraffe by Library Hotel Collection**

$$$ | HOTEL | Friendly service, large rooms, a convenient but peaceful location, and nice extras, such as a complimentary Continental breakfast until 10 am, draws lots of repeat customers (particularly business travelers) to the Hotel Giraffe. **Pros:** comfortable and friendly lobby to relax in; free coffee and healthy snacks in the lobby; many rooms have (small) balconies. **Cons:** street noise near lower levels; location a bit off the beaten path; no gym on-site. *Rooms from: $475 ✉ 365 Park Ave. S, at 26th St., Flatiron District ☎ 212/685–7700 🌐 www.hotelgiraffe.com 72 rooms Free Breakfast Ⓜ 6 to 28th St.*

★ **Hyatt Union Square New York**

$$$ | HOTEL | You'd be hard-pressed to find a more conveniently located hotel than this hip Hyatt a block south of Union Square, near New York University and at the hub of major subway lines. **Pros:** convenient and vibrant location; solid lobby dining and drinking options; welcoming staff. **Cons:** busy neighborhood means some street noise; room decor a bit bland; high-traffic area. *Rooms from: $599 ✉ 134 4th Ave., between 12th and 13th Sts., Union Square ☎ 212/253–1234 🌐 www.hyatt.com 178 rooms No Meals Ⓜ 4, 5, 6, L, N, Q, R, W to 14th St.–Union Sq.*

The James New York – NoMad

$$ | **HOTEL** | Sleek but comfortable, with a playful design aesthetic, the James is an easy spot to relax into for a few nights. **Pros:** sleek version of mid-century design; comfy beds; excellent on-site dining options. **Cons:** some rooms have views of brick walls; inconsistent service; street noise can be an issue. *Rooms from: $443* *22 E. 29th St., at Madison Ave., Flatiron District* *212/532–4100* *www.jameshotels.com/new-york/nomad* *337 rooms* *No Meals* *6, N, R, W to 28th St.*

MADE Hotel

$$ | **HOTEL** | You'll feel like you made the right choice with a stay at MADE, which takes everything people love about the designer boutique hotel trend (hip design, lobby and rooftop bars, buzzy restaurant) and doubles down on the luxury and comfort. **Pros:** cool design; on-site dining and year-round rooftop bar; inviting public spaces. **Cons:** little storage space; scant in-room amenities (no fridge or iron); some rooms have platform beds that can be hazardous if you get up at night. *Rooms from: $389* *44 W. 29th St., between Broadway and 6th Ave., Flatiron District* *212/213–4429* *www.madehotels.com* *108 rooms* *No Meals* *N, R, W to 28th St.*

The Ned

$$$$ | **HOTEL** | The first stateside location of London's Ned Hotel is run by Soho House so the property doubles as a private-member venue but, unlike many Soho House properties, anyone can book its elegant prewar rooms and guests and members alike get priority access to the hotel's northern Italian restaurant, Cecconi's, and Little Ned bar, where the cocktail list is helmed by Chris Moore, whose mixology credits include Dante and the Savoy. **Pros:** priority access to hotel restaurants and bars; top-shelf toiletry kit in every room ($85 value); large rooms by Manhattan standards. **Cons:** no spa on-site; medium-size rooms feel dated and have open claw-foot tubs; in-room coffee- and teamaker only upon request. *Rooms from: $850* *1170 Broadway, at W. 28th St., Flatiron District* *212/722–0555* *www.thened.com/nomad* *167 rooms* *No Meals* *N, R, W to 28th St.*

★ The New York EDITION

$$$$ | **HOTEL** | The landmarked clock tower in the 1909 Metropolitan Life building that overlooks Madison Square Park also houses an ultrasleek hotel—masterminded by renowned hotelier Ian Schrager—with neutral-tone rooms, a luxurious lobby bar, and a highly regarded restaurant, The Clocktower, helmed by British chef Jason Atheron. **Pros:** on-site spa; classy atmosphere; upscale restaurant options. **Cons:** very pricey; neighborhood a bit sedate;

windowless gym. *Rooms from: $980 ✉ 5 Madison Ave., at 24th St., Flatiron District ☎ 212/413–4200 🌐 www.editionhotels.com/new-york 273 rooms No Meals Ⓜ N, R, W to 23rd St.*

Park South Hotel

$$ | **HOTEL** | In a beautifully transformed 1906 office building, this contemporary hotel is a great vacation base: comfortable and convenient but basic enough to be good value. **Pros:** expansive (seasonal) rooftop bar; comfortable lobby; good value for NYC. **Cons:** bland room decor; small rooms and bathrooms; neighborhood might be too quiet for some. *Rooms from: $359 ✉ 124 E. 28th St., between Lexington and Park Aves., Flatiron District ☎ 212/448–0888 🌐 www.parksouthhotel.com 131 rooms No Meals Ⓜ 6 to 28th St.*

The Ritz-Carlton Hotel, NoMad

$$$$ | **HOTEL** | Occupying a new, luxury 50-story building at the northern end of NoMad, this sleek, all-glass hotel is a departure for the Ritz brand, thanks to its emerging neighborhood, versus tried and true, location. **Pros:** 6,800-square-foot Ritz-Carlton Spa; José Andrés–run restaurants and rooftop bar; high-floor rooms have fab downtown views. **Cons:** expensive for the location; the neighborhood still has some grit; dress code for Nubeluz restaurant. *Rooms from: $1255 ✉ 25 W. 28th St., at Broadway, Flatiron District ☎ 212/404–8400 🌐 www.ritzcarlton.com 250 rooms No Meals Ⓜ R, W to 28th St.*

★ The Standard, High Line

$$ | **HOTEL** | This modern architectural statement is perpetually one of New York's hottest hotels, with the High Line running underneath it, a lobby full of glamorous types, an authentic beer garden (open year-round; dig the table tennis), and an 18th-floor nightclub that is one of the toughest doors in town. **Pros:** nice building with sweeping views; beautiful people; impressive restaurant space. **Cons:** noisy at night; tight rooms; can be too trendy. *Rooms from: $445 ✉ 848 Washington St., between 13th and Little W. 12th Sts., Meatpacking District ☎ 212/645–4646 🌐 www.standardhotels.com 338 rooms No Meals Ⓜ A, C, E to 14th St.; L to 8th Ave.*

Nightlife

City Winery

LIVE MUSIC | It's a restaurant. It's a bar. It's a winery. But above all the new-ish location of City Winery at Pier 57 is a music venue, attracting top-notch artists and comedians. The 350-seat auditorium is an intimate spot to catch a show. Singer Rufus Wainwright, comedian John Mulaney, and musician Norah Jones have graced the stage. Even the late, great Prince put on unannounced shows at City Winery. The in-house eatery serves everything from burgers to seafood to flatbreads and the bar has 12 different wines on tap. ✉ *25 11th Ave., at W. 15th St., Chelsea* ☎ *646/751–6033* 🌐 *www.citywinery.com* Ⓜ *A, C, E to 14th St.; L to 8th Ave.*

Dear Irving

COCKTAIL BARS | This cocktail parlor invites you inside with its name, the beginning of an imaginary love letter to Irving Place, on which the bar resides. Interiors themed for different eras are chic and refined, and just as at sister property Raines Law Room, there are private sections of tables and couches for intimate conversations. Reservations are recommended (make them online), but you can sometimes get a table if you just show up. ✉ *55 Irving Pl., between 17th and 18th Sts., Gramercy* 🌐 *www.dearirving.com* Ⓜ *4, 5, 6, L, N, Q, R, W to 14th St.–Union Sq.*

★ Raines Law Room

COCKTAIL BARS | There's no phone number or big sign for this speakeasy; just ring the bell to enter. Wood-burning fireplaces, deep banquettes, and curtains for privacy all contribute to the intimate vibe—perfect for a date or small group gathering. The little candlelit garden out back is lovely and put to use: herbs grown here are used in the carefully crafted cocktails. You can make reservations through the website but walk-ins are welcome. ✉ *48 W. 17th St., between 5th and 6th Aves., Flatiron District* 🌐 *www.raineslawroom.com* Ⓜ *F, M to 14th St.; 4, 5, 6, L, N, Q, R, W to 14th St.–Union Sq.*

Shopping

★ Strand

BOOKS | Opened in 1927 and still run by the same family, this vast book emporium—home to 2 million volumes, or "18 Miles of Books"—is a symbol of a bygone era, a mecca for serious bibliophiles, and a local institution. The stock includes new and secondhand books, foreign-language titles, and thousands of collector's items—some of which are found in the third-floor rare-book room. The basement has discounted, sometimes barely touched review copies of new books organized by author. If you're looking for souvenirs, there's lots of New York–centric literature as well as T-shirts and totes. Check the store's events calendar for live readings. ✉ *828 Broadway, at 12th St., Union Square* ☎ *212/473–1452* 🌐 *www.strandbooks.com* Ⓜ *4, 5, 6, L, N, Q, R, W to 14th St.–Union Sq.*

Chapter 6

6

MIDTOWN

Updated by
Arabella Bowen

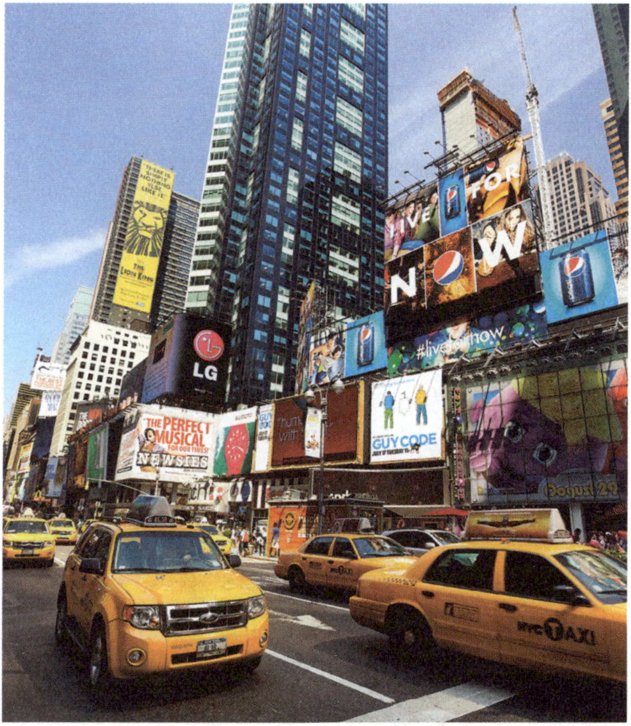

Sights	Restaurants	Hotels	Shopping	Nightlife
★★★★★	★★★★☆	★★★★★	★★★☆☆	★★★☆☆

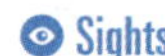

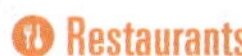

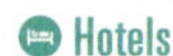

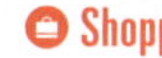

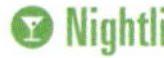

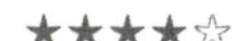

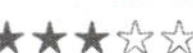

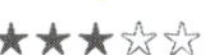

The Museum of Modern Art Tour

Some of the world's most famous paintings hang at the MoMA, including Monet's *Water Lilies.* Renovations in 2019 prompted a complete re-hang of its permanent collection, which now changes much more often—so there's always something new to see.

1 Enter the MoMA via its 53rd Street entrance. Once you have your ticket, turn right to locate the South Entrance escalator across from the Member Desk and head all the way up to the fifth floor. Turn right at the landing and head behind the escalators to the sixth floor (reserved for special exhibits) to find a sculpture court with spectacular Midtown rooftop views from its floor-to-ceiling windows on the right.

2 Enter the Alfred H. Barr, Jr. Galleries on your left to scout the highlights of the museum's fabulous collection of works from the 1880s–1940s. New works appear on the walls every month, but the MoMA's stalwarts—Picasso, Van Gogh, Monet, and Matisse—are always here.

3 Gallery 501, with its focus on French Landscapes and Interiors, starts with a bang. Look for Vincent van Gogh's *The Starry Night* (1889)—often with crowds before it. Here, the night sky swirls in vivid blues and yellows around one of Van Gogh's beloved cypress trees.

Walking Tour 101

HIGHLIGHTS

Van Gogh's *The Starry Night*, Picasso's *Les Demoiselles D'Avignon*, works from Jackson Pollock, Mark Rothko, Henri Matisse, and Andy Warhol, just to name a few

WHERE TO START

Alfred H. Barr, Jr. Galleries on the fifth floor

LENGTH

1½ hours

WHERE TO END

Abby Aldrich Rockefeller Sculpture Garden

INSIDER TIPS

Go in the early afternoon during the week, especially if you want to see Henri Matisse's *The Swimming Pool*, which only opens at 1 pm to help preserve it. Weekends and rainy days are insanely crowded; avoid them if you can.

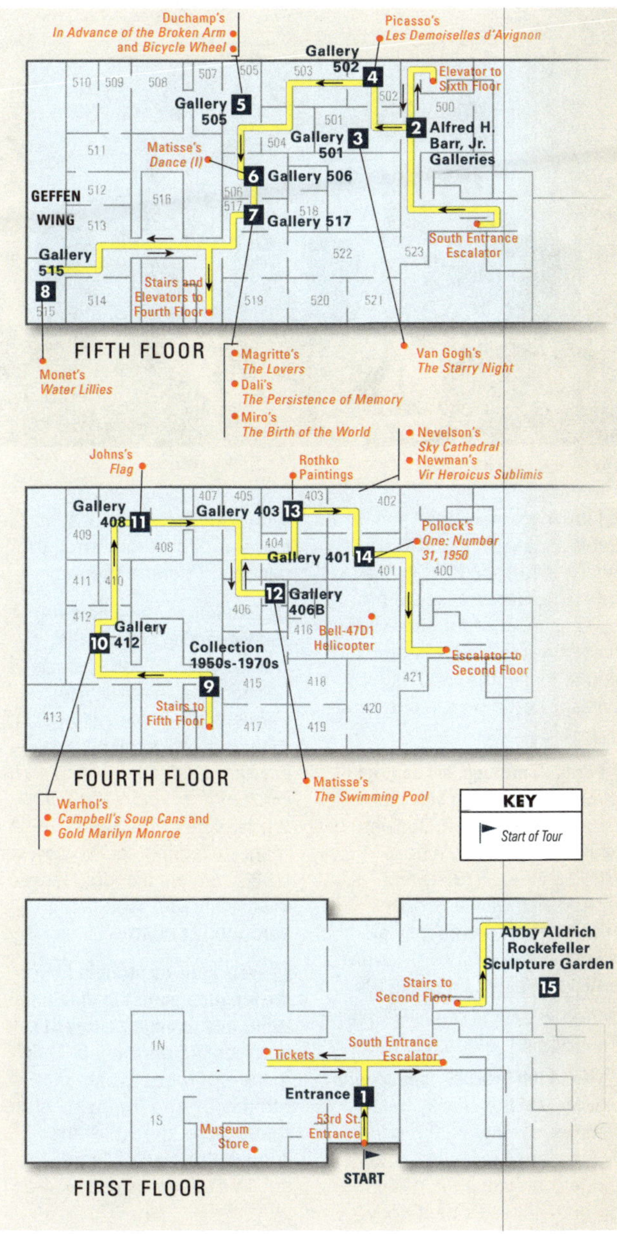
Duchamp's
In Advance of the Broken Arm
and Bicycle Wheel
Picasso's
Les Demoiselles d'Avignon
Gallery 502
4
Elevator to Sixth Floor
Gallery 505
5
Gallery 501
3
2 Alfred H. Barr, Jr. Galleries
Matisse's
Dance (I)
6 Gallery 506
GEFFEN WING
7 Gallery 517
South Entrance Escalator
Gallery 515
8
Stairs and Elevators to Fourth Floor
FIFTH FLOOR
Monet's
Water Lillies
Magritte's
The Lovers
Dali's
The Persistence of Memory
Miro's
The Birth of the World
Van Gogh's
The Starry Night
Nevelson's
Sky Cathedral
Newman's
Vir Heroicus Sublimis
Johns's
Flag
Rothko
Paintings
Gallery 408 11
Gallery 403 13
Pollock's
One: Number 31, 1950
Gallery 401 14
12 Gallery 406B
Bell-47D1 Helicopter
Gallery 412
10
Collection 1950s-1970s
9
Escalator to Second Floor
Stairs to Fifth Floor
FOURTH FLOOR
Warhol's
Campbell's Soup Cans and
Gold Marilyn Monroe
Matisse's
The Swimming Pool
KEY
Start of Tour
Abby Aldrich Rockefeller Sculpture Garden
15
Stairs to Second Floor
Tickets
South Entrance Escalator
Entrance 1
53rd St. Entrance
Museum Store
START
FIRST FLOOR

Les Demoiselles d'Avignon

4 Turn right into 502 to see Pablo Picasso's *Les Demoiselles d'Avignon* (1907). The monumental work is said to have scandalized those who first saw it in his Paris studio. If you're lucky, the studies for it will still be up on the surrounding walls.

5 Cut left through 503 and right through 504 to enter 505. Here, pause for the great Dadaist Marcel Duchamp, whose *Bicycle Wheel* (1951) and *In Advance of the Broken Arm* (1964)—essentially an everyday snow shovel—were both conceived in the 1910s in response to the era's increasing mechanization.

6 Head left into 506, loaded with vibrant, joyful works by Henri Matisse, the early-20th-century master of form and color. Linger on *Dance (I)* (1909), one of Matisse's best-known works: the artist reduced line, color, and form to portray the dancers' "life and rhythm."

7 Turn into 517 for a best-in-show grouping of Surrealist works by Miró, Dalí, and more. Salvador Dalí's small *The Persistence of Memory* (1931), with its famously limp watches, hangs near Joan Miró's *The Birth of the World* (1925). On the far side of the room, René Magritte's gripping *The Lovers* (1928) depicts a couple locked in an embrace, their faces shrouded in cloth.

8 From here, go straight from the Magritte across to the Geffen Wing, and through Gallery 513, to enter 515 on the left. This is the last room to visit on the fifth floor—and it's an absolute must. Here, the walls are lined with Claude Monet's sublime *Water Lilies* (1914–26), depicting the Impressionist artist's lush Giverny gardens.

9 Return half-way to the Magritte to find the stairs and elevator bank on the right. Head down to the fourth floor to explore Collection 1950s–1970s, with unmissable works by Abstract Expressionists Jackson Pollock and Mark Rothko at its core, along with big-hitters like Jasper Johns, and more.

10 Take a left from the landing into Gallery 412, where Andy Warhol's monumental *Campbell's Soup Cans* (1962) depicts 32 cans of every flavor sold by Campbell's at the time. Another signature Warhol motif, *Gold Marilyn Monroe* (1962), hangs nearby.

11 Exit 412 and head through 410 to 408. Here, you'll find one of Jasper Johns' trademark American *Flag* paintings, composed of newspaper scraps painted over with hot wax and color. It depicts just 48 stars—Alaska and Hawaii had yet to join the United States when he painted it in 1954–55.

The Starry Night

12 Continue through 407 and 405, and duck into 406 on the right. On the left in 406B is a room devoted entirely to Matisse's *The Swimming Pool* (1952), the site-specific cut-out of cavorting divers, swimmers, and sea creatures he created for his dining room at the Hôtel Régina in Nice. (Note: the room is only open from 1 pm daily, to preserve the work.)

13 Backtrack to 405, go straight through 404, and left into 403 to find the MoMA's extraordinary collection of Mark Rothko paintings. The AbEx artist was known for his vivid large-scale canvases layered with dense color fields of reds, purples, oranges, yellows, and greens.

14 Head right into 402—dominated by Barnett Newman's bold-red *Vir Heroicus Sublimis* (1950–51) and Louise Nevelson's immense *Sky Cathedral* (1958) sculpture made of found objects—to reach 401, the last room on this floor. Here, Jackson Pollock's *One: Number 31, 1950* (1950) epitomizes his renowned "drip" technique.

15 Turn right on exit and take the escalators back down to the second floor. Then take the stairs next to the Atrium to finish your visit in the Abby Aldrich Rockefeller Sculpture Garden. Before you go, spend some time in the excellent gift shop.

NEIGHBORHOOD SNAPSHOT

TOP EXPERIENCES

- Standing in the center of the main concourse in Grand Central Terminal and taking in the LED-lit map of the constellations overhead
- Soaking in the art and serenity at MoMA's Sculpture Garden
- Checking out the views from the Top of the Rock; opinions vary on whether the vistas are better from here or from the Empire State Building. Either way, if you go at night, the city spreads out below in a mesmerizing blanket of lights
- Strolling along 5th Avenue, where some of the world's top luxury brands have flagship stores—especially around the holidays, when store windows are dressed to impress
- Ice-skating in the Rockefeller Center rink or just strolling and admiring the stunning Art Deco architecture

GETTING HERE

You can get to Midtown via almost every subway. For Midtown West, the 1, 2, 3, 7, A, C, E, N, Q, R, and W serve Times Square and West 42nd Street. The S, or Shuttle, travels back and forth between Times Square and Grand Central Terminal. The B, D, F, and M trains serve Bryant Park and Rockefeller Center.

To get to the east side of Midtown, take the 4, 5, 6, or 7 to Grand Central. The S, or Shuttle, travels back and forth between Grand Central and Times Square.

You can reach the Empire State Building via the B, D, F, M, N, Q, R, and W trains to 34th Street or the 6 to 33rd Street.

PAUSE HERE

- **Summit of Manhattan.** Created by Australian artist Todd Stuart, this sculpture crafted from high-grade stainless steel polished to a mirror finish is a reimagining of the infinity symbol. ✉ *222 E. 44th St.* 🚇 *4, 5, 6, 7, S to Grand Central Terminal–42nd St.*
- **New York Public Library Main Branch Plaza.** Behind the library's historic lions is an often overlooked shaded seating area with tables, perfect for a break from the Midtown bustle. ✉ *476 5th Ave.* 🌐 *www.NYPL.org* 🚇 *B, D, F, M to 42nd St.–Bryant Park; 7 to 5th Ave.*

Love it or hate it, Times Square is the flashy and fluttering heart of Midtown, and a visit to New York demands a turn here. Just don't forget there's plenty more to see and experience beyond this famous crossroads at 7th Avenue and Broadway.

Luckily you needn't go far to find eclectic restaurants, the huge Hudson Yards complex with even more eateries and shops around 34th Street and Hudson Boulevard, or Bryant Park's zen green space stretched out behind the New York Public Library.

Although people think of Broadway as the heart of the theater scene, few theaters actually line the thoroughfare. Instead, head west on 45th Street for grand dames like the Booth, Schoenfeld, Jacobs, Music Box, and Imperial. You can score good seats to some of the hottest shows for half the going rate at the TKTS booth in Duffy Square at 47th Street and Broadway.

Meanwhile, some of the city's most historic buildings lie east of Fifth Avenue, Manhattan's dividing line, including the Chrysler Building, Grand Central Terminal, and the Empire State Building. Midtown East's skyline has been changing dramatically in recent years, and now includes such supertall buildings as One Vanderbilt. While it's somewhat more laid back than Midtown West, the area has lots to keep you busy.

Sights

★ Bryant Park

CITY PARK | FAMILY | This lovely green space spread out among landmarks and skyscrapers is one of Manhattan's most popular parks. Tall London plane trees line the perimeter of the sunny central lawn, overlooking stone terraces, flower beds, and snack kiosks. The garden tables scattered about fill with lunching office workers and folks enjoying the park's free Wi-Fi. In summer, there are free readings, live jazz, and "Broadway in Bryant Park" musical theater performances. Most popular of all is the summer film festival: locals leave work early to snag a spot on the lawn for the outdoor screenings each Monday at dusk.

At the east side of the park, near a bronze cast of Gertrude Stein, is the stylish Bryant Park Grill, which has a rooftop garden, and the adjacent open-air Bryant Park Café, open seasonally. On the

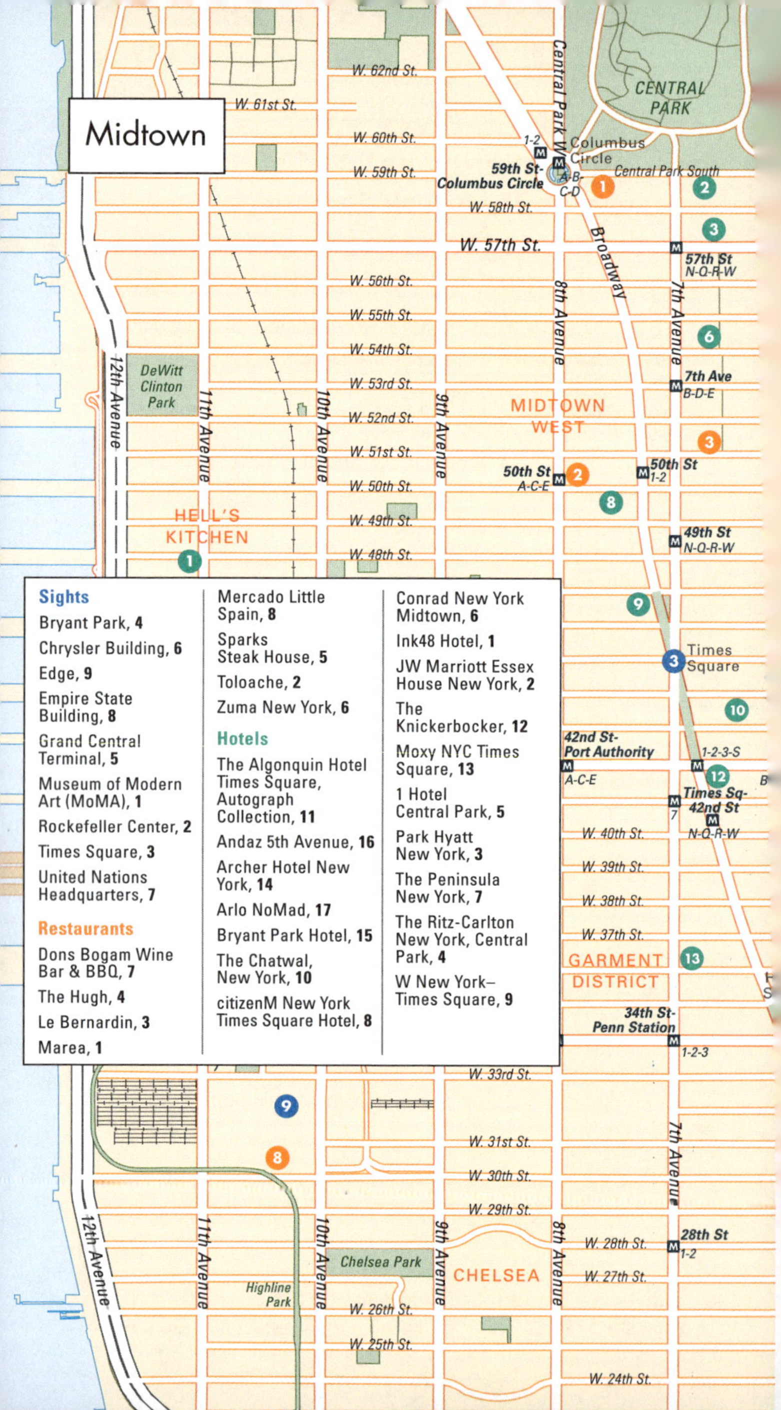

Midtown
Sights
Bryant Park, 4
Chrysler Building, 6
Edge, 9
Empire State Building, 8
Grand Central Terminal, 5
Museum of Modern Art (MoMA), 1
Rockefeller Center, 2
Times Square, 3
United Nations Headquarters, 7
Restaurants
Dons Bogam Wine Bar & BBQ, 7
The Hugh, 4
Le Bernardin, 3
Marea, 1
Mercado Little Spain, 8
Sparks Steak House, 5
Toloache, 2
Zuma New York, 6
Hotels
The Algonquin Hotel Times Square, Autograph Collection, 11
Andaz 5th Avenue, 16
Archer Hotel New York, 14
Arlo NoMad, 17
Bryant Park Hotel, 15
The Chatwal, New York, 10
citizenM New York Times Square Hotel, 8
Conrad New York Midtown, 6
Ink48 Hotel, 1
JW Marriott Essex House New York, 2
The Knickerbocker, 12
Moxy NYC Times Square, 13
1 Hotel Central Park, 5
Park Hyatt New York, 3
The Peninsula New York, 7
The Ritz-Carlton New York, Central Park, 4
W New York–Times Square, 9
CENTRAL PARK
Columbus Circle
Central Park South
59th St-Columbus Circle
A-B-C-D
1-2
Central Park W.
Broadway
57th St
N-Q-R-W
7th Avenue
8th Avenue
7th Ave
B-D-E
MIDTOWN WEST
50th St
A-C-E
50th St
1-2
49th St
N-Q-R-W
Times Square
42nd St-Port Authority
A-C-E
1-2-3-S
Times Sq-42nd St
7
N-Q-R-W
GARMENT DISTRICT
34th St-Penn Station
1-2-3
28th St
1-2
CHELSEA
Chelsea Park
Highline Park
HELL'S KITCHEN
DeWitt Clinton Park
12th Avenue
11th Avenue
10th Avenue
9th Avenue
W. 62nd St.
W. 61st St.
W. 60th St.
W. 59th St.
W. 58th St.
W. 57th St.
W. 56th St.
W. 55th St.
W. 54th St.
W. 53rd St.
W. 52nd St.
W. 51st St.
W. 50th St.
W. 49th St.
W. 48th St.
W. 40th St.
W. 39th St.
W. 38th St.
W. 37th St.
W. 33rd St.
W. 31st St.
W. 30th St.
W. 29th St.
W. 28th St.
W. 27th St.
W. 26th St.
W. 25th St.
W. 24th St.

Lexington Ave-63rd St
F-Q
LENOX HILL
E. 62nd St.
E. 61st St.
The Pond
Lexington Ave-59th St
N-R-W
5th Ave-59th St
N-R-W
4-5-6
E. 60th St.
Queensboro Br.
E. 59th St.
E. 58th St.
E. 57th St.
57th St
F
Park Avenue
Lexington Avenue
3rd Avenue
2nd Avenue
1st Avenue
5th Avenue
Avenue of the Americas (6th Ave.)
E. 56th St.
E. 55th St.
E. 54th St.
E. 53rd St.
E. 52nd St.
E. 51st St.
E. 50th St.
E. 49th St.
E. 48th St.
E. 47th St.
E. 46th St.
E. 45th St.
E. 44th St.
E. 43rd St.
5th Ave-53rd St
E-M
Lexington Ave-53rd St
E-M
51st St
4-6
0
1,000 ft
0
200 m
47th-50th Sts-Rockefeller Ctr
B-D-F-M
W. 47th St.
W. 46th St.
W. 45th St.
W. 44th St.
W. 43rd St.
MIDTOWN EAST
Madison Avenue
Grand Central-42nd St
42nd St-Bryant Pk
5th Ave
7
B-D-F-M
S
4-5-6
7
E. 42nd St.
Bryant Park
E. 41st St.
E. 40th St.
E. 39th St.
E. 38th St.
E. 37th St.
E. 36th St.
E. 35th St.
MURRAY HILL
Herald Square
34th St-Herald Sq
B-D-F-M-N-Q-R-W
E. 34th St.
33rd St
PATH
33rd St
4-6
E. 33rd St.
E. 32nd St.
E. 31st St.
E. 30th St.
E. 29th St.
E. 28th St.
E. 27th St.
E. 26th St.
E. 25th St.
E. 24th St.
FDR Drive
Broadway
28th St
N-Q-R-W
28th St
4-6
FLATIRON DISTRICT
Madison Square Park
KEY
Sights
Restaurants
Hotels

south side of the park is an old-fashioned carousel ($4) where kids can also attend storytellings and magic shows. Come late October, the park rolls out the artificial frozen "pond" (October–March, daily 8 am–10 pm; skate rental starts at $18) for free ice-skating (bring your own padlock for the lockers). Surrounding the ice rink are the Christmas-market stalls of the holiday shops, selling handcrafted goods and local foods. ✉ *6th Ave., between 40th and 42nd Sts., Midtown West* ☎ *212/768–4242* 🌐 *www.bryantpark.org* Ⓜ *B, D, F, M to 42nd St.–Bryant Park; 7 to 5th Ave.*

Chrysler Building

NOTABLE BUILDING | A monument to modernity and the mighty automotive industry, the former Chrysler headquarters wins many New Yorkers' vote for the city's most marvelous and beloved skyscraper, despite the fact that you can only love it from a distance. Architect William Van Alen, who designed this 1930 Art Deco masterpiece, incorporated car details into its form: American eagle gargoyles, made of chromium nickel and resembling hood ornaments used on 1920s Chryslers, sprout from the 61st floor; winged urns festooning the 31st floor reference the car's radiator caps. Most breathtaking is the pinnacle, with tiered crescents and spiked windows that radiate out like a magnificent steel sunburst. While the current owner has been given permission to reopen an observation deck on the 71st floor that closed in 1945, for now you have to make do with appreciating it from afar or ducking in for a quick look at the amazing time-capsule lobby replete with chrome "grillwork," intricately patterned wood elevator doors, marble walls and floors, and an enormous ceiling mural saluting transportation and human endeavor. You may enter the lobby during business hours (8 am–6 pm). **TIP→ For a great view/photo, walk to the northeast corner of 44th Street and 3rd Avenue.** ✉ *405 Lexington Ave., at 42nd St., Midtown East* 🌐 *chryslerbuilding.com* 🎫 *Free* 🕒 *Closed weekends* Ⓜ *4, 5, 6, 7, S to Grand Central–42nd St.*

Edge

VIEWPOINT | Opened in 2020, Edge is the gleaming new observation deck at the Hudson Yards development, and at 1,131 feet, it is the highest outdoor sky deck in the western hemisphere. Its walled triangular floor juts 80 feet from the tower's edge. The views here are truly panoramic, from those of the streets 100 stories below to those of Central Park, the Empire State Building, the Statue of Liberty, and beyond. An outdoor staircase connects Floor 100, home to a gift shop and indoor champagne bar, with Floor 101's Peak restaurant and cocktail bar (🌐 *www.peaknyc.com*). Besides regular adult timed-tickets, there are packages with extras, such as the Flex Pass ($60), which includes

The lights on the top of the Empire State Building often change color to support different holidays and causes.

flexible-arrival-time tickets and a digital souvenir photo. ✉ *30 Hudson Yards, near 33rd St., between 10th and 11th Aves., Midtown West* ☎ *332/204–8500* 🌐 *www.edgenyc.com* 🎫 *$40 for regular timed tickets; packages available* Ⓜ *7 to 34th St.–Hudson Yards.*

★ Empire State Building

NOTABLE BUILDING | FAMILY | With a legendary silhouette recognizable virtually worldwide, the Empire State Building is an Art Deco monument to progress, a symbol of NYC, and a star in many romantic scenes—on- and off-screen. Built in 1931 at the peak of the skyscraper craze, this 103-floor limestone giant opened after 13 months of construction. The framework rose at a rate of 4½ stories per week, making the Empire State Building the fastest-rising skyscraper ever built, to date.

Enter the visitor experience in the building's designated Observatory lobby—a two-story hall off 34th Street—and exit through the building's illustrious 5th Avenue lobby. Purchase or retrieve prepurchased timed tickets at kiosks, then head to the 10,000-square-foot Second Floor Galleries to learn all about the skyscraper—from its engineering to its role in modern culture (including a fun photo op with King Kong himself). There are interactive experiences, along with marvelous Art Deco design details throughout.

Rise from Floor 2 to reach Floor 80's enclosed observatory, with interactive kiosks to create custom NYC itineraries and an impressive NYC skyline drawing by memory artist Steven Wiltshire. Then head to the 86th-floor observatory (1,050 feet high) to find another enclosed area and the spectacular wraparound outdoor deck. The views from the compact 102nd-floor observatory are better still, though it comes with an extra price tag. A new Sunrise@ESB experience ($135) provides preopening access to the 86th floor observation deck on Saturday morning to watch the sunrise with pastries and a custom Starbucks coffee. A Starbucks Reserve Store opened inside the building in 2022.

Expect long lines during peak tourist times/seasons—best avoided with weekday morning or winter visits. Plan for three-plus hours to absorb the full experience and to pass through security. Save time by purchasing tickets online in advance. ■TIP→ **The building opens the stairs from the 86th floor down to the 80th floor on busy days so visitors can bypass any potential lines.** ✉ *20 W. 34th St., between Broadway and 5th Ave., Murray Hill* ☎ *212/736–3100* 🌐 *www.esbnyc.com* 🎟 *$44 for 86th fl.; $79 to add 102nd fl.; $120 for Express Pass to 86th and 102nd fls.* Ⓜ *B, D, F, M, N, Q, R, W to 34th St.–Herald Sq.; 6 to 33rd St.*

★ Grand Central Terminal

TRAIN/TRAIN STATION | Grand Central is not only the world's largest railway station by area (at 49 acres and 44 platforms), but also one of the world's most magnificent public spaces, the majesty of its 1913 building preserved, in part, by Jacqueline Kennedy Onassis's 1975 campaign to save it as a landmark. The main concourse stands roughly 12 stories high and is modeled after an ancient Roman public bath. Overhead, an LED-lit map of the constellations covers the ceiling. Of course, Grand Central still functions primarily as a transit hub: underground, trains travel to Connecticut and through various New York counties and the Bronx via the Metro-North commuter rail and to Long Island via the Long Island Rail Road through Grand Central Madison; the subway connects here as well.

To best admire Grand Central's exquisite Beaux-Arts architecture, avoid rush hour and head up one of the staircases at either end, where an Apple store occupies the top of one of the balcony spaces. From this level, you can survey the concourse and feel the terminal's dynamism. Then head to the southwest corner to reach the tucked-away The Campbell cocktail lounge. The on-site Vanderbilt Tennis Club is a best kept secret; court time can be reserved there. Around and below the main concourse are fantastic shops and eateries—including the New York Transit Museum gallery annex, Grand Central Market and Grand Central Oyster Bar. ■TIP→ **If you're with a friend, position yourselves in opposite corners of the tiled passageway just outside the Oyster Bar, facing away from each other, and murmur your secrets to the wall. Or just**

The restoration and cleaning of Grand Central Terminal in the late 1990s uncovered the elaborate astronomical design on the ceiling of the main concourse.

stand and watch others indulge in the delightful acoustic oddity that is the whispering gallery. Take Walks NYC (🌐 *www.takewalks.com/new-york-tours/grand-central-tours*) leads two official daily walking tours for $35 at 11 am and 3 pm. ✉ *Main entrance, 42nd St. and Park Ave., Midtown East* ☎ *212/935–3960* 🌐 *www.grandcentralterminal.com* Ⓜ *4, 5, 6, 7, S to Grand Central–42nd St.*

★ Museum of Modern Art (MoMA)

ART MUSEUM | Housing one of the world's finest collections of modern art, MoMA is renowned for its permanent collection, which includes masterpieces by Picasso, Van Gogh, Monet, Kahlo, Warhol, and Dalí, as well as its first-rate multimedia exhibitions. MoMA completed a $450 million renovation and expansion in 2019, and the building now features walkways between old and new galleries, each organized to showcase familiar masters alongside great, but lesser-known, artists—many of them women and people of color. Contemporary works and those of varied media also are strategically exhibited beside familiar classics. The displays breathe new life into the institution's curatorial experience.

MoMA spans six levels, and it's helpful to explore from top to bottom. See the most famous works on Floors 4 and 5; installations on 6; and galleries of photography, drawings, architecture projects, and special exhibitions on the lower floors. Level 1 remains home to the delightful Abby Aldrich Rockefeller Sculpture Garden. Within the museum, dine at high-end The Modern; snack at cafés on Floor 2; and enjoy outdoor views from the Terrace café on Floor 6. The cellar-level cinema screens international films and theme

Ice-skating under the sculpture of Prometheus at Rockefeller Center is a winter ritual for many local and visiting families.

series (museum entry is included with your film ticket). Browse at the famous MoMA Store and MoMA Design Store (across 53rd Street). ■ **TIP→ Entry is free for NYC residents the first Friday of each month, 4–8 pm. The first-floor galleries are free and open to the public. The museum is open until 7 pm on Saturday.** ✉ *11 W. 53rd St., between 5th and 6th Aves., Midtown West* ☎ *212/708–9400* 🌐 *www.moma.org* 🎟 *$28* Ⓜ *E, M to 5th Ave.–53rd St.; F to 57th St.; B, D, E to 7th Ave.*

Rockefeller Center

NOTABLE BUILDING | Comprising more than 100 shops and 50 eateries, the Rockefeller Center complex runs from 47th to 52nd Street between 5th and 6th Avenues; special events dominate the central plazas in spring and summer. In December an enormous, twinkling tree towers above the ice-skating rink, causing crowds of visitors from across the country and the globe to shuffle through with cameras flashing.

The world's most famous ice-skating rink occupies Rockefeller Center's sunken lower plaza from October through mid-April and converts to a roller-skating rink in summer. A gold-leaf statue of the Greek hero Prometheus hovers above. The lower plaza also provides access to the marble-lined concourse underneath Rockefeller Center, which houses restaurants, a post office, and clean public restrooms.

Rising from the Lower Plaza's west side is the 70-story Art Deco GE building. Here John D. Rockefeller Jr. commissioned and then destroyed a mural by Diego Rivera. He replaced it with the monumental *American Progress* by José María Sert, still on view in the lobby, flanked by additional murals by Sert and English artist Frank Brangwyn. Up on the 65th floor is the landmark Rainbow Room, a glittering big-band ballroom dating from 1934. Higher up, Top of the Rock has what many consider the finest panoramas of the city. Rockefeller Center guided walking tours are available several times daily (tickets start at $27), with the option to add a visit to the observation deck. ✉ *47th to 52nd St. between 5th and 6th Aves., Midtown West* ☎ *212/588–8601* 🌐 *www.rockefellercenter.com* Ⓜ *B, D, F, M to 47th–50th Sts./Rockefeller Center; E, M to 5th Ave.–53rd St.*

Times Square

BUSINESS DISTRICT | **FAMILY** | This is the most energetic part of New York City, a cacophony of flashing lights and shoulder-to-shoulder crowds that many New Yorkers studiously avoid. Originally named after the *New York Times* (whose headquarters has since relocated to 8th Avenue), the area has seen many changes since the first subway line, which included a 42nd Street station, opened in 1904. The area was once a bastion of the city's unseemly side, but today it's a vibrant, family-friendly destination, with pedestrian stretches that have lined Broadway Plaza with tables, chairs, and granite benches. There's no longer a visitor center here, since the official NYC Information Center is down at 151 West 34th Street in Herald Square, with maps, brochures, coupons, and a bilingual staff.

The focus of the entertainment might have shifted over the years, but live shows are still the heart of Midtown's theater scene, and there are 40 Broadway theaters nearby. (A few of the most historic theaters are spotlighted in this chapter's introduction.) Learn about Broadway's history and architecture on a two-hour walking tour by Manhattan Walking Tours (🎫 *$50* ⏲ *Daily at 10:30 am* 🌐 *www.manhattanwalkingtour.com*) or join the two-hour guided Inside Broadway tour (🎫 *$39* ⏲ *Daily at 4 pm* 🌐 *www.insidebroadwaytours.com*) that leaves from the George M. Cohan statue at West 46th Street and Broadway. ✉ *Broadway between 42nd and 48th Sts., Midtown West* ☎ *212/768–1560 for Times Square Alliance* 🌐 *www.timessquarenyc.org* Ⓜ *1, 2, 3, 7, N, Q, R, S, W to Times Sq.–42 St.*

United Nations Headquarters

GOVERNMENT BUILDING | Officially an "international zone" in the city's heart, the UN Headquarters sits on an 18-acre tract on the East River, fronted by flags of its 193 member states, who are charged with helping maintain international security and peace.

Built between 1949 and 1961, the complex completed an overhaul in 2015—the 70th anniversary of the UN's founding—that retained the 1950s look while upgrading its infrastructure. The only way to enter the UN Headquarters is with the hourlong weekday standard guided tour, available in all six UN official languages; reservations can be made online, and you'll need a security pass from the visitors office at 801 1st Avenue. ⚠ **Arrive 60 minutes before your tour's start for security screening.** The tour includes the General Assembly, Security Chamber Council, and exhibitions and educational details. Youngsters under five are not admitted. Other scheduled tours cater to different aspects of the UN such as art and architecture, or emphasize Black history or women and children; virtual versions are also available.

The complex's buildings (the slim, 550-foot-tall green-glass Secretariat Building; the much smaller, domed General Assembly Building; and the Dag Hammarskjöld Library) evoke the influential Swiss-born French modernist architect Le Corbusier, and the surrounding park and plaza remain visionary. The public concourse has a visitor center with a gift shop, a bookstore, and a post office where you can mail postcards with UN stamps; bring your passport to add the commemorative UN stamp. ✉ *Visitor entrance, 1st Ave. and 46th St., Midtown East* ☎ *212/963–8687* 🌐 *www.un.org/en/visit/tour* 🎟 *Tour $26* 🕒 *No tours on weekends* Ⓜ *4, 5, 6, 7, S to Grand Central–42nd St.*

Restaurants

Dons Bogam Wine Bar & BBQ

$$$ | KOREAN BARBECUE | Meat lovers in particular will enjoy Korean barbecue, and Dons Bogam is a venerable, quality option with a variety of meats (including American Wagyu) and seafood, cooked for you on a grill embedded in your table. Dishes are served with assorted condiments, sauces, and embellishments. **Known for:** spicy Korean stews and noodle dishes (both cold and hot); long list of wines and sakes; reservations necessary, even on weeknights. $ *Average main: $40* ✉ *17 E. 32nd St., between 5th and Madison Aves., Murray Hill* ☎ *212/683–2200* 🌐 *www.donsbogam.com* Ⓜ *6 to 33rd St.; B, D, F, M, N, Q, R, W to 34th St.–Herald Sq.*

The Hugh

$ | FOOD HALL | Named after architect Hugh Stubbins, who designed the Citicorp Center building in which it's based in, this food court is across from the E line subway stop at Lexington and 53rd. Fifteen-plus tenants consist of a mix of eateries, bars, and restaurants whose culinary offerings are as diverse as the city itself. **Known for:** different seating areas; adjacent to subway;

a good mix of restaurants. *Average main: $14 The Atrium, 157 E. 53rd St., Midtown East www.thehughnyc.com Closed weekends E, M to Lexington Ave.–53rd St.*

★ Le Bernardin

$$$$ | SEAFOOD | Enter the serene, teak-paneled dining room at this trendsetting French seafood restaurant, and let chef Eric Ripert work his magic with anything that swims—at times preferring not to cook it at all. Deceptively simple dishes are typical of his style, which has earned this restaurant many James Beard and other awards, including a rank among the world's top 20 restaurants and an incredible three Michelin stars. **Known for:** splurge-worthy prix-fixe only; impeccable service; reservations essential well in advance. *Average main: $210 155 W. 51st St., between 6th and 7th Aves., Midtown West 212/554–1515 www.le-bernardin.com Closed Sun. Jacket required 1 to 50th St.; N, R, W to 49th St.; B, D, E to 7th Ave.*

Marea

$$$$ | SEAFOOD | Large picture windows look out to expansive views of Central Park South at this elegant, seafood-focused Italian eatery. No expense is spared in importing the very best of the ocean's bounty, beginning with the crudo dishes—think scallops with orange, wild fennel, and arugula—that are the restaurant's signature. **Known for:** baked branzino for two; memorable homemade pastas; reservations essential. *Average main: $45 240 Central Park S, between 7th Ave. and Broadway, Midtown West 212/582–5100 www.marea-nyc.com 1, A, B, C, D to 59th St.–Columbus Circle.*

Mercado Little Spain

$$ | SPANISH | At the base of the Shops at Hudson Yards, this is a 35,000-square-foot, multifaceted love letter to Spanish food helmed by chef José Andrés and team. You can eat at self-serve tables; dine in full-service restaurants, Mar, Spanish Diner, or Leña; or pull up a stool at La Barra to sample delectable tapas (with vegetarian and seafood selections) and terrific wine and cocktails. **Known for:** bustling market-style shopping and dining; rich, authentic choices for different palates; stands selling ham, seafood, pastries, and more. *Average main: $23 10 Hudson Yards, 10th Ave. at 30th St., Midtown West 646/495–1242 www.littlespain.com 7 to 34th St.–Hudson Yards.*

Sparks Steak House

$$$$ | STEAK HOUSE | Brace yourself to spend indulgently at this famed steak house, where the dining rooms are festooned with pricey magnums of wines and have walls lined with pictures and tables draped in white linens. Although tasty, fresh seafood is given more than fair play on the menu—and the extra-thick lamb and veal chops are noteworthy—Sparks is really about dry-aged steak. **Known for:** notably long wine list; reservations essential; the spot where, in 1985, members of the Gambino crime family were gunned down. *Average main: $60 210 E. 46th St., between 2nd and 3rd Aves., Midtown East 212/687–4855 sparkssteakhouse.com No lunch weekends 4, 5, 6, 7, S to Grand Central–42nd St.*

Toloache

$$$ | MEXICAN | The bi-level eatery at this bustling Mexican cantina just off Broadway has a festive vibe, with several seating options: bar, balcony, main dining room, and ceviche bar. Foodies flock here for three types of guacamole (traditional, fruited, and spicy), well-executed ceviches, Mexico City–style tacos with Negra Modelo–braised brisket, and quesadillas with black truffle and *huitlacoche* (a corn fungus known as "the Mexican truffle"). **Known for:** contemporary Mexican cuisine; standout ceviche menu; broad tequila selection. *Average main: $30 251 W. 50th St., near 8th Ave., Midtown West 212/581–1818 www.toloachenyc.com 1, C, E to 50th St.; N, R, W to 49th St.*

Zuma New York

$$$ | JAPANESE FUSION | With an emphasis on presentation, the dishes at Zuma are authentically Japanese yet not bound by tradition, and designed to be shared at the table. You can choose sushi or items prepared on the robata grill, or, should you arrive on an empty stomach and with an adventurous spirit, go big with one of three omakase experiences. **Known for:** delicious cocktails; upstairs lounge can be noisy on weekends; good for special occasions. *Average main: $40 261 Madison Ave., between 38th and 39th Sts., Murray Hill 212/544–9862 www.zumarestaurant.com Closed Sun. No lunch Sat. 4, 5, 6, 7, S to Grand Central–42nd St.; 7 to 5th Av.*

Hotels

★ The Algonquin Hotel Times Square, Autograph Collection

$$ | HOTEL | One of Manhattan's most historic properties, the Algonquin is a landmark of literary history made famous by the luminaries of the famed Round Table (now the hotel restaurant's moniker). **Pros:** historic character but modernized rooms; good rates for the central location; hotel cat keeps guests company. **Cons:** some small rooms; busy street traffic; no in-room minibar. *Rooms from: $389 59 W. 44th St., between 5th and 6th Aves., Midtown West 212/840–6800 www.algonquinhotel.*

com 181 rooms No Meals *7 to 5th Ave.; B, D, F, M to 42nd St.–Bryant Park.*

★ Andaz 5th Avenue

$$$ | HOTEL | The name of this Hyatt brand means "personal style" in Hindi, and the serene and spacious modern rooms evoke that coveted New York loft feel, with floor-to-ceiling windows overlooking 5th Avenue and the New York Public Library. **Pros:** proximity to Bryant Park, Grand Central and Midtown attractions; high ceilings, tall windows, and suites have outdoor space; complimentary wine hour and morning coffee and tea. **Cons:** check-in at 4 pm (an hour later than most NYC hotels); not all rooms have notable views; rooms could do with more storage space. *Rooms from: $519 485 5th Ave., at 41st St., Midtown East 212/601–1234 www.hyatt.com 184 rooms No Meals 4, 5, 6, 7, S to Grand Central–42nd St.*

Archer Hotel New York

$$ | HOTEL | Rooftop bar Spyglass, with its killer view of the Empire State Building, is the star of this boutique property just south of Bryant Park, with its subtly industrial-inspired look that nods to the neighborhood's past. **Pros:** whimsical design and ambience; nice bathrooms and robes; reasonably priced for Manhattan. **Cons:** small rooms; lack of amenities, including gym or spa; convenient but unglamorous location. *Rooms from: $399 45 W. 38th St., between 5th and 6th Aves., Midtown West 212/719–4100, 855/200–9061 www.archerhotel.com 180 rooms No Meals B, D, F, M, 7 to 42nd St.–Bryant Park.*

Arlo NoMad

$ | HOTEL | With the Empire State Building just two blocks north, Koreatown a few blocks west, the Flatiron District seven blocks south, and easy access to subway lines, bars, and restaurants, the compact but stylish Arlo NoMad is perfectly positioned for the visitor who cares more about proximity and value than floor space and amenities. **Pros:** on-site activities and amenities; convenient location; Empire State Building views from the rooftop bar and Sky Rooms. **Cons:** no room service; glass-walled bathrooms; compact rooms. *Rooms from: $285 11 E. 31st St., Murray Hill 212/806–7000 arlohotels.com/nomad 239 rooms No Meals 6 to 33rd St.*

Bryant Park Hotel

$$ | HOTEL | A city landmark towering over the New York Public Library and Bryant Park in a Midtown sweet spot, this sleek hotel has rooms featuring padded leather headboards with decorative bolster pillows and marble bathrooms with rainfall shower heads and Molton Brown products. **Pros:** historic building on Bryant Park;

fashionable crowd and setting; stylish, spacious rooms. **Cons:** bustling traffic outside; not kid-friendly; limited nightlife in the area. *Rooms from: $365 40 W. 40th St., between 5th and 6th Aves., Midtown West 212/869–0100 www.bryantparkhotel.com 128 rooms No Meals B, D, F, M to 42nd St.–Bryant Park; 7 to 5th Ave.*

★ The Chatwal, New York

$$$$ | **HOTEL** | A lavishly refurbished reincarnation of a classic Manhattan theater club, the Chatwal delivers a stylish, luxury experience with a matching price tag. **Pros:** sophisticated furnishings; state-of-the-art room controls and amenities; excellent service. **Cons:** pricey even for Times Square; small pool; in-room lighting controls are confusing. *Rooms from: $625 130 W. 44th St., between Broadway and 6th Ave., Midtown West 212/764–6200 www.thechatwalny.com 76 rooms No Meals 1, 2, 3, 7, N, Q, R, S, W to Times Sq.–42nd St.*

★ citizenM New York Times Square Hotel

$$ | **HOTEL** | Part of a modern European chain, citizenM prizes a more eclectic, youthful style that puts technology and art at the forefront. **Pros:** cool indoor-outdoor rooftop bar; rooms are surprisingly quiet for Midtown; 21st-floor gym has great views. **Cons:** all rooms are for two people max only; high-traffic area; iPad room controls can be hard to navigate. *Rooms from: $329 218 W. 50th St., between Broadway and 8th Ave., Midtown West 212/461–3638 www.citizenm.com 230 rooms No Meals 1, C, E to 50th St.; N, R, W to 49th St.*

Conrad New York Midtown

$$$ | **HOTEL** | Sophisticated and spacious, the Conrad New York Midtown is a reasonably priced, business-oriented option just blocks from Central Park and Times Square. **Pros:** good location near Central Park; excellent fitness center; reliable concierge service. **Cons:** no bathtubs in most rooms; room decor is basic; lackluster restaurant. *Rooms from: $450 151 W. 54th St., between 6th and 7th Aves., Midtown West 212/307–5000 www.conradnewyorkmidtown.com 562 suites No Meals B, D, E to 7th Ave.; N, Q, R, W to 57th St.–7th Ave.*

Ink48 Hotel

$ | **HOTEL** | If you want to be near Midtown but a bit removed from the hustle and bustle, this hotel is a great option, with spacious, reasonably priced rooms, expansive views, and solid service that make up for a long walk from most subways. **Pros:** friendly staff; skyline and Hudson River views; large rooms. **Cons:** out-of-the-way location; lobby can feel overly quiet; street noise in lower-floor rooms. *Rooms from: $229 653 11th Ave., at 48th St.,*

Midtown West ☎ 212/757–0088 🌐 www.ink48.com 222 rooms 🍽 No Meals Ⓜ C, E to 50th St.

JW Marriott Essex House New York

$$$ | **HOTEL** | With Central Park views and an Art Deco masterpiece of a lobby dating to 1931, the JW Marriott Essex House is a comfortable Midtown hotel full of character. **Pros:** great service; amazing views and easy access to Central Park; gorgeous, timeless architecture and decor. **Cons:** overly complex room gadgetry; expensive bar; traffic jams during rush hours. *$ Rooms from: $465 ✉ 160 Central Park S, between 6th and 7th Aves., Midtown West ☎ 212/247–0300 🌐 www.marriott.com 426 rooms 🍽 No Meals Ⓜ N, Q, R, W to 57th St.–7th Ave.; F to 57th St.*

The Knickerbocker

$$ | **HOTEL** | An oasis of urban sophistication in the heart of Times Square, the Knickerbocker is a soothing counterpoint to the mass of people, lights, and excitement that converge nearby at Broadway and 42nd Street. **Pros:** in Times Square but aesthetically apart from it; spacious gym; fabulous rooftop bar. **Cons:** glowing lights surround the building; small lobby; resort fee for Wi-Fi. *$ Rooms from: $390 ✉ 6 Times Sq., entrance on 42nd St., east of Broadway, Midtown West ☎ 212/204–4980 🌐 www.theknickerbocker.com 330 rooms 🍽 No Meals Ⓜ 1, 2, 3, 7, N, Q, R, S, W to Times Sq.–42nd St.*

Moxy NYC Times Square

$ | **HOTEL** | Among Midtown's trendy lodging choices is this good-value hotel (part of a stylish chain) designed with modern boutique swagger and a vibrant dining and drinking scene. **Pros:** affordable rates; central location near public transit; vibrant on-site restaurants and bars. **Cons:** small rooms with minimal storage; street noise and bright lights flashing outside; sink is in main room instead of bathroom. *$ Rooms from: $260 ✉ 485 7th Ave., at 36th St., Midtown West ☎ 212/967–6699 🌐 www.moxytimessquare.com 612 rooms 🍽 No Meals Ⓜ 1, 2, 3, A, C, E to 34th St.–Penn Station.*

1 Hotel Central Park

$$$ | **HOTEL** | A commitment to next-level eco-friendly policies is evident in the smallest details at this hotel, from in-room chalkboards (instead of notepads) to triple-filtered water straight from the taps that eliminates the need for bottled water. **Pros:** green policies and convenient amenities; room are surprisingly quiet; cozy window seats with great city views. **Cons:** some service inconsistencies; rooms are on the small side; no spa. *$ Rooms from: $489 ✉ 1414 Ave. of the Americas, at 58th St., Midtown*

West ☎ 212/703–2001 ⊕ 1hotels.com/central-park ⇨ 229 rooms 🍴 No Meals Ⓜ F to 57th St; N, R, W to 5th Ave.–59th St.

★ Park Hyatt New York

$$$$ | **HOTEL** | Occupying the first 25 floors of a towering Midtown skyscraper, this luxury property is the flagship of the global Park Hyatt brand and features one of the best spas in New York. **Pros:** large guest rooms; luxurious furnishings throughout the hotel; city views from the fitness center and spa. **Cons:** disappointing views from guest rooms; pricey even for the neighborhood; street noise audible from lower floors. *$ Rooms from: $895 ✉ 153 W. 57th St., between 6th and 7th Aves., Midtown West ☎ 646/774–1234 ⊕ www.hyatt.com ⇨ 210 rooms 🍴 No Meals Ⓜ N, Q, R, W to 57th St.–7th Ave.*

★ The Peninsula New York

$$$$ | **HOTEL** | Stepping through the Peninsula's Beaux-Arts facade onto the grand staircase beneath a monumental chandelier, you know you're in for a glitzy treat. **Pros:** prime location; luxurious rooms with convenient controls; award-winning spa. **Cons:** extremely pricey; high-traffic area, especially on weekends; service can be inconsistent. *$ Rooms from: $1200 ✉ 700 5th Ave., at 55th St., Midtown West ☎ 212/956–2888 ⊕ www.peninsula.com/newyork ⇨ 235 rooms 🍴 No Meals Ⓜ E, M to 5th Ave.–53rd St.*

★ The Ritz-Carlton New York, Central Park

$$$$ | **HOTEL** | **FAMILY** | It's all about the park views here, though the above-and-beyond service, accommodating to a fault, makes this renowned hotel popular with celebs and other guests who can afford premier luxury travel. **Pros:** personalized service; lavish furnishings; stellar location with Central Park views. **Cons:** guests can be pretentious; pricey pet fee; overly expensive dining and bar menus. *$ Rooms from: $915 ✉ 50 Central Park S, at 6th Ave., Midtown West ☎ 212/308–9100 ⊕ www.ritzcarlton.com/central-park ⇨ 259 rooms 🍴 No Meals Ⓜ F to 57th St.; N, R, W to 5th Ave.–59th St.*

W New York – Times Square

$$ | **HOTEL** | The W Times Square stands out in the craziness of Midtown, thanks to its infamous 57-story exterior—if you want to be in the thick of the action, this is the place to stay. **Pros:** vibrant nightlife and happy-hour scene; sleek rooms; 24-hour room service. **Cons:** if you want quiet, head elsewhere; no bathtubs in the smaller rooms; extra fees for pets. *$ Rooms from: $389 ✉ 1567 Broadway, at 47th St., Midtown West ☎ 888/627–9102 ⊕ www.wnewyorktimessquare.com ⇨ 509 rooms 🍴 No Meals Ⓜ 1, 2, 3, 7, N, Q, R, S, W to Times Sq.–42th St.*

★ Carnegie Hall

MUSIC | FAMILY | Internationally renowned Carnegie Hall has incomparable acoustics that make it one of the world's best venues for music—classical as well as jazz, pop, cabaret, and folk. Since the opening-night concert on May 5, 1891, which Tchaikovsky conducted, virtually every important musician in the world has appeared in this Italian Renaissance–style building. The world's top orchestras perform in the grand and fabulously steep 2,804-seat Isaac Stern Auditorium; the 268-seat Weill Recital Hall often features young talents making their New York debuts; and the subterranean 599-seat Judy and Arthur Zankel Hall attracts big-name artists such as the Kronos Quartet and Milton Nascimento to its stylish modern space. A noted roster of family concerts is also part of Carnegie's programming.

The box office releases $10 rush tickets for some shows on the day of performance, or you can buy partial-view seating in advance at 50% off the full ticket price. Head to the second-floor Rose Museum (open by appointment) to learn more about the famous hall's history through its archival treasures, or join an insider's guided tour (available most days; $20 for adults). ✉ *881 7th Ave., at 57th St., Midtown West* ☎ *212/247–7800* 🌐 *www.carnegiehall.org* Ⓜ *N, Q, R, W to 57th St.–7th Ave.; B, D, E to 7th Ave.; F to 57th St.*

★ Radio City Music Hall

PERFORMANCE VENUES | This landmark was built shortly after the stock market crash of 1929, when John D. Rockefeller Jr. wanted to create a symbol of hope in what was a sad, broke city. When the hall opened, some said there was no need for performances, because people would get more than their money's worth simply by sitting there and enjoying the grand space. Despite being the largest indoor theater in the world, with its city-block-long marquee and nearly 6,000 seats, it feels warm and intimate. Hour-long Stage Door walking tours run year-round with limited availability.

There are big-name concerts and major events year-round, but the biggest draw is the Radio City Christmas Spectacular: more than a million visitors every year come to see the renowned Rockettes dance. Make reservations early, especially if you want to attend near Christmas or on a weekend (many performances can sell out by October). Tickets are affordable for the 90-minute show, with promotional and matinee deals available. ✉ *1260 6th Ave., between 50th and 51st Sts., Midtown West* ☎ *866/858–0007 for tickets, 212/465–6000 🌐 www.msg.com/radio-city-music-hall Ⓜ B, D, F, M to 47th–50th Sts./Rockefeller Center; N, R, W to 49th St.*

Shopping

★ Saks Fifth Avenue

DEPARTMENT STORE | This 660,000-square-foot-flagship store remains a high-fashion force and continually revamps its modish offerings with contemporary designer lines, such as Proenza Schouler and Victoria Beckham, and legacy brands including Gucci, Louis Vuitton, and Chanel. The Vault, with a 1920s-inspired grandiose bank interior, caters to fine jewelry and luxury watches and has Hōseki, a six-seat, modern omakase counter spearheaded by Michelin-star Chef Daniel Kim. The second-level beauty department stocks an incredible array of products, from classics to edgy. The department store also has a designer sneaker shop, and Barneys at Sax, featuring fashion-forward designers. This store's extravagant Holiday Light Show is one of the city's top attractions from late November to early January. ✉ *611 5th Ave., between 49th and 50th Sts., Midtown East* ☎ *212/753–4000* 🌐 *www.saksfifthavenue.com* Ⓜ *E, M to 5th Ave.–53rd St.; B, D, F, M to 47–50th Sts./Rockefeller Center.*

Tiffany & Co.

JEWELRY & WATCHES | It's hard to think of a more quintessentially New York jewelry store than Tiffany, along with its unmistakable robin's egg blue box. Daydream among the displays of platinum-and-diamond bracelets and massive engagement rings, or head to the sterling-silver floor for more affordable baubles. The first level's "Diamond Sky," a marvelous 22-foot-art installation, glistens among displays of gold and platinum crafted pieces and assorted gemstones. This flagship is among the world's most famous stores, thanks in part to Truman Capote's 1958 novella *Breakfast at Tiffany's* and the 1961 classic film starring Audrey Hepburn as Holly Golightly. It's now possible to have breakfast or some high tea within the store's Blue Box Café by Daniel Boulud. ✉ *727 5th Ave., at 57th St., Midtown East* ☎ *212/755–8000* 🌐 *www.tiffany.com* Ⓜ *N, R, W to 5th Ave.–59th St.; E, M to 5th Ave./53rd St.*

Chapter 7

UPPER EAST AND WEST WITH HARLEM

Updated by
Arabella Bowen

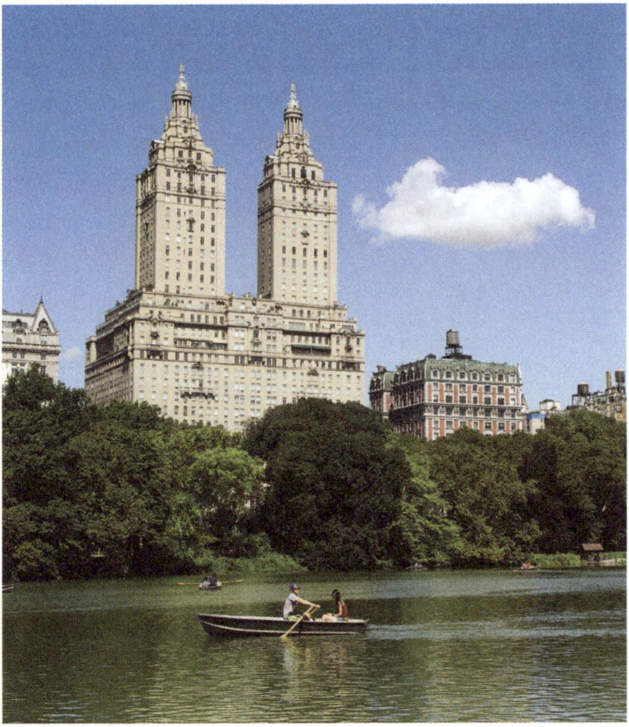

Sights	Restaurants	Hotels	Shopping	Nightlife
★★★★★	★★★☆☆	★★☆☆☆	★★★☆☆	★★★☆☆

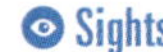

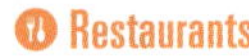

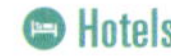

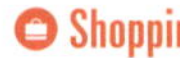

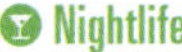

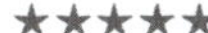

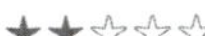

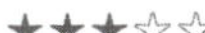

The Metropolitan Museum of Art Tour

If the city held no other museum than the colossal Metropolitan Museum of Art, you could still occupy yourself for days roaming its labyrinthine corridors. With more than 2 million works of art representing 5,000 years of history, this is the one not to miss.

1 Begin at the 82nd Street entrance, where the Met's granite steps lead up to its majestic Great Hall. On any given day, you'll see hundreds of people hanging out here under the museum's grand facade.

2 Head to the opposite end to enter the Egyptian Art Collection. The galleries cover 4,000 years of history, with tombs and papyrus pages from the Egyptian Book of the Dead (circa 332–200 BC). Walk through them clockwise from Gallery 138 until you reach Gallery 123, dominated by the Harkhebit sarcophagus (595–526 BC).

3 Next door in Gallery 121 is the entrance to the major star: the Temple of Dendur (completed by 10 BC). Egypt gifted it to the U.S. in 1965, and it now sits by itself in a sun-lit atrium with a moat-like pool to represent its original locale near the Nile.

4 Access the American Wing via the back of the room, then head through a set of glass doors on the right. You'll be plunged into the hushed galleries with much to see, from Colonial furniture to great master works by John

Walking Tour 101

HIGHLIGHTS

The Temple of Dendur; Emanuel Leutze's *Washington Crossing the Delaware*; the Frank Lloyd Wright Room; Impressionist and Post-Impressionist art

WHERE TO START

Egyptian Art

LENGTH

Two hours

WHERE TO END

Greek and Roman art

INSIDER TIPS

Weekday mornings (except Wednesday, when it's closed) and Friday and Saturday evenings are the best times to go. Be sure to grab a printed map to stay oriented. Don't hesitate to ask one of the many docents for directions when you get lost (which you will); they know the place intimately and are unfailingly helpful.

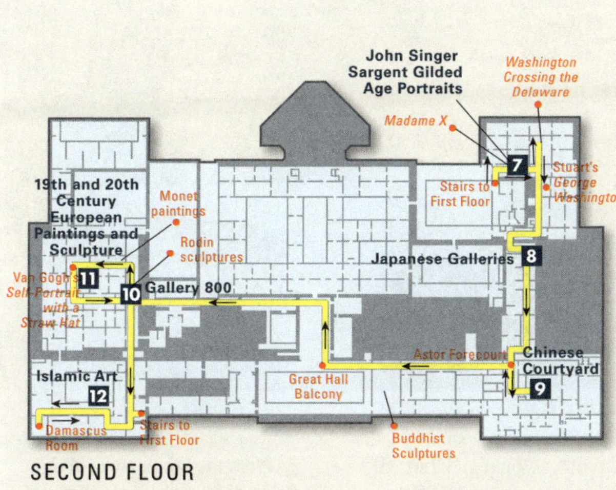

SECOND FLOOR

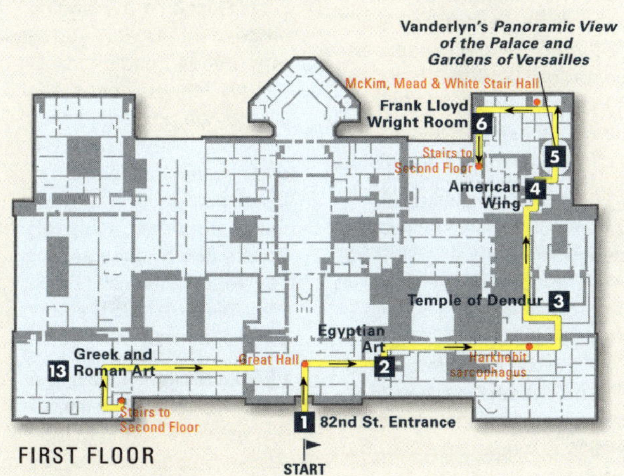

FIRST FLOOR

KEY

Start of Tour

Temple of Dendur

Singleton Copley, Gilbert Stuart, Winslow Homer, and more.

5 Find Gallery 735 off a hall to the right. The oval room contains Vanderlyn's *Panoramic View of the Palace and Gardens of Versailles* (1818–1819), a rare surviving example of 19th-century public art that invited vicarious travel.

6 Continue straight through Gallery 736, then left for two showstoppers. First: a Stair Hall designed by architects McKim, Mead & White for a Buffalo house in 1882–84 (Gallery 741), then, on the left side of Gallery 743 (full of decorative arts by Louis Comfort Tiffany), a brick walkway wraps around to the entrance of a glorious Frank Lloyd Wright Room rebuilt from floor plans for a Minnesota lake house he designed in 1912 (Gallery 745).

7 From the Frank Lloyd Wright Room, take a short set of steps straight ahead through Gallery 744, then take the stairs on the left to Floor 2. At the landing, proceed into Gallery 772, and turn right to head into Gallery 771 for John Singer Sargent's Gilded Age portraits, especially *Madame X* (1883–84), a once-scandalous portrait of a Parisian socialite. Cut through the next room and turn left into Gallery 760 to gape at Emanuel Leutze's *Washington Crossing the Delaware* (1851) in a massive gilded frame.

8 From 760, turn around, and walk straight through the next four galleries—looking for Gilbert Stuart's seminal portrait of George Washington as you exit the second—and turn right at the end. An unassuming entrance to Asian Art, a few steps down on the left, accesses the Japanese galleries. Skirt them all and go through the glass doors at the end to arrive in Gallery 209, aka the Astor Forecourt.

9 Head left into Gallery 217 to experience a Ming Dynasty-style Chinese courtyard, assembled here by 26 Chinese craftsmen over a six-month period. Once you've looped through, backtrack to Gallery 209 and continue to the end of the forecourt. Gallery 241 contains an ornate teak dome and balconies from a Jain meeting hall in western India, carved in the 16th century.

10 Retrace your steps back to the start of Gallery 209, and turn left. Walk through Gallery 207, down a short set of stairs, and through Gallery 206, with its towering Buddhist sculptures, to join the Great Hall Balcony. From here, trace the top of the museum's grand staircase on the right, turn left, and walk to the end of a long hallway, to reach Gallery 800, studded with Rodin statues.

The Met entrance

11 Gallery 800 is the heart of the Met's renowned 19th and Early 20th Century European Paintings and Sculpture collection. The warren of galleries to the left burst with sensational Impressionist and Post-Impressionist works by Picasso, Monet, Renoir, Cézanne, and Van Gogh. Enter via Gallery 819 for Monet's greatest hits—haystacks, water lilies, and the Rouen Cathedral. Take a quick spin by Vincent van Gogh's celebrated *Self-Portrait with a Straw Hat* (1887) in a glass case in Gallery 825.

12 Return to the Rodins and turn right. Keep going until you see Cypriot Galleries and an elevator bank. Turn right into one of the world's premier collections of Islamic art, 15 galleries known as Art of the Arab Lands, Turkey, Iran, Central Asia, and Later South Asia that traces the course of Islamic civilization over 13 centuries. Head to Gallery 461 to bask in the Damascus Room, an opulent 18th-century Ottoman reception room from Syria.

13 Exit the way you came in and take the stairs, or elevator, down to Floor 1, where you'll arrive in Greek and Roman Art, with works ranging from 4500 BC to AD 312. Turn right into Gallery 153 and wander among the Greek statuary—some of them marble copies made during the Roman period—to return to the Great Hall.

NEIGHBORHOOD SNAPSHOT

TOP EXPERIENCES

- Exploring the staggering collection of the Metropolitan Museum of Art
- Window-shopping on Madison Avenue
- Taking a stroll in Central Park
- Spending an evening at the prestigious Apollo Theater in Harlem
- Standing beneath the blue whale at the American Museum of Natural History

GETTING HERE

For the Upper East Side, take the Lexington Avenue 4 or 5 express train to 59th or 86th Street. The 6 local train stops at 59th, 68th, 77th, 86th, and 96th Streets and the Q train stops at 72nd, 86th, and 96th Streets.

The A, B, C, D, and 1 subway lines take you to Columbus Circle at the Upper West Side's southern edge. From there, the B and C lines make local stops along Central Park. Along Broadway, the 1 train runs local, while the express 2 and 3 trains stop at 72nd and 96th Streets. The 1 makes local stops along Broadway and St. Nicholas Avenue. The A train runs express from 59th Street and along Fort Washington Avenue; the 190th Street stop places you at entrance to Fort Tryon Park.

The 2 and 3 subway lines stop on Lenox Avenue; the 1 goes along Broadway, to the west; and the A, B, C, and D trains travel along St. Nicholas and 8th Avenues (note: the B train does not run on weekends). And yes, as the song goes, the A train is still usually "the quickest way to Harlem."

PAUSE HERE

- **Conservatory Garden.** Take a respite inside this formal garden in Central Park. This tranquil setting consists of the North (French-style), Center (Italianate) and South (English-style) gardens. ✉ *5th Ave., between 104th and 106th Sts.* 🌐 *www.centralparknyc.org* 🚇 *6 to 96th St. or 103rd St.*
- **Revson Fountain.** The magnificent central fountain in the main plaza of Lincoln Center for the Performing Arts, with its dancing water display, is a popular resting and meeting point year-round. ✉ *Plaza, Columbus Ave. between 63rd and 64th Sts.* 🌐 *www.lincolncenter.org* 🚇 *1 to 66th St.–Lincoln Center.*

To many New Yorkers, the Upper East Side connotes old money and high society. Alongside Central Park, between Fifth and Lexington Avenues as far up as East 96th Street, the trappings of wealth are apparent everywhere from posh doorman buildings to Madison Avenue's flagship boutiques.

It's also a key destination for visitors because some of the country's finest museums are here—including the Metropolitan Museum of Art; the Solomon R. Guggenheim Museum; and the Cooper Hewitt, Smithsonian Design Museum—on a stretch of Fifth Avenue called "Museum Mile." For a taste of the luxe life, catwalk down Madison Avenue for its lavish boutiques, especially the platinum-card corridor between 60th and 82nd Streets, where global fashion houses showcase their luxe threads in exquisite settings.

Meanwhile, across Central Park—one of the city's top attractions, no matter the season or time of day—the Upper West Side's lovely, tree-lined streets shelter their fair share of cultural institutions, from the 16-acre Lincoln Center performing-arts complex to the much-loved American Museum of Natural History.

To the north, Harlem is known throughout the world as a vibrant center of Black culture, music, and life. The neighborhood brims with historic jewels such as the Apollo Theater, splendid churches, and and beautiful brownstones. And yes, as the song goes, you should still "Take the 'A' Train" to get there.

★ American Museum of Natural History

SCIENCE MUSEUM | FAMILY | With more than 40 exhibition halls and 34 million artifacts and specimens, the world's largest and most important museum of natural history can easily keep you occupied for more than a day. The dioramas might seem a bit dated but are still fun; dinosaur fossils and exhibits, including a massive *T. rex*, are highlights for many people, especially kids. A 94-foot model of a blue whale, another museum icon, is suspended from the ceiling in the Milstein Hall of Ocean Life. Attached to the museum

Sights
American Museum of Natural History, 4
Central Park, 5
The Frick Collection, 2
The Jewish Museum, 9
Lincoln Center for the Performing Arts, 1
The Metropolitan Museum of Art, 6
Neue Galerie New York, 7
New-York Historical Society, 3
Solomon R. Guggenheim Museum, 8
Strivers' Row, 10
Restaurants
Bad Roman, 1
Café Sabarsky, 6
Daniel, 3
Harlem Shake, 7
Heidelberg Restaurant, 5
Jean-Georges, 2
Jones Wood Foundry, 4
Red Rooster Harlem, 8
Hotels
Aloft Harlem, 5
The Empire Hotel, 2
The Gardens Sonesta ES Suites New York, 3
Mandarin Oriental, New York, 1
The Mark Hotel, 4
MORNINGSIDE HEIGHTS
NEW JERSEY
James J. Braddock Park
79th St.
WOODCLIFF
River Rd.
HUDSON RIVER
Riverside Park
Henry Hudson Pkwy.
Riverside Dr.
W. 110th St.
W. 106th St.
Broadway
W. 96th St.
Amsterdam Ave.
West End Ave.
W. 86th St.
UPPER WEST SIDE
Jacqueline Kennedy Onassis Reservoir
W. 79th St.
9A
Columbus Ave.
CENTRAL PARK
W. 72nd St.
12th Ave.
The Lake
5th Ave.
Central Park W.
10th Ave.
E. 72nd St.
Park Ave.
Madison Ave.
W. 57th St.
11th Ave.
9th Ave.
8th Ave.
Central Park S.
The Pond
HELL'S KITCHEN
0
0.5 mi
0
0.5 km
KEY
Sights
Restaurants
Hotels

Upper East and West with Harlem
MANHATTANVILLE
THE BRONX
MOTT HAVEN
HARLEM
EAST HARLEM
RANDALLS ISLAND
YORKVILLE
UPPER EAST SIDE
LENOX HILL
ROOSEVELT ISLAND
ASTORIA
QUEENS
EAST RIVER
Harlem River
Broadway
W. 145th St.
W. 135th St.
W. 125th St.
E. 125th St.
E. 120th St.
E. 116th St.
E. 110th St.
E. 106th St.
E. 96th St.
E. 86th St.
E. 79th St.
E. 138th St.
St. Nicholas Park
St. Nicholas Ave.
St Nicholas Ave.
Frederick Douglass Blvd.
Adam Clayton Powell Jr. Blvd.
Lenox Ave.
5th Ave.
Madison Ave.
Park Ave.
Lexington Ave.
3rd Ave.
2nd Ave.
1st Ave.
York Ave.
East End Ave.
FDR Dr.
Amsterdam Ave.
Morningside Ave.
Manhattan Ave.
Morningside Park
Marcus Garvey Park
Harlem River Dr.
Grand Conc.
Morris Ave.
Randalls Island Park
Wards Island Park
Astoria Park
19th St.
27th Ave.
Astoria Blvd.
31st St.
Vernon Blvd.
87
278

is the Rose Center for Earth and Space featuring various exhibits, the Hayden Planetarium, a giant-screen theater, and the *Worlds Beyond Earth* space show, which takes you on a cosmic journey to the inner reaches of our solar system. Do your bling thing at the dazzling Mignone Halls of Gems and Minerals, displaying giant geodes, diamonds, and sapphires, and explore the revitalized Northwest Coast Hall, where you will find exhibits on the history and creativity of the cultures of the Pacific Northwest. The latest addition to this ever-changing museum is the Richard Gilder Center for Science, Innovation, and Education, which opened in mid-2023 adding an organic canyon-like atrium with large skylights to create a welcoming new space for discovery; new galleries dedicated to insects; a permanent butterfly vivarium; classrooms; a research library; and a state-of-the-art theater-in-the-round.

Many family-friendly events, including storytelling and dance performances, are included with admission. Purchase timed entry tickets in advance, and check the website for special programs, including sleepovers for kids. ✉ *200 Central Park W, at 79th St., Upper West Side* ☎ *212/769–5100* 🌐 *www.amnh.org* 🎫 *$28 includes admission to Rose Center for Earth and Space; $34 includes one ticketed exhibition, giant-screen film, or space show* Ⓜ *B, C to 81st St.–Museum of Natural History; 1 to 79th St.–Broadway.*

★ Central Park

CITY PARK | FAMILY | Central Park's creators, landscape architects Frederick Law Olmsted and Calvert Vaux, had a simple goal when they submitted their plan in 1858: to design a place where city dwellers could go to forget the city. Even though New York eventually grew far taller than the trees planted to hide it, the park has always been an urbanized Eden that gives residents and visitors alike a bite of the apple. Indeed, without Central Park's 843 acres of meandering paths, tranquil lakes, ponds, and open meadows, New Yorkers (especially Manhattanites) might be a lot less sane. Olmsted and Vaux also designed Brooklyn's Prospect Park and the grounds of the White House.

The busy southern section of Central Park, from 59th to 72nd Street, is where most people get their first impression. But no matter how many people congregate around here, you can always find a spot to picnic, ponder, or just take in the foliage, even on a sunny weekend day. Playgrounds, lawns, jogging and biking paths, and striking buildings populate the midsection of the park, from 72nd Street to the reservoir. You can soak up the sun, take in the public art, take pictures at Bethesda Fountain, visit the penguins at the Central Park Zoo, or join the runners huffing counterclockwise on the dirt track that surrounds the reservoir. North of the reservoir and up to 110th Street, Central Park is less crowded and feels more rugged. The Central Park Conservancy is currently revitalizing the area around the Harlem Meer (a man-made lake) at the north end of the park to add a full-scale ice rink, an additional new skating experience on the meer, a larger-than-Olympic-size pool, and revamp the parkland around it. The new facility is called the Harlem Meer Center (formerly the Lasker Rink and Pool site) and is expected to be open by winter 2024. To find out about park events and year-round walking tours, check the website of the Central Park Conservancy (🌐 *www.centralparknyc.org*).

If you're taking the subway to the park's southernmost parts, the stops at either Columbus Circle (southwest corner) or 5th Avenue–59th Street (southeast corner) are handy. If headed for points north, the A, B, C, and D subway lines travel along Central Park West (beware of local versus express stops); the 4, 5, and 6 lines travel along Lexington Avenue, three blocks east of 5th Avenue and the park.

There are many paved pedestrian entrances into the park from 5th Avenue, Central Park North (110th Street), Central Park West, and Central Park South (59th Street). Four roads, or transverses, for cars and city busses cut through the park from east to west—66th, 79th, 86th, and 96th Streets. The East and West drives are both along the north–south axis; Center Drive enters the south edge of the park at 6th Avenue and connects with East Drive around 66th Street. Cars are no longer allowed on the drives, which are exclusively for pedestrians, cyclists and horse-drawn carriages. Along the main loop, lampposts are marked with location codes that include a letter—always "E" (for east) or "W" (for west)—followed by numbers, the first two of which tell you the nearest cross street. For example, E7803 means you're near 78th Street; above 99, the initial "1" is omitted, so W0401 is near West 104th Street. Download the Central Park Conservancy's free app for a GPS-enabled map to help you navigate the park. The app also includes an audio guide, self-guided tours, and current events in the park, as well as a new interactive Cherry Blossom Tracker Map to help visitors and locals track when and where the flowers will peak in the park in spring.

If you haven't packed a picnic and you want a snack, you can usually find one of those rather tired-looking food carts selling hot dogs, pretzels and ice-cream sandwiches. Specialty food carts are often around, too, mostly in the park's southern half, especially when there are concerts or other major events—your taste buds

Many Beatles fans come to Strawberry Fields in Central Park to pay their respects to John Lennon, who was murdered across the street at the Dakota apartments.

will thank you. Other reliable options include the café next to the Boathouse Restaurant (midpark at 74th Street), or the park's newly renovated branch of Le Pain Quotidien (midpark at 69th Street). Both serve sandwiches, soups, pastries, and other satisfying on-the-go grub (and Le Pain also has free Wi-Fi). For something a little more elegant, you can stop for brunch, lunch, or dinner at the Tavern on the Green.

As part of a parkwide restoration project named Plan for Play, all 21 playgrounds have undergone (or are still scheduled to receive) updates. Most have seen renovations to play structures, plus other improvements that will ensure each one's structural stability and ongoing maintenance for years to come. ⊠ *Bounded by Central Park South and Central Park North, and Central Park West and 5th Ave., Upper West Side* ☎ *212/794–6564 for Dairy Visitor Center, 212/360–2726 for custom walking tours, 212/310–6600 for Central Park Conservancy* 🌐 *www.centralparknyc.org* Ⓜ *1, A, B, C, D to 59th St.–Columbus Circle; N, R, W to 5th Ave.–59th St.*

★ The Frick Collection

ART MUSEUM | Late 2024 is when the Frick Collection plans to return to its opulent 5th Avenue mansion location, which was being renovated and modernized with new technology and accessibility features. Before then, some of the museum's treasures were temporarily shown in a modernist building on Madison Avenue that once housed The Met Breuer (named for the building's architect, Marcel Breuer). Its namesake, Henry Clay Frick (1849–1919) made his fortune amid the smoke of Pittsburgh, where he was a coke (a coal fuel derivative) and steel baron, but his amazing art collection of Old Masters is decidedly far removed from soot. Exceptional pieces from the Renaissance through the late 19th century include paintings by Holbein, Vermeer, and Rembrandt and works by El Greco, Goya, Van Dyck, Hogarth, Degas, and Turner. The museum also has 18th-century French furniture, delicate Chinese ceramics and other decorative arts. Children under 10 are not admitted. At its East 70th Street address, the museum will become equipped with ADA-accessible entrance ramps, elevators and bathrooms, publicly open its second floor and add a café overlooking its restful garden. ✉ *1 E. 70th St., Upper East Side* ☎ *212/288–0700* 🌐 *www.frick.org* 🎫 *$22; pay-what-you-wish Thurs. 4–6* ⏲ *Closed Mon.–Wed.* Ⓜ *6 to 68th St.–Hunter College or 77th St.*

★ The Jewish Museum

ART MUSEUM | Housed in a circa 1908 French-Gothic, chateau-style mansion that was once the home of German-Jewish immigrant and businessman Felix Warburg, the Jewish Museum draws on an impressive collection of art and ceremonial objects to explore Jewish identity and culture over spanning more than 4,000 years. The wide-ranging artifacts include the world's largest collection of Hanukkah lamps, a 3rd–4th century Roman burial plaque, 20th-century sculpture by George Segal, and works by such artists as Camille Pissarro, Deborah Kass, Lee Krasner, and Kehinde Wiley. The museum's changing exhibitions are well curated and lively. Purchasing timed admission tickets in advance is recommended. The museum's gift shop carries Judaica, ceremonial objects and suggested gift ideas but it's closed on Saturdays. ✉ *1109 5th Ave., at 92nd St., Upper East Side* ☎ *212/423–3200* 🌐 *thejewishmuseum.org* 🎫 *$18 (free Sat. and select Jewish holidays)* ⏲ *Closed Tues. and Wed.* Ⓜ *6 to 96th St.*

★ Lincoln Center for the Performing Arts

ARTS CENTER | **FAMILY** | Internationally renowned, this cultural destination attracts more than 6.5 million visitors annually to its massive, white-travertine-clad complex of buildings, including the homes of the New York Philharmonic, Metropolitan Opera, New York City Ballet, the Juilliard School, the Film Center, a branch of the New York Public Library specializing in the performing arts, and the Damrosch Park outdoor performance space. All of this makes Lincoln Center one of the nation's most concentrated destinations for the performing arts. The16-acre campus, containing 30 venues in all, was designed by prolific New York architect Wallace Harrison and was built over the course of several years from 1962 to 1969. When David Geffen Hall reopened in fall 2022 after a two-year $550 million renovation, the acoustically superior venue—home to the New York Philharmonic, the oldest symphony orchestra in the United States—evoked and honored the vibrant Black and Puerto Rican neighborhood that had been razed to make way for the complex with a multimedia piece by the composer Etienne Charles called "San Juan Hill." The opening included a commitment to making programming more accessible to all audiences: performances from within the Wu Tsai Theater are simulcast on the lobby's Hauser Digital Wall for anyone to experience and rotating visual artworks are also be shown on the digital wall as well as on the facade on 65th Street at Broadway. You can also get a glimpse of artists working and rehearsing in the new Sidewalk Studio facing Broadway.

The Metropolitan Opera House, notable for its arched entrance, features immense chandeliers and Marc Chagall paintings, both of which can be seen from outside. Even the fountain in the central plaza puts on a show, with performances that include spouts of water 40-feet high. From mid-May to mid-August, Lincoln Center's "Summer for the City" presents hundreds of mostly free events.

Guided tours (weekdays 2 pm and 3:45 pm) are 75 minutes and include backstage access to Geffen and Tully halls where visitors can enjoy a unique look behind the scenes at rehearsals, technical work, backstage areas, and theaters. Book tickets online or at Geffen Hall Box Offices. ✉ *From 62nd St. to 66th St., between Broadway/Columbus and Amsterdam Aves., Upper West Side* ☎ *212/875–5456 for general inquiries, 212/721–6500 for tickets* 🌐 *www.lincolncenter.org* 🎫 *Tickets vary by venue; guided tour $20* Ⓜ *1 to 66th St.–Lincoln Center.*

★ The Metropolitan Museum of Art

ART MUSEUM | If Manhattan had no museums other than the colossal Metropolitan Museum of Art, you could still occupy yourself for days—even a week—roaming its labyrinthine corridors. It is the largest museum in the Western Hemisphere, with more than 1.5 million works of art representing 5,000 years of world history, so plan ahead and be selective. The famous Egyptian Art collection (including the Temple of Dendur) is reason enough to visit. Other don't-miss sections include the extensive European Paintings galleries, the magnificent Islamic Art galleries, the vibrant collection of Impressionist paintings, The American Wing, the Anna Wintour Costume Center (named for the celebrated *Vogue* editor-in-chief and holding The Costume Institute's fashionable collection), and tons (literally) of ancient Greek and Roman statues. Kids will love the Arms and Armor displays.

Be aware of ongoing renovations. A rebuild of the Ancient Near Eastern and Cypriot Art galleries will continue into early 2026;

check the website and museum map to plan your visit around gallery closures. In between exhibits, take a break at the Cantor Roof Garden, open late April through late October, or at one of five cafés and lounges offering light bites and cocktails. Or book a reservation for The Met Dining Room, an upscale restaurant with Central Park views and a seasonal menu. Admission includes same-day entry to The Met Cloisters, a combination of medieval European art, architecture and gardens in Fort Tryon Park in Upper Manhattan. Make the most of your visit by downloading a free digital or audio guide from the Met's website or take advantage of guided tours available in 10 different languages. ✉ *1000 5th Ave., at 82nd St., Upper East Side* ☎ *212/535–7710* 🌐 *www.metmuseum.org* 🎟 *$30 (includes same-day admission to Met Cloisters); New York State residents have a pay-what-you-wish option* ⏲ *Closed Wed.* Ⓜ *4, 5, 6 to 86th St.*

Neue Galerie New York

ART MUSEUM | Early-20th-century German and Austrian art and design are the focus here, with works by Ernst Ludwig Kirchner, Egon Schiele, and designers from the Wiener Werkstätte. It's perhaps best known for having Gustav Klimt's portrait, *Adele Bloch-Bauer I* or *Woman in Gold*. Inside a 1914 Carrère and Hastings mansion, where Mrs. Cornelius Vanderbilt III once lived, the Neue Galerie was founded by the late art dealer Serge Sabarsky and cosmetics heir and art collector Ronald S. Lauder. Children under 12 are not admitted, and teens 12–16 must be accompanied by an adult. The first-floor Café Sabarsky is popular for its elegant Viennese coffeehouse setting and menu. If busy, try the basement-level Café Fledermaus, which has much the same offerings. ✉ *1048 5th Ave., at 86th St., Upper East Side* ☎ *212/628–6200* 🌐 *neuegalerie.org* 🎟 *$25; free 5–8 pm on 1st Fri. of month* ⏲ *Closed Tues. and Wed.* Ⓜ *4, 5, 6 to 86th St.*

★ **New-York Historical Society**

HISTORY MUSEUM | **FAMILY** | New York City's oldest (and perhaps most under-the-radar) museum, founded in 1804, has an extensive research library in addition to sleek interactive technology, a children's museum, and inventive exhibitions that shed light on America's history, art, and architecture. The eclectic permanent collection includes more than 14 million pieces of art, literature, prints, photographs, and memorabilia, and special exhibitions showcase the museum's unique voice and ability to provide fresh insight on all things related to New York and the nation. The Henry Luce III Center for the Study of American Culture includes 100 dazzling Tiffany lamps on display and historic treasures that tell the American story in a novel way. Also part of the Luce Center is the Center for Women's History, examining the untold stories of

Did You Know?

The Upper East Side has some of the most expensive apartment buildings in Manhattan. Fifth Avenue in particular is a coveted location among business moguls, socialites, and celebrities. Jackie Kennedy famously lived at 1040 5th Avenue between 85th and 86th streets.

women who have impacted and continue to shape the American experience. The DiMenna Children's History Museum on the lower level invites children to become "history detectives" and explore New York's past through interactive displays, hands-on activities, and the stories of notable New York children through the centuries. **TIP→ The gift shop offers excellent New York–specific gifts and souvenirs.**

In late 2023, the museum began construction of its Democracy Wing, scheduled to open in 2026 to celebrate the 250th anniversary of the United States of America. The new wing will include expanded space for educational programs, state-of-the-art preservation facilities, a new exhibition gallery, a courtyard, and rooftop garden terraces. The museum will remain open during construction.

Clara, the light-filled restaurant on the first floor (separate entrance), serves contemporary takes on classic New York dishes at lunch, dinner, and brunch on weekends; Cafe 77 sells beverages, pastries, and snacks. ✉ *170 Central Park W, at 77th St., Upper West Side* ☎ *212/873–3400* 🌐 *www.nyhistory.org* 🎫 *$24; pay-as-you-wish admission Fri. 6 pm–8 pm* ⏲ *Closed Mon.* Ⓜ *B, C to 81st St.–Museum of Natural History.*

★ Solomon R. Guggenheim Museum

ART MUSEUM | Frank Lloyd Wright's landmark nautilus-like building is renowned as much for its famous architecture as for its superlative collection of modern and contemporary art and well-curated shows, some of which utilize the entire museum. Opened in 1959, shortly after Wright's death, the Guggenheim is acclaimed as one of the greatest buildings of the 20th century. Inside, under a 96-foot-high skylight, just over a quarter-mile long ramp spirals down past current exhibits. The museum has strong holdings of works by Vasily Kandinsky (over 150 paintings), Josef Albers, Pawel Althamer, Paul Klee, Marc Chagall, Pablo Picasso, and Robert Mapplethorpe. **TIP→ In 2023, the museum hired its first associate curator of art and technology to promote artists working with technology.**

Wright's superior design was criticized by some who believed that the distinctive building detracted from the art, but the spiraling layout allows artwork to be viewed from different angles and distances. On permanent display, the museum's Thannhauser Collection is made up primarily of works by French impressionists and postimpressionists Van Gogh, Degas, Cézanne, Renoir, and Manet. **TIP→ Escape the crowded lobby by taking the elevator to the top and working your way down the spiral.** The Cafe Rebay offers snacks, salads, and sandwiches, while the gift shop is

This Harlem block, lined with spectacular Georgian and Italian Renaissance townhouses, is known as Strivers' Row.

near the main entrance. ✉ *1071 5th Ave., between 88th and 89th Sts., Upper East Side* ☎ *212/423–3500* 🌐 *www.guggenheim.org* 🎫 *$30; pay-what-you-wish Sat. 5–8* Ⓜ *4, 5, 6 to 86th St.*

Strivers' Row

NEIGHBORHOOD | This block of gorgeous 1890s Georgian and Italian Renaissance Revival homes earned its nickname in the 1920s from less-affluent Harlemites who felt its residents were "striving" to become well-to-do. Some of the few remaining private service alleys, used when deliveries arrived via horse and cart, lie behind these houses and are visible through iron gates. Note the gatepost between Nos. 251 and 253 on 138th Street that reads, "Private Road. Walk Your Horses." These houses were built by the contractor David H. King Jr., whose developments also include Madison Square Garden and the Washington Arch. When the houses failed to sell to white people, the properties on these blocks were sold to Black doctors, lawyers, and other professionals; composers and musicians W.C. Handy and Eubie Blake were also among the residents. If you have the time, detour a block north to see the palazzo-style group of houses designed by Stanford White, on the north side of 139th Street. ✉ *138th and 139th Sts., between Adam Clayton Powell Jr. and Frederick Douglass Blvds., Harlem* 🌐 *www.striversrownyc.org* Ⓜ *B, C to 135th St.; A, B, C, D to 145th St.*

Restaurants

★ Bad Roman

$$$ | **MODERN ITALIAN** | Set on the third floor of the Deutsche Bank center at Columbus Circle, and one floor down from the temple of haute cuisine, Per Se, this irreverent, playful, maximalist, authentic, inauthentic, gimmicky, and just plain fun Italian restaurant is not bad at all; in fact, it's very good. Any illusions that this is a traditional and polite Italian dining experience are left at the door where you are met with a half-ton wild boar statue wearing a neon necklace and a dining room that is a feast of color and texture with red and white travertine, trompe l'oeil mosaics, and lush greenery suspended from wood coffered ceilings above orange banquettes. **Known for:** playful setting and crowds; 2-pound lobster with a mound of pasta between the claws; great wine list and reasonably priced by-the-glass wines. *Average main: $40* *Deutsche Bank Center, 10 Columbus Circle, 3rd fl., Upper West Side* *212/970–2033* *www.badromannyc.com* *1, A, B, C, D to 59th St.-Columbus Circle.*

★ Café Sabarsky

$$ | **AUSTRIAN** | In the Neue Galerie, this stately coffeehouse—open for breakfast, lunch, and dinner—offers a Viennese café experience, with art deco furnishings; a selection of daily newspapers; and cases with cakes and strudels. The menu of heartier sandwiches and goulash or sausage dishes is under the direction of German-born executive chef Christopher Engel, who worked at Wallsé and Aureole, earning a Michelin star. **Known for:** a slice of Vienna on the UES; delicious Sacher torte; goulash soup and Bavarian sausage. *Average main: $25* *Neue Galerie, 1048 5th Ave., near 86th St., Upper East Side* *212/288–0665* *www.neuegalerie.org* *Closed Tues. and Wed. No dinner Mon.* *4, 5, 6 to 86th St.*

★ Daniel

$$$$ | **FRENCH** | At his namesake restaurant, celebrity-chef Daniel Boulud offers one of the most refined dining experiences in Manhattan in an equally elegant dining room with a formal dress code (men's jacket required). A predominantly French-driven, four-course, prix-fixe menu is served within the main dining room. **Known for:** special-occasion haute fare; superb cheeses and desserts; reservations essential. *Average main: $188* *60 E. 65th St., At Park Ave., Upper East Side* *212/288–0033* *www.danielnyc.com* *Closed Mon. No lunch* *Jacket required* *6 to 68th St.–Hunter College.*

★ Harlem Shake

$ | **AMERICAN** | **FAMILY** | This family-friendly burger joint on the bustling, brownstone-lined corner of 124th Street and Malcolm X Boulevard has a retro malt-shop interior adorned with headshots of Black entertainers, vintage *Jet* magazine covers, and even a Wall of Fro dedicated to customers with afros. The name is a clever take on the world-famous Harlem Shake dance made popular by Harlem resident Al B, and also gives a nod to its rich organic milk shakes—such as the signature Red Velvet, locally made with real cake and Blue Marble ice cream. **Known for:** tasty fries including jerk or chili-cheese; organic milk shakes; wide variety of burgers and hotdogs. *Average main: $9* *100 W. 124th St., at Lenox Ave. (Malcolm X Blvd.), Harlem* *212/222–8300* *www.harlemshake.com* *2, 3 to 125th St.*

Heidelberg Restaurant

$$$ | **GERMAN** | Family-owned for three generations, the Heidelberg is a throwback to when Yorkville was a bustling German community more than a century ago. A thriving remnant of this past, the restaurant's exterior reflects German (half-timbered) facade. **Known for:** sausages and wursts; good schnitzels; plenty of German beer on tap. *Average main: $34* *1648 2nd Ave., between 85th and 86th Sts., Upper East Side* *212/628–2332* *www.heidelberg-nyc.com* *4, 5, 6, Q to 86th St.*

★ Jean-Georges

$$$$ | **FRENCH** | Chef célèbre Jean-Georges Vongerichten's prix-fixe–only culinary flagship focuses wholly on his spectacular dishes, which either approach the limits of the taste universe (perhaps foie-gras brûlée with fig jam and ice-wine reduction) or are models of simplicity (say, toasted egg yolk and caviar). The dining room is sleek but understated, with floor-to-ceiling windows adding sparkle to the white leather furnishings, white walls, and white linens; fresh-cut flowers adorn every table. **Known for:** exquisite cuisine and service; award-winning dining; lunch in Nougatine, the less-pricey front room. *Average main: $298* *1 Central Park W, at 60th St., Upper West Side* *212/299–3900* *www.jean-georges.com* *No lunch* *Jacket required* *1, A, B, C, D to 59th St.–Columbus Circle.*

Jones Wood Foundry

$$ | **BRITISH** | This British-style gastropub with exposed brick walls and wooden tables and floors is named for—and located in—the iron foundry that was located here in the late 1800s, when it created staircases, doors, and even manhole covers for a growing city. There's an extensive list of beers, ales, and wines, and the Euro-style menu includes beef bourguignon alongside light and

flaky fish-and-chips. **Known for:** British beers and ales; classic British pub food; hidden garden dining area. $ *Average main: $29* ✉ *401 E. 76th St., at 1st Ave., Upper East Side* ☎ *212/249–2700* 🌐 *www.joneswoodfoundry.com* Ⓜ *6 to 77th St., Q to 72nd St.*

★ Red Rooster Harlem

$$$ | **AMERICAN** | Marcus Samuelsson, who earned his celebrity chefdom at Aquavit in Midtown for his take on Ethiopian-accented Scandinavian cuisine (fusing the food of his birthplace with that of where he grew up), moved to Harlem in 2010, creating a culinary hot spot in this casual, jazzy-looking space with wall murals, wooden tables, and bistro chairs. The comfort-food menu reflects the ethnic diversity of modern-day New York City, from spicy jerk salmon to the shrimp and grits with tomato-okra stew. **Known for:** lines for Sunday brunch with gospel music; chicken (with maple hot sauce) and waffles; lively scene. $ *Average main: $32* ✉ *310 Lenox Ave. (Malcolm X Blvd.), between 125th and 126th Sts., Harlem* ☎ *212/792–9001* 🌐 *www.redroosterharlem.com* Ⓜ *2, 3 to 125th St.*

Hotels

Aloft Harlem

$$ | **HOTEL** | A reasonably priced option in an increasingly popular area of Harlem with plenty of access to public transportation at 125th Street, this branch of the Aloft chain delivers cheerful service and a fun atmosphere. **Pros:** good room size; convenient to subways; ever-increasing local shopping and dining options. **Cons:** rooms have minimal space for hanging clothes; rooms get some street noise; decor is outdated. $ *Rooms from: $314* ✉ *2296 Frederick Douglass Blvd., between 123th and 124th Sts., Harlem* ☎ *212/749–4000* 🌐 *www.aloftharlem.com* *125 rooms* *No Meals* Ⓜ *2, 3, A, B, C, D to 125th St.*

The Empire Hotel

$$ | **HOTEL** | **FAMILY** | Overlooking Lincoln Center, one block from Central Park, and convenient to midtown shopping and sights, the showstopper of this hotel is a seasonal outdoor pool and a rooftop lounge with live music and entertainment. **Pros:** outdoor pool, a rarity in Manhattan hotels; rooftop bar with splashy red neon sign; great location for culture, sights, and Central Park. **Cons:** located at a busy traffic intersection; daily "residence fee" for bottled water and Wi-Fi; no on-site restaurant. $ *Rooms from: $350* ✉ *44 W. 63rd St., between Broadway and Columbus Ave., Upper West Side* ☎ *212/265–7400* 🌐 *www.empirehotelnyc.com* *427 rooms* *No Meals* Ⓜ *A, B, C, D to 59th St.–Columbus Circle; 1 to 66th St.–Lincoln Center.*

The Gardens Sonesta ES Suites New York

$$$ | **HOTEL** | **FAMILY** | This extended-stay hotel on a quieter residential-feeling street has spacious, well-maintained rooms and amenities which makes it an excellent option for families or visitors who like to retreat to a patio or terrace and order in after a day of exploring nearby Central Park, the Met, or Bloomingdale's. **Pros:** some rooms have patios or terraces; modern, fully equipped kitchenettes; convenient to subway and Grand Central Terminal. **Cons:** bathrooms are well maintained but could use an update; public spaces are compact; no room service or restaurant. *Ⓢ Rooms from: $541 ✉ 215 E. 64th St., Upper East Side ✣ Between 3rd and 2nd Aves. ☎ 212/355–1230 ⊕ www.sonesta.com/sonesta-es-suites/ny/new-york/gardens-sonesta-es-suites-new-york 🛏 132 suites 🍽 No Meals Ⓜ E, F, Q to Lexington Ave.–63rd. St.*

Mandarin Oriental, New York

$$$$ | **HOTEL** | The Mandarin chain's commitment to excess and luxury is evident in the lobby, on the 35th floor of the Deutsche Bank Center, where dramatic floor-to-ceiling windows look out over Columbus Circle and Central Park across the way. **Pros:** vibrant location at the southern entrance to Central Park; destination-worthy cocktails, dining, and spa; expansive suites. **Cons:** long elevator rides; river or park views will cost you; mall-like surroundings on street level. *Ⓢ Rooms from: $1300 ✉ 80 Columbus Circle, at 60th St., Upper West Side ☎ 212/805–8800 ⊕ www.mandarinoriental.com/newyork 🛏 198 rooms 🍽 No Meals Ⓜ 1, A, B, C, D to 59th St.–Columbus Circle.*

The Mark Hotel

$$$$ | **HOTEL** | Within this 1927 landmark building, The Mark personifies lavish comforts coupled with modern guest amenities. **Pros:** private pedicabs; 24-hour in-room dining; walking distance to Central Park and Museum Mile. **Cons:** caters to more of an older and business crowd; street noise might be an issue; bar can get crowded. *Ⓢ Rooms from: $1425 ✉ 25 E. 77th St., Upper East Side ☎ 212/744–4300 ⊕ www.themarkhotel.com 🛏 153 rooms 🍽 No Meals Ⓜ 4, 6 to 77th St.*

Nightlife

★ The Carlyle

PIANO BAR | Amid music-themed murals by Marcel Vertès, the hotel's discreetly sophisticated supper club, Café Carlyle, hosts such top cabaret and jazz performers as Alan Cumming, Christine Ebersole, Judy Collins, Jon Batiste, John Pizzarelli, Steve Tyrell, and comedians Mario Cantone and Tony Danza. The less fancy-schmancy (though still pricey) Bemelmans Bar features a rotating cast of pianist-singers. Bemelmans is known also for its wall murals and lampshades painted by the author of the *Madeline* books, who is said to have traded the artwork for lodging. Both nightspots feature old-fashioned cocktails and trendy new-fashioned ones. Chic attire only (no active sportswear permitted in either one). ✉ *35 E. 76th St., between Madison and Park Aves., Upper East Side* ☎ *212/744–1600* 🌐 *www.rosewoodhotels.com/en/thecarlyle-new-york* Ⓜ *6 to 77th St.*

Performing Arts

★ Apollo Theater

CONCERTS | Arguably the most famous landmark in the neighborhood, no visit to Harlem is complete without stopping by the legendary Apollo Theater. Michael Jackson, Ella Fitzgerald, and James Brown are just a few of the world-class performers who have appeared on this equally famed stage. This year, Apollo's Amateur Night begins their 90th season, with shows every Wednesday night. Perhaps bigger than the 90th season of Amateur Night, the Apollo is slated to undergo renovation to expand into the Apollo Performing Arts Center, with a restoration of the Apollo Theater, and the opening of the Apollo's Victoria Theater. The Apollo Stages at the Victoria are accessible via the third floor of the newly-opened Renaissance New York Harlem Hotel. Safe to say, the Apollo is a history buff's treat with more room to explore than ever, so to dive in deeper, take a tour, held on Monday at 11 am and 1 pm, Wednesday at 11 am, and Saturday at 11 am and 1 pm, and must be reserved in advance. ✉ *253 W. 125th St., between Frederick Douglass and Adam Clayton Powell Jr. Blvds., Harlem* ☎ *212/531–5300* 🌐 *www.apollotheater.org* 🎟 *Varies* Ⓜ *2, 3, A, B, C, D to 125th St.*

Shopping

★ Bonpoint

CHILDREN'S CLOTHING | **FAMILY** | Upper East Siders shop at this pricey French children's boutique for the beautiful designs and impeccable workmanship—think leather baby booties, hand-embroidered jumpers, and cashmere onesies. The NYC flagship has a loftlike design with whimsical touches, such as a large indoor tree and a cloud sculpture. ✉ *805 Madison Ave., between 67th and 68th Sts., Upper East Side* ☎ *212/879–0900* 🌐 *www.bonpoint.com* Ⓜ *6 to 68th St.–Hunter College.*

Ralph Lauren

CLOTHING | Even if you can't afford the clothes here, come just to soak up the luxe lifestyle. The four-story designer's flagship store for women's and home collections is housed in a 22,000-square-foot building in a former historic Beaux-Arts mansion, complete with its own curving marble staircase and stone floors. In addition to the complete women's collection, the brand's lingerie, housewares, and fine-jewelry and watch salon and upscale café are here. You can find the men's flagship directly across the street. ✉ *888 Madison Ave., at 72nd St., Upper East Side* ☎ *212/434–8000* 🌐 *www.ralphlauren.com* Ⓜ *6 to 68th St.–Hunter College.*

Tom Ford

CLOTHING | Famous for revamping Gucci, among other accomplishments, Ford does not disappoint with either his eponymous line or his Madison Avenue flagship, a sleek, grandiose temple to glamorous fashion. Women's stilettos and clutches are unabashedly sexy; men's selections encompass made-to-measure along with traditional and impeccably tailored. Shirts come in more than 300 hues, and off-the-rack suits start at around $5,000. His Black Orchid unisex fragrance is a cult favorite. ✉ *672 Madison Ave., at 61st St., Upper East Side* ☎ *212/359–0300* 🌐 *www.tomford.com* Ⓜ *F, Q to Lexington Ave.–63rd St.; N, R, W to Lexington Ave.–59th St.*

★ Zabar's

FOOD | When it comes to authentic New York food, it's hard to beat this local-favorite specialty food emporium. Best known for its smoked fish counter, not limited to lox (smoked salmon), sliced to order, Zabar's also features one of the largest selections of domestic and imported cheeses and salamis in town, bakery items including cheesecake, ground-to-order coffees, and prepared foods like soups and stuffed cabbage the way Grandma made them. And that's only the ground floor. Upstairs are housewares, from espresso makers to fondue pots to serving dishes. Head next door, to the Zabar's Cafe, to score a cup of gourmet coffee and a bagel and lox with cream cheese. ✉ *2245 Broadway, at 80th St., Upper West Side* ☎ *212/787–2000* 🌐 *www.zabars.com* Ⓜ *1 to 79th St.*

Chapter 8

8

THE OUTER BOROUGHS

Updated by
Arabella Bowen

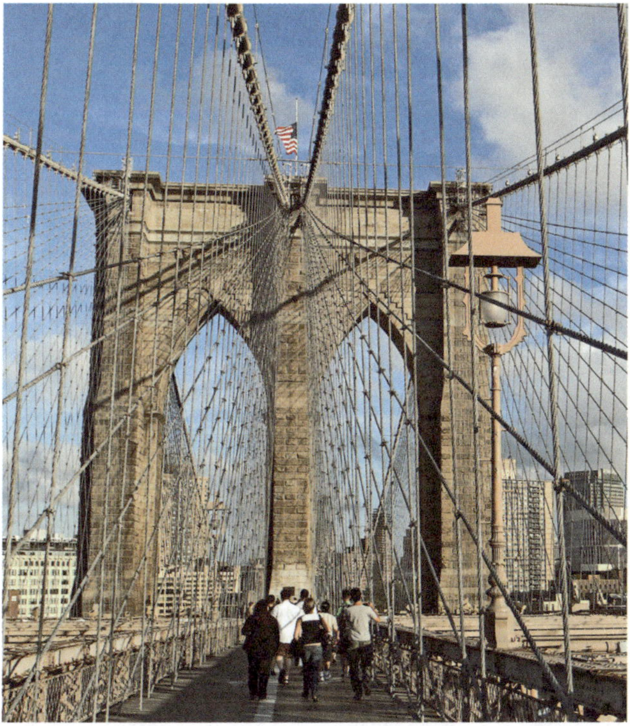

Sights ★★★☆☆ Restaurants ★★★★☆ Hotels ★★☆☆☆ Shopping ★★☆☆☆ Nightlife ★★☆☆☆

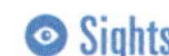

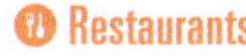

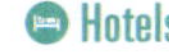

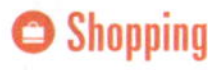

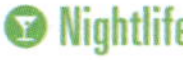

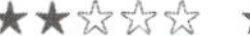

DUMBO Walking Tour

For sheer jaw-dropping drama, few city walks rival the one along the DUMBO waterfront. The photogenic area pairs turn-of-the-20th-century warehouses on cobblestone streets with Brooklyn and Manhattan bridges overhead.

1 The most picturesque way to get here is via the East River Ferry to Fulton Landing, the only vestige that remains of the two-million square feet of real estate purchased in 1979 by controversial New York engineer and developer David Walentas. He spent the next decade transforming the area, then called the Fulton Landing waterfront, into what's now known as DUMBO.

2 Once you've arrived on the wood-planked pier, you'll spot Bargemusic on the right, the legendary River Café on the left, and an outpost of Brooklyn's Van Leeuwen ice-cream parlor straight ahead, all of it suffused by the sounds of cars and subways rumbling overhead along the neighborhood's two dominant bridges—Brooklyn and Manhattan.

3 Tack left on Water Street to enter Brooklyn Bridge Park. What started as a scenic but small hilltop park beneath the Manhattan Bridge has turned into a sweeping feat of green urban renewal stretching from the Manhattan to Brooklyn Bridge

Walking Tour 101

HIGHLIGHTS
Famed bridge and Lower Manhattan views; cinematic photo ops; atmospheric cobblestone blocks; refurbished brick warehouses

WHERE TO START
Fulton Ferry Landing

LENGTH
1½–2 hours

WHERE TO END
The Prospect Street stairs to the Brooklyn Bridge (if you're planning to walk across), High Street subway or, back to the ferry landing

BEST TIME TO GO
Weekday mornings or the first Thursday night of the month, when local galleries stay open late

WORST TIME TO GO
Saturday and Sunday afternoons

and beyond to the south. The park has playgrounds, food concessions, a beach, and lots of grass for lounging. But the real reason to visit is for its astounding views of Lower Manhattan and both bridges overhead.

4 After you walk under the Brooklyn Bridge, head left to the Emily Warren Roebling Plaza along the waterfront for a knockout view. The last piece of the park to be completed, the plaza opened in December 2021 and features concrete pavers that echo the pattern of the bridge overhead. Fittingly, given its up-close views, the space honors the woman who did much of the work to complete the engineering marvel after her husband, its chief engineer, was paralyzed by an accident in 1872. (In recognition, Mrs. Roebling was the first to cross it on its opening day in 1883.)

5 Take the wooden boardwalk along the East River towards the Manhattan Bridge. As you wind along the boardwalk, the stunning Jane's Carousel comes into view on the right. Set inside a glass box designed by Pritzker Prize–winning French architect Jean Nouvel, the fully restored—and

Jane's Carousel

functional—carousel dates from 1922, with 48 horses and two chariots off to the races year-round. If it's open, go for a spin.

6 The enormous 19th-century Empire Stores building (Nos. 53–83 Water Street) behind the carousel dates back to the area's heyday as one of the world's busiest waterfronts, where Brazilian coffee, Argentinian cattle hides, Kentucky tobacco, and Cuban sugar arrived to be stored. Today, it houses a collection of 21st-century shops and restaurants, including West Elm's global HQ at one end (the home-furnishings giant was founded in DUMBO in 2002) and Time Out Market, a great spot to grab a quick bite, on the other. There are rotating art exhibits and pop-ups throughout (and: public restrooms).

7 Flanking Empire Stores on the right, the cutting-edge St. Ann's Warehouse theater at No. 45 Water Street occupies the stunningly refurbished Tobacco Warehouse that dates from 1860. Even if you're not seeing a performance, the triangular Max Family Garden on its rightmost end is worth a stop: The open-air space is contained within the building's original brick walls and archways.

8 Head back out to the boardwalk and continue along the East River to reach tiny Pebble Beach for killer views of the Brooklyn Bridge, Lower Manhattan, and Jane's Carousel all in one. The best are found from the top of the steps behind the beach.

9 From the top of the steps, turn right and exit the park via the path to the left of the Main Street playground. Look up as you go to see the Manhattan Bridge peeping above the treetops. (Fans of the OG *Gossip Girl* will recognize the building immediately below as the location of Dan Humphrey's Brooklyn apartment.)

10 From the Plymouth Street exit, take Washington Street one block to the intersection at Water Street. Turn around when you get there to see a classic city photo op: a cobblestone street flanked with redbrick warehouses and the Manhattan Bridge soaring above, with the faraway Empire State building "peeking" through its supports. It'll be immediately obvious why it's such an arresting backdrop for wedding proposals, fashion shoots, and, of course, innumerable selfies.

11 Turn right onto Water Street Walk past the famous Gleason's Gym at No. 130, which counts Mohammed Ali and Jake LaMotta—the real-life boxer whose life is depicted in the movie *Raging Bull*—among its illustrious boxing alumni.

DUMBO Walls

12 Cross Adams Street to enter the DUMBO Archway. What was once an industrial storage lot is now a soaring 8,000-square-foot venue for seasonal dance parties and performances, with artist David Crumley's *DUMBO Reflector* installation spelling out DUMBO right as you enter. On summer weekends, you might catch a Brooklyn DJ spinning tracks and food trucks besides.

13 Turn right as you exit the Plaza, take a left on Front Street, and turn right onto Jay Street, the area's most commercial artery. The newer buildings aren't the draw here; the street art is. Known collectively as DUMBO Walls, fabulous murals line the underpasses below the Brooklyn-Queens Expressway along York Street from Jay to Washington streets. Start at the Jay Street Underpass and duck in and out as you head west.

14 Turn left when you reach Washington Street. Take the Brooklyn Bridge Steps (just on the right past Prospect Street) to access the Brooklyn Bridge—if you're up for a scenic 40-minute walk back to Manhattan. Ready to sit a spell? The High Street subway stop is just another block up, or you can head back to the ferry landing.

NEIGHBORHOOD SNAPSHOT

TOP EXPERIENCES

- Walking across the Brooklyn Bridge
- Seeing a baseball game at Yankee Stadium
- Being awestruck by DUMBO's architecture and skyline views
- Stopping to smell the roses at the New York Botanic Garden
- Spending the day relaxing at Rockaway Beach or Coney Island

GETTING HERE

Brooklyn is very accessible by subway or ferry service from Manhattan. Brooklyn Heights, Downtown Brooklyn, DUMBO, Red Hook, Williamsburg, and Greenpoint are the closest neighborhoods to Manhattan. You can reach Coney Island in about an hour if you're traveling from Midtown via subway.

Queens is served by many subway lines. To get to Astoria, take the N or W train. For Long Island City, take the E, M, G, or 7 train. The A train (or NYC ferry from Wall Street/Pier 11 in Manhattan) will take you out to Rockaway Beach.

The Bronx is serviced by the 1, 2, 4, 5, 6, B, and D trains. Attractions are spread out across the borough, though, so you need to take different lines to get where you want to go—and rideshares and some MTA buses can fill the void. From Manhattan, the B, D, and 4 trains go to Yankee Stadium and the 2 and 5 trains take you close to the Bronx Zoo.

PAUSE HERE

- **Pepsi-Cola Sign.** On the Queens waterfront, your instinct is to aim your camera toward Manhattan. But you'll definitely want to snap this giant red sign; a favorite backdrop since 1936, marking the site of a now-shuttered Pepsi bottling plant. ✉ *46th Ave. and Center Blvd.* 🚇 *E, M to Court Sq.–23rd St., 7, G to Court Sq.*

- **Orchard Beach.** It can be hard to believe there's a beach in the Bronx, but this public strip of sand, part of Pelham Bay Park, is a beloved respite in summer, with plenty of snack bars and sports courts. ✉ *Pelham Bay* 🚇 *6 to Pelham Bay Park, Bx29 bus to Orchard Beach Circle at City Island Rd.*

At 71 square miles—more than three times the area of Manhattan—Brooklyn is hardly Manhattan's sidekick but a destination in its own right. The best-known of the city's outer boroughs offers so many diverse neighborhoods and a seemingly endless number of compelling sights and fabulous places to eat and drink and shop, you'll never be able to see all of it in one day or even two—so don't even try.

Brooklyn Heights and DUMBO are easily accessible from Manhattan by subway, ferry, or via the Brooklyn Bridge; both neighborhoods have compelling but different architecture (brownstones versus 19th-century warehouses). Trendy Williamsburg has become a destination of its own, spawning many hotels and restaurants, while Park Slope and Prospect Park invite laid-back, family-friendly activities. Coney Island hosts Brooklyn's beaches, boardwalks, and amusement park attractions, including the legendary Cyclone roller coaster.

The city's easternmost borough, Queens, is also its largest. Here, dozens of ethnically rich neighborhoods offer something for visitors—especially culinary-wise—along with a smattering of major art must-sees, including MoMA PS1, the Noguchi Museum, and the Museum of the Moving Image.

Up in the Bronx, New York City's northernmost borough, there's plenty of fun to be had, whether you're eating a hot dog and sipping a beer at a Yankees game or scoping out exotic species at the Bronx Zoo.

Sights

★ Bronx Zoo

ZOO | FAMILY | With 265 acres and more than 11,000 animals representing 700-plus species, this is the largest metropolitan zoo in the United States, opened in 1899. See exotic creatures in natural settings that re-create native habitats; you're often separated from the animals by no more than a moat or wall of glass. Don't miss

Sights
Bronx Zoo, 2
Brooklyn Bridge (Entrance), 5
Brooklyn Bridge Park, 4
Brooklyn Museum, 6
Coney Island Beach, 8
New York Botanical Garden, 1
Prospect Park, 7
Rockaway Beach and Boardwalk, 9
Yankee Stadium, 3
Restaurants
Brooklyn Crab, 6
Casa Enrique, 2
Nathan's Famous, 8
Olmsted, 7
Peter Luger Steak House, 4
The River Café, 5
Roberta's, 3
Taverna Kyclades, 1
Hotels
1 Hotel Brooklyn Bridge, 2
The Rockaway Hotel + Spa, 3
Wythe Hotel, 1
Inwood
Fort Lee
Washington Heights
Harlem
North Bergen
North Arlington
NEW JERSEY
West New York
Hudson River
Broadway
Upper East Side
MANHATTAN
Central Park
Secaucus
Hackensack
Kearny
Union City
FDR Dr.
Astoria
Midtown
Harrison
Hoboken
Chelsea
Long Island City
Greenwich Village
Lower East Side
East River
Greenpoint
Ironbound
Journal Square
Newport
West St.
Williamsburg
Jersey City
Liberty State Park
Dumbo
Ellis I.
Greenville
Governors I.
Liberty I.
Downtown Brooklyn
Bedford-Stuyvesant
Newark Bay
Atlantic Ave.
Bayonne
Red Hook
Park Slope
Crown Heights
Upper New York Bay
Green-Wood Cem.
Linden Blvd.
Sunset Park
Flatbush
Randall Manor
St. George
Port Richmond
BROOKLYN
Bay Ridge
Tompkinsville
Borough Park
Ocean Pkwy.
Flatbush Ave.
West Brighton
Clifton
Bensonhurst
Midwood
STATEN ISLAND
Fort Wadsworth
Gravesend
Sheepshead Bay
Belt Pkwy.
Midland Beach
Lower New York Bay
Brighton Beach
KEY
Sights
Restaurants
Hotels

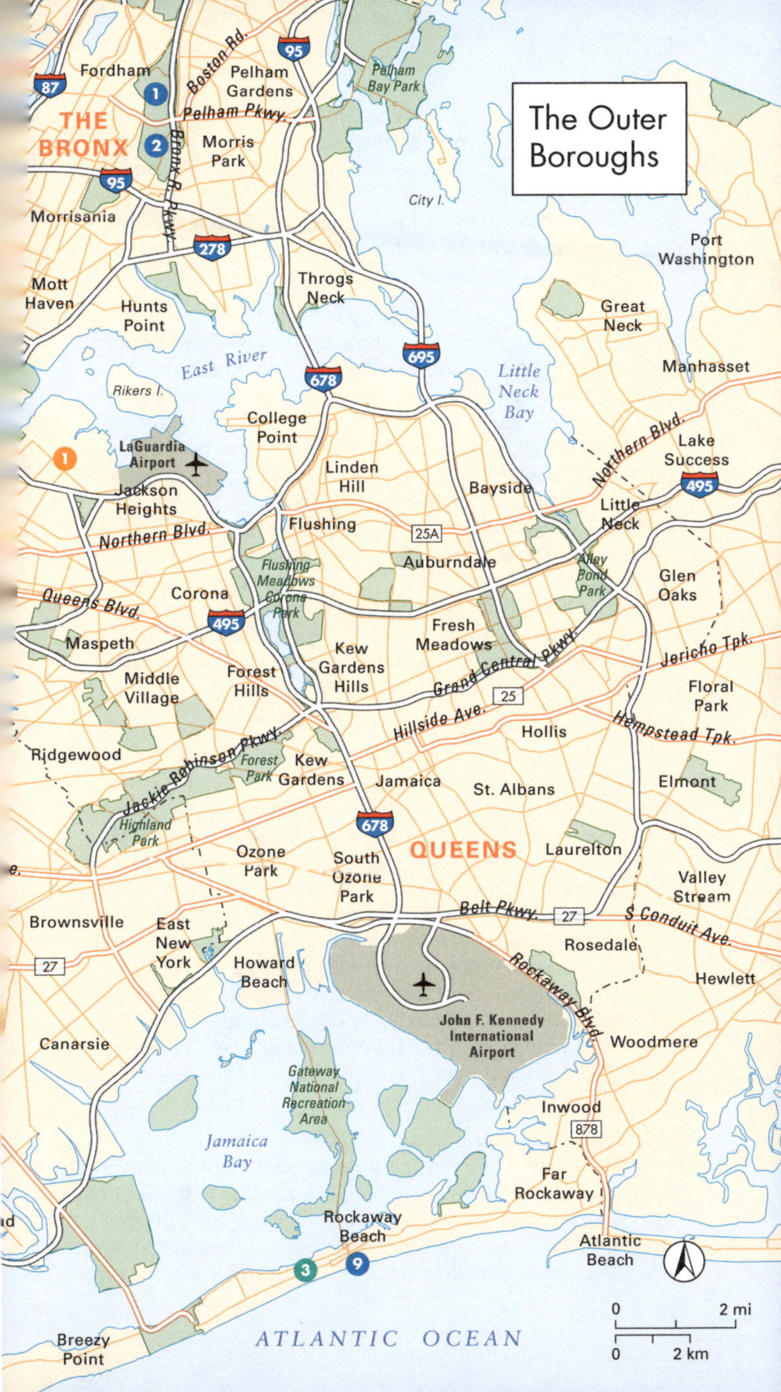
The Outer Boroughs
THE BRONX
QUEENS
Fordham
Pelham Gardens
Pelham Bay Park
Morris Park
Morrisania
Mott Haven
Hunts Point
Throgs Neck
City I.
East River
Rikers I.
College Point
LaGuardia Airport
Jackson Heights
Linden Hill
Flushing
Bayside
Auburndale
Corona
Flushing Meadows Corona Park
Maspeth
Middle Village
Forest Hills
Kew Gardens Hills
Fresh Meadows
Ridgewood
Forest Park
Kew Gardens
Jamaica
Hollis
St. Albans
Highland Park
Ozone Park
South Ozone Park
Laurelton
Brownsville
East New York
Howard Beach
Canarsie
John F. Kennedy International Airport
Gateway National Recreation Area
Jamaica Bay
Rockaway Beach
Breezy Point
ATLANTIC OCEAN
Port Washington
Great Neck
Manhasset
Little Neck Bay
Lake Success
Little Neck
Alley Pond Park
Glen Oaks
Floral Park
Elmont
Valley Stream
Rosedale
Hewlett
Woodmere
Inwood
Far Rockaway
Atlantic Beach
Boston Rd.
Pelham Pkwy.
Bronx R. Pkwy.
Northern Blvd.
Queens Blvd.
Grand Central Pkwy.
Hillside Ave.
Jackie Robinson Pkwy.
Jericho Tpk.
Hempstead Tpk.
Belt Pkwy.
S Conduit Ave.
Rockaway Blvd.
87
95
278
678
695
495
25A
25
27
878
0
2 mi
2 km

the Congo Gorilla Forest, a 6½-acre re-creation of a lush African rain forest with western lowland gorillas, as well as mandrills, okapis, and red river hogs. At Tiger Mountain an open viewing shelter lets you get incredibly close to Siberian tigers. As the big cats nap at midday, visit in the morning or afternoon. *Madagascar!* is a verdant re-creation of one of the world's most threatened natural habitats, with six species of lemurs and more.

Go on a mini-safari via the Wild Asia Monorail, May through October, weather permitting. Here you can view Asian elephants, Indo-Chinese tigers, Indian rhinoceroses, and other species. Try to visit the popular exhibits early to avoid lines later in the day. In winter, some outdoor exhibitions have fewer animals on view, but there's plenty to savor indoors. Some exhibits have an extra charge; to see everything, consider purchasing the Total Experience ticket. ✉ *2300 Southern Blvd., near 187th St., Belmont* ☎ *718/220–5100* 🌐 *www.bronxzoo.com* 🎫 *Flex pricing from $31 (depending on date of visit)* ✍ *No walk-in admission; all guests must purchase date-specific tickets online in advance* ☞ *Wed. free with advanced reservations made after 5 pm the Mon. before; parking $20* Ⓜ *2, 5 to Pelham Pkwy.; BxM11 express bus to Bronx River entrance; Metro-North (Harlem or New Haven local line) to Fordham.*

★ Brooklyn Bridge (Entrance)

BRIDGE | Most visitors cross the Brooklyn Bridge from Manhattan, but you'll get better views traversing the span from the Brooklyn side. It's a surprisingly long walk (more than a mile) that normally takes about 40 minutes, but the exhilarating views are worth the exertion. No need to look out for cyclists; a separated bike lane on the vehicle road has made the pedestrian walkway much more pleasant. The bridge is most magical and quiet in the early morning, but if you don't mind the crowds, it's worth making the trip at sunset in summer, when the lights of Manhattan come to life. There are two pedestrian access points for the bridge on the Brooklyn side: at the intersection of Tillary Street and Adams Street, and another in DUMBO from a staircase at the underpass where Cadman Plaza East intersects Prospect Street. ✉ *Brooklyn Heights* Ⓜ *A, C to High St.; F to York St.; 2, 3 to Clark St.*

★ Brooklyn Bridge Park

CITY PARK | **FAMILY** | This sweeping feat of green urban renewal stretches from the Manhattan Bridge in DUMBO to the Brooklyn Bridge and south all the way to Pier 6, carpeting old industrial sites along the waterfront with scenic esplanades and lush meadows. The park has playgrounds, sports fields, food concessions, and the wonderfully restored Jane's Carousel, plus lots of grass for lounging. In the summer, there are outdoor movies on the Harbor View Lawn. You can access the park at various points; just head down the hill toward the East River and you can't miss it. ✉ *Brooklyn Waterfront, Brooklyn Heights* ☎ *718/222–9939* 🌐 *www.brooklynbridgepark.org* Ⓜ *2, 3 to Clark St.; A, C to High St.; F to York St.; NYC Ferry to DUMBO.*

★ Brooklyn Museum

ART MUSEUM | FAMILY | New York's second-largest museum (after Manhattan's Metropolitan Museum of Art) is also one of the largest in America, with 560,000 square feet of exhibition space. The colossal Beaux-Arts structure houses a world class collection of Egyptian art, as well as impressive collections of African, pre-Columbian, Native American, pan-Asian, and feminist art. In addition, you'll find works by Georgia O'Keeffe, Winslow Homer, John Singer Sargent, George Bellows, Thomas Eakins, and Milton Avery. The museum is also well known for its contemporary, cutting-edge special exhibits. The monthly (except September and November through January) First Saturday free-entry night is a neighborhood party of art, music, and dancing, with food vendors and several cash bars. ✉ *200 Eastern Pkwy., Prospect Heights* ☎ *718/638–5000* 🌐 *www.brooklynmuseum.org* 🎟 *$20 suggested donation, $25 combo ticket with Brooklyn Botanic Garden* 🕒 *Closed Mon. and Tues.* Ⓜ *2, 3 to Eastern Pkwy.–Brooklyn Museum.*

Coney Island Beach

BEACH | FAMILY | This 2½-mile beach, flanked by the Riegelmann Boardwalk and the amusement park rides beyond, has become an essential part of New York legend. Although open (and visited) year-round, the beach really heats up in summer, when it can feel like the entire population of New York is out sunning and swimming. In winter, you'll see Russian, Eastern European, and Central Asian inhabitants of neighboring Brighton Beach strolling the boardwalk in their Sunday best. Moreover, the annual Polar Bear Plunge on January 1 sees thousands of revelers greet the new year by diving into the frigid waters of the Atlantic. Run by the Coney Island Polar Bear Club (🌐 *www.polarbearclub.org*), a winter bathing club founded in 1903, it's free and open to everyone as long as they've registered on the website—although donations are highly-encouraged at registration, to benefit local non-profits and the community. **Amenities:** toilets; snack bars; sports facilities. **Best for:** swimming; sunbathing; people-watching. ✉ *Coney Island* Ⓜ *D, F, N, Q to Coney Island–Stillwell Ave.; B, Q to Brighton Beach; Q to Ocean Pkwy.*

The Boathouse in Prospect Park, built in 1905, was one of the first buildings in New York City to be declared a historic landmark.

★ New York Botanical Garden

GARDEN | FAMILY | Considered one of the world's leading botany centers, this beautiful, 250-acre campus is also one of the best reasons to make a trip to the Bronx. Built around the dramatic gorge of the Bronx River, it's home to lush indoor and outdoor gardens and acres of natural forest, and it offers classes, concerts, and special exhibits. Be captivated by the seasonal fragrance of the Peggy Rockefeller Rose Garden's 4,000 blooms, which represent more than 650 varieties. Relax in the leafy Thain Family Forest, or explore the Everett Children's Adventure Garden, a 12-acre, indoor-outdoor museum with a boulder maze, giant animal topiaries, and a plant discovery center. The Victorian-style Enid A. Haupt Conservatory houses re-creations of misty tropical rain forests and arid African and North American deserts, as well as exhibitions such as the annual Holiday Train Show and the winter-into-spring Orchid Show, which showcases flowers that look like the stuff of science fiction. The All-Garden Pass gives you access to the conservatory, adventure garden, special exhibitions, and more. ✉ *2900 Southern Blvd., Belmont* ☎ *718/817–8700* 🌐 *www.nybg.org* 🎟 *All Garden Pass $35; check website as pricing varies for special exhibitions and events; parking $22* ⏱ *Closed Mon.* Ⓜ *4, B, D to Bedford Park Blvd.; then walk about 8 blocks downhill to the garden (or take the Bx26 bus). Metro-North (Harlem local line) to Botanical Garden.*

★ Prospect Park

CITY PARK | FAMILY | Brooklyn residents are passionate about Prospect Park, and with good reason: lush green spaces, gently curved walkways, summer concerts, vivid foliage in autumn, and an all-season skating rink make it a year-round getaway. In 1859, the New York Legislature decided to develop plans for a park in the fast-growing city of Brooklyn. After landscape architects Frederick Law Olmsted and Calvert Vaux completed the park in the late 1880s, Olmsted remarked that he was prouder of it than any of his other works—including Manhattan's Central Park—and many critics agree. On weekends, those not jogging the 3.35-mile loop gravitate to the rolling hills of the Long Meadow to picnic, fly kites, or play cricket, flag football, or Frisbee. On summer Sundays, foodies flock to Breeze Hill, site of outdoor food market Smorgasburg's second Brooklyn location. The park's north entrance is at Grand Army Plaza, where the Soldiers' and Sailors' Memorial Arch (patterned on the Arc de Triomphe in Paris) honors Civil War veterans. On Saturday, year-round, a greenmarket at the plaza throngs with shoppers.

A good way to experience the park is to walk the Long Meadow—or stop in for the occasional free yoga class—and then head to the eastern side and south toward the lake. Along the way, you'll encounter attractions including Brooklyn's last remaining forest, including the Lefferts Historic House (now closed for renovations), Prospect Park Audubon Center, and the LeFrak Center. The Prospect Park Carousel, built in 1912, still thrills the kids. The Boathouse, dating from 1905, is a stunning example of Beaux-Arts architecture. The annual Celebrate Brooklyn! Festival takes place at the Prospect Park Bandshell from early June through mid-August. ✉ *Prospect Park W, Flatbush Ave., Prospect Park* ☎ *718/965–8951* 🌐 *www.prospectpark.org* 🎫 *Carousel $3* 🕒 *Carousel closed Mon.–Wed. and winter months* Ⓜ *2, 3 to Grand Army Plaza; F, G to 7th Ave. or 15th St.–Prospect Park; B, Q to 7th Ave.–Prospect Park/Parkside Ave.*

★ Rockaway Beach and Boardwalk

BEACH | Stretching almost the entire length of the peninsula, this beach is separated into sections according to and labeled with the nearest cross street. In order to prevent erosion that worsened after Hurricane Sandy, certain sections of the beach are closed on various days, so check the website for details. The adjoining concrete boardwalk becomes a see-and-be-seen bazaar in the height of summer. Bikers, strollers, joggers, and rollerbladers all share space with day trippers trying to spot their friends on the sand. There are also plenty of eateries and some swimsuit and surf shops for browsing. **Amenities:** food and drink; toilets; lifeguards (in season). **Best for:** swimming; walking; surfing; partiers. ✉ *Beach 3rd St., to Beach 153rd St., Rockaway Beach* 🌐 *www.nycgovparks.org/parks/rockaway-beach-and-boardwalk* ☞ *Beach and boardwalk open year-round; many shops and restaurants only in summer* Ⓜ *A to Beach 90th St.*

★ Yankee Stadium

SPORTS VENUE | FAMILY | From April through October, you can see one of baseball's great franchises, the "Bronx Bombers," in action at their $1.5 billion Yankee Stadium, opened in 2009 right across the street from the site of the original (aka "the House that Ruth Built"), which is now parkland. Tickets can be pricey, but the experience is like watching baseball in a modern-day coliseum. It's quite opulent: a traditional white frieze adorns the stadium's top; inside, limestone-and-marble hallways are lined with photos of past Yankee greats. History buffs and hard-core fans should visit the museum (set on the main level and open 'til the end of the eighth inning), filled with team memorabilia, and Monument Park (closes 45 minutes prior to first pitch), with plaques of past Yankee legends, by center field. **■ TIP→ Pregame and off-season one-hour stadium tours are held on a near-daily basis year-round; visit the Yankees website for more info on times and ticketing.** ✉ *1 E. 161st St., at River Ave., South Bronx* ☎ *718/293–4300* 🌐 *www.yankees.com* Ⓜ *4, B, D to 161st St.–Yankee Stadium.*

Restaurants

Brooklyn Crab

$$ | SEAFOOD | FAMILY | If you see the fiberglass head of a hammerhead shark in the front yard, you've arrived at this three-story restaurant where the nautical paraphernalia continues inside and out. Fashioned to be a beach house down the shore, there's an indoor restaurant component serving up crabs and other seafood, which spills out to the large seating area in the back. **Known for:** lively beach bar vibe; miniature golf; huge backyard. Ⓢ *Average main: $27* ✉ *24 Reed St., Red Hook* ☎ *718/643–2722* 🌐 *www.brooklyncrab.com* ⊙ *Closed Mon.–Wed.* Ⓜ *NYC Ferry to Red Hook.*

Casa Enrique

$$ | MEXICAN | Come for the tacos, stay for the margaritas: that's what a lot of local Long Island City folks do at this popular Mexican standout. The chef is from Chiapas, but expect pan-Mexican fare, with tacos crammed with slow-cooked beef tongue or rich chorizo, among other options like a seasonal vegan taco. **Known for:** different margaritas; Michelin-rated cuisine; delicious mole. Ⓢ *Average main: $25* ✉ *5–48 49th Ave., between Vernon Blvd.*

A stroll on the boardwalk at Coney Island is a New York summer tradition.

and 5th St., Long Island City ☎ *347/448–6040* 🌐 *casaenriquelic.com* ⏲ *No lunch weekdays* Ⓜ *7 to Vernon Blvd.–Jackson Ave.*

★ Nathan's Famous

$ | HOT DOG | Nathan Handwerker, a Polish immigrant with a $300 loan and his wife Ida's secret spice recipe, founded this Coney Island hot dog stand in 1916. Fast forward over a century, and this New York City institution has endured with a cultlike following among celebrities and heads of state, paving the way for international franchises. **Known for:** world-famous hot dogs; seafood counter serving fried frog legs; annual hot-dog-eating contest. Ⓢ *Average main: $10* ✉ *1310 Surf Ave., Coney Island* ☎ *718/333–2202* 🌐 *www.nathansfamous.com* Ⓜ *D, F, N, Q to Coney Island–Stillwell Ave.*

Olmsted

$$$$ | INTERNATIONAL | Named after one of the two masterminds behind the design of Central Park and Prospect Park—Frederick Law Olmsted that is, of Olmsted & Vaux—this restaurant caused a stir when it first opened in 2016, for keeping live farm animals in its backyard. Today, the animals are gone, but you can still sip a cocktail there before enjoying seasonal farm-to-table, prix-fixe tasting menus of sophisticated international courses ($125 dinner, $38 brunch). **Known for:** à la carte and prix-fixe tasting menus; heated backyard garden; popular brunch. Ⓢ *Average main: $50* ✉ *659 Vanderbilt Ave., Prospect Heights* ☎ *718/552–2610* 🌐 *www.olmstednyc.com* ⏲ *Closed Tues. No lunch weekdays* Ⓜ *2, 3 to Grand Army Plaza; B, Q to 7 Ave.*

★ Peter Luger Steak House

$$$$ | STEAK HOUSE | Despite scathing food critic reviews in recent years, steak lovers (and food bloggers) continue to embrace to this steak institution that's endured since 1887. It's known for dry-aged cuts of meat and classic steak-house sides, as much as its old school, high-handed waiters. **Known for:** being a steak institution for over 135 years; historic Brooklyn environs; no credit cards. *Average main: $80* *178 Broadway, Williamsburg* *718/387–7400* *www.peterluger.com* *No credit cards* *J, M, Z to Marcy Ave.; NYC Ferry to South Williamsburg.*

★ The River Café

$$$$ | MODERN AMERICAN | A deservedly popular special-occasion destination, this waterfront institution complements its exquisite Brooklyn Bridge views with memorable top-shelf cuisine served by an unfailingly attentive staff. Lobster, lamb, duck, and steak are among the staples of the prix-fixe menu. **Known for:** unforgettable location; top-shelf cuisine; refined atmosphere. *Average main: $195* *1 Water St., Brooklyn Heights* *718/522–5200* *www.rivercafe.com* *Closed Mon. and Tues.* *Jackets and collared shirts required for men* *2, 3 to Clark St.; A, C to High St.; F to York St.; NYC Ferry to DUMBO.*

★ Roberta's

$$ | PIZZA | Roberta's completely transformed this industrial district in 2007 with its destination wood-fired pizzas topped with hyperlocal ingredients—many herbs come from their garden on-site, a former garage and yard. Their acclaimed pies with innovative combinations and signature crusts have wowed pizza connoisseurs so successfully, Roberta's has expanded well beyond this groundbreaking original location, with a frozen pizza line and outposts as far as Singapore. **Known for:** internationally recognized pizza; patio with tiki bar; hyperlocal ingredients. *Average main: $21* *261 Moore St., Bushwick* *718/417–1118* *www.robertaspizza.com* *L to Morgan Ave.*

★ Taverna Kyclades

$$$ | GREEK | You won't need to jump on the next flight to Athens or the next ferry to Santorini to indulge in some of the best Greek food in the world. Instead, you'll find it right here in Astoria in this brightly lit eatery. **Known for:** most authentic Greek fare this side of the Acropolis; seafood and lamb chops; no reservations. *Average main: $30* *36–01 Ditmars Blvd., Astoria* *718/545–8666* *www.tavernakyclades.com* *N, W to Astoria–Ditmars Blvd.*

Hotels

★ 1 Hotel Brooklyn Bridge

$$$$ | **HOTEL** | A sustainable ethos drives this hip, beautifully designed outpost of the 1 Hotels brand, as evidenced by a 20-foot plant wall punctuating the Brooklyn-inspired lobby, and filtered water bottle-filling stations in many guest rooms. **Pros:** fine dining at on-site restaurant, The Osprey; stellar views of the Brooklyn Bridge; rooftop pool and bar. **Cons:** east-facing rooms overlook busy thoroughfare; pool closed in winter; uneven service. *Rooms from: $699* *60 Furman St., Brooklyn Heights* *347/696–2500* *1hotels.com/brooklyn-bridge* *195 rooms* *No Meals* *2, 3 to Clark St.; A, C to High St.*

★ The Rockaway Hotel + Spa

$$$ | **HOTEL** | The Rockaways had been gaining popularity for years but its status was cemented with this trendy newcomer, giving surfers and sunbathers a reason to stay overnight—guests can expect a beachy and mid-century modern decor, with lots of light teak wood, rattan and linen accents, and marine blues and grays that catch the sunlight. **Pros:** great pool and spa; Manhattan skyline restaurant views; high-end accents. **Cons:** breakfast not included; isolated from the rest of NYC; neighborhood lacks amenities. *Rooms from: $500* *108–10 Rockaway Beach Dr., Rockaway Beach* *718/474–1216* *www.therockawayhotel.com* *61 rooms, including 8 bungalows* *No Meals* *A to Beach 105th St.*

★ Wythe Hotel

$$ | **HOTEL** | A former cooperage on the Brooklyn waterfront has found new life as the Wythe Hotel, a stunner for its Manhattan-skyline views, locally sourced design touches and amenities. **Pros:** Brooklyn-based design and environmentally friendly products; fabulous views from rooms or terrace bar; destination-worthy restaurant. **Cons:** somewhat removed from the subway; not all rooms have a skyline view; the rooftop bar gets crowded. *Rooms from: $361* *80 Wythe Ave., at N. 11th St., Williamsburg* *718/460–8000* *www.wythehotel.com* *72 rooms* *No Meals* *L to Bedford Ave.; NYC Ferry to North Williamsburg.*

Nightlife

Brooklyn Brewery

BREWPUBS | This brewery resurrected the borough's once-active craft beer scene when it opened in a former matzo factory in 1996. There are free tours on Sunday, while weekday Small Batch

Tours offer an in-depth look and a chance to try and give feedback on new experimental beers. Tap offerings in its sizable, congenial taproom include their signature Brooklyn Lager and crowd favorite Pulp Art Hazy IPA. ✉ *79 N. 11th St., Williamsburg* ☎ *718/486–7422* 🌐 *www.brooklynbrewery.com* Ⓜ *L to Bedford Ave.; G to Nassau Ave.; NYC Ferry to North Williamsburg.*

★ Dutch Kills

COCKTAIL BARS | The dark bartop with cozy wooden booths at Dutch Kills—a cocktail den with a nod to the neighborhood's historic roots—serves finely crafted drinks for $17 each. Try Tiger Chilled Coffee, made with rum, cold brew, and cinnamon syrup, or Whiskey Fix, which is simply your choice of bourbon or rye with fresh lemon juice and sugar, served on crushed ice. Expect precisely chiseled chunks of ice and skilled bartenders who, with a few queries into your preferences and curiosities, can create a concoction just to your taste. ✉ *27–24 Jackson Ave., Long Island City* ☎ *718/383–2724* 🌐 *www.dutchkillsbar.com* Ⓜ *E, M, R to Queens Plaza; 7, G to Court Sq.; 7, N, W to Queensboro Plaza.*

★ Maison Premiere

COCKTAIL BARS | Transport yourself to New Orleans in this dimly lit yet lively cocktail and oyster bar, known for an extensive absinthe selection, a menu spanning light fare to hearty braised beef cheeks, and above all, an impressive selection of oysters hailing from both coasts. Cozy up at the horseshoe-shape bar or dine at a cast-iron table inside—or in the back garden on warm days. ✉ *298 Bedford Ave., Williamsburg* ☎ *347/889–5710* 🌐 *www.maisonpremiere.com* Ⓜ *L to Bedford Ave.; NYC Ferry to North Williamsburg.*

Performing Arts

★ Brooklyn Academy of Music *(BAM)*

PERFORMANCE VENUES | Founded in 1861 and operating at its current location since 1908, BAM is a more than music; it's multidisciplinary performing arts center that now encompasses three edifices, including the Beaux-Arts, seven-story Peter Jay Sharp building. It's known for innovative performances within its facilities, including an unadorned "black box" theater, dance venues, a four-screen cinema, an opera house, a gallery, and an open-plan performance and restaurant space. ✉ *Peter Jay Sharp Bldg., 30 Lafayette Ave., Fort Greene* ☎ *718/636–4100* 🌐 *www.bam.org* Ⓜ *2, 3, 4, 5, B, D, N, Q, R to Atlantic Ave.–Barclays Ctr.; G to Fulton St.; C to Lafayette Ave.*

Index

Photo Credits

Front cover: Peter Unger/Getty Images [Descr.: The Statue of Liberty, 1886, UNESCO World Heritage Listed, Liberty Island, New York, USA.] **Back cover, from left to right:** Tonyshi.Photos/GettyImages. Sborisov/iStockphoto. Frankpeters/iStockphoto. **Spine:** Frankpeters/iStockphoto. **Interior, from left to right:** Jodi Nasser (1). GagliardiPhotography/Shutterstock (2). **Chapter 1: Experience New York City:** IM_photo/Shutterstock (6-7). Christopher Postlewaite/NYC & Co (8-9). Spyarm/Shutterstock (9). Tagger Yancey IV/ NYC & Company (9). Marley White (10). Gang Liu/Shutterstock (10). TJ Muzeni (11). Kate Glicksberg/NYC & Company (12). Kate Glicksberg (12). Stockinasia/Shutterstock (12). Alexandr Spatari/GettyImages (13). Patrick Michael Chin (18). Courtesy of Roberta's (18). Danielle Adams (18). Russ & Daughters (18). Evan Sung (19). Anton_Ivanov/Shutterstock (20). Qiwoman01/Dreamstime (20). EqRoy/Shutterstock.com (20). The Solomon R. Guggenheim Foundation, NY (20). Andersphoto/Shutterstock (21). Maurizio De Mattei/Shutterstock (21). Courtesy of Brooklyn Museum (21). Courtesy of The Jewish Museum (21). Strand Books (22). Choongky/Shutterstock (23). Nadya Kubik/Shutterstock (24). Richard Green/Alamy Stock Photo (25). John Randazzo/GetyyImages (26). Andrew F Kazmierski/iStockphoto (27). **Chapter 3: Lower Manhattan:** Spyarm/Shutterstock (79). Ian Dagnall/Alamy Stock Photo (82). Philip Scalia/Alamy Stock Photo (83). Almaz888/Dreamstime (89). Estormiz/Wikimedia Commons (92). Philip Lange/Shutterstock (94). **Chapter 4: The Village and Lower East Side:** Lazyllama/Alamy Stock Photo (99). Tracey Whitefoot/Alamy Stock Photo (102). Felix Lipov/Shutterstock (103). Scott Raichilson/iStockphoto (108). Tenement Museum Lower East Side Manhattan (110). Jennifer Arnow (112). **Chapter 5: Union Square and Chelsea:** Lerka555/Dreamstime (117). Marco Rubino/Shutterstock (122). Mandritoiu/Shutterstock (125). **Chapter 6: Midtown:** Dibrova/Dreamstime (133). Bumble Dee/Shutterstock (136). Bumble Dee/Shutterstock (137). Sanjay Dalvi/Dreamstime (143). Stuart Monk/iStockphoto (145). Kasto80/iStockphoto (146). **Chapter 7: Upper East and West with Harlem:** Mary Robnett/Boating (157). Maurizio De Mattei/Shutterstock (160). Spiroview Inc/Shutterstock (161). Kmiragaya/Dreamstime (168). Jon Baran/istockphoto (172). Here Now/Shutterstock (174). **Chapter 8: The Outer Boroughs:** Olga Bogatyrenko/Shutterstock (181). T photography/Shutterstock (184). Reid Dalland/Shutterstock (185). Littleny/Dreamstime (192). Pio3/Shutterstock (195). **About Our Writers:** All photos are courtesy of the writers.

*Every effort has been made to trace the copyright holders, and we apologize in advance for any accidental errors. We would be happy to apply the corrections in the following edition of this publication.

Fodor's Pocket Guides NEW YORK CITY

Publisher: Stephen Horowitz, *General Manager*

Editorial: Douglas Stallings, *Editorial Director;* Jill Fergus, Amanda Sadlowski, *Senior Editors;* Brian Eschrich, Alexis Kelly, *Editors;* Angelique Kennedy-Chavannes, Yoojin Shin, *Associate Editors*

Design: Tina Malaney, *Director of Design and Production;* Jessica Gonzalez, *Senior Designer;* Jaimee Shaye, *Graphic Design Associate*

Production: Jennifer DePrima, *Editorial Production Manager;* Elyse Rozelle, *Senior Production Editor;* Monica White, *Production Editor*

Maps: Rebecca Baer, *Map Director;* Mark Stroud (Moon Street Cartography), *Cartographer*

Photography: Viviane Teles, *Director of Photography;* Namrata Aggarwal, Neha Gupta, Payal Gupta, Ashok Kumar, *Photo Editors;* Jade Rodgers, Shanelle Jacobs, *Photo Production Intern*

Business and Operations: Chuck Hoover, *Chief Marketing Officer;* Robert Ames, *Group General Manager*

Public Relations and Marketing: Joe Ewaskiw, *Senior Director of Communications and Public Relations*

Fodors.com: Jeremy Tarr, *Editorial Director;* Rachael Levitt, *Managing Editor*

Technology: Jon Atkinson, *Executive Director of Technology;* Rudresh Teotia, *Associate Director of Technology;* Alison Lieu, *Project Manager*

Writer: Arabella Bowen

Editor: Jill Fergus

Production Editor: Monica White

16th Edition

ISBN 978-1-64097-789-1

ISSN 1056-7712

PRINTED IN CANADA

10 9 8 7 6 5 4 3 2 1

About Our Writers

Arabella Bowen is a New York City–based arts and travel writer. Formerly the editor-in-chief of Fodor's and digital content director at AFAR, her work has also appeared in the *New York Times*, Digital Party, Christie's, and more. Arabella began her travel career writing guidebooks for Rough Guides and still loves getting beneath the surface of a place. Creating the walking tours for this Pocket guide allowed her to rediscover NYC with fresh eyes. Follow her on Instagram @arabynyc.

In addition, the listings in this book were updated with the help of our New York City guidebook team: **Kelsy Chauvin, David Farley, Michele Herrmann, Jacinta O'Halloran, Kaitlyn Rosati,** and **Erik Trinidad.**